Federal Aid to Depressed Areas

✦✦✦✦✦✦✦✦✦✦✦✦✦✦✦✦✦✦✦✦✦✦✦

Federal Aid
to Depressed Areas

An Evaluation of the
Area Redevelopment Administration

++

BY
SAR A. LEVITAN

JOHNS HOPKINS PRESS   BALTIMORE

To
Brita Ann

Preface

++++++++++++++++++++++++++

On May 1, 1961, President John F. Kennedy signed a bill designed to help depressed areas that had relatively high levels of unemployment and underemployment. The euphemistic title of the new law was the Area Redevelopment Act of 1961.

As much as any piece of legislation can be, the Area Redevelopment Act is largely a product of one man, Senator Paul H. Douglas, of Illinois. He formulated the intellectual underpinnings of the program and played a leading role in the shaping of the coalition which supported the legislation. It was largely due to his perseverance that the Act survived two presidential vetoes and was finally signed into law under a friendly Administration in 1961.

The economic climate was favorable to sustain the prolonged struggle over the legislation. The country had experienced creeping unemployment since Douglas introduced his original bill in 1955, and the growing number of depressed areas and their intensifying problems were increasingly perceived as major public-policy issues.

This study examines the various components of the area redevelopment program, describes its operations, mainly from a Washington vantage point, and evaluates the activities of the Area Redevelopment Administration during its first two years. The public controversy surrounding the program has not abated during the two years, and hence its scope and future direction remain in doubt. An attempt is made to place the controversy in perspective by appraising the contradictory claims relating to area redevelopment and by raising, though not necessarily answering, the major issues implicit in the program.

The provisions of the Area Redevelopment Act are loosely drawn, reflecting the usual compromises over controversial legislation and the gaps in knowledge about appropriate programs for rehabilitating depressed areas. The study therefore opens with an analysis of the economic and political issues underlying the prolonged legislative hassle over the bill.

The formal legislative provisions establish, at best, only a viable framework for a governmental program, and the administrative instrument evolved to implement the enabling act is critical to an understanding of the program. Moreover, the Area Redevelopment Act permits the administrators considerable flexibility in implementing the legislation. Attention is focused in Chapter 2 on the peculiar organizational structure under which the Area Redevelopment Administration has operated. The socioeconomic characteristics of the areas the program is supposed to help are discussed in the subsequent chapter.

The substantive ingredients of the Area Redevelopment Act (which are discussed in Chapters 4–7) are four related programs:

1. Long-term loans at low rates of interest providing venture capital to attract new business to locate in depressed areas or to help expand established businesses.

2. Financial aid to help communities develop the public facilities needed to attract business.

3. Training programs to help the unemployed and underemployed secure jobs.

4. Technical assistance to help communities plan constructive development programs which will stimulate their economic growth.

Separate chapters are devoted to each of the above-listed programs. The legislative history of the appropriate provision is traced, and the supplementary measures adopted by the Area Redevelopment Administration are reviewed. The major measures pertaining to depressed areas, enacted by Congress during the two years following the passage of the Area Redevelopment Act, are discussed in Chapter 8. In addition, other proposals that were considered but not included in the Act are examined—including preferential treatment in government procurement, tax incentives aimed at stimulating economic growth in depressed areas, and subsidies for relocating the unemployed. The final chapter assesses the package of tools which Congress put together to combat unemployment in depressed areas, examines the limitations of the program, and considers alternative approaches for its extension.

The area redevelopment program is a long-term effort aimed at expanding economic growth in chronic labor-surplus areas; it should therefore be stressed that an evaluation of its first two years of operations is necessarily tentative.

There is little in this study that touches upon the current "great debate" among economists as to the causes of the disturbingly high level of unemployment which the American economy has experienced during the past six years. I believe that measures aimed at stimulating over-all expansion of demand as well as specially tailored programs are needed to combat unemployment in depressed areas. The two types of measures are complementary, and in a slack economy the policy implications of the debate among the "inadequate demand" and "structural" schools are extremely limited.

I want to express my gratitude to the many persons who have contributed to the preparation of this study. Officials of the ARA and other government agencies involved in the program were most cooperative and tolerant of an outside kibitzer looking over their collective shoulders while they were engaged in developing and administering the program. Dr. Roger Davidson collaborated on Chapter 2 and offered a valuable critical review of the whole study. Mrs. Ethel W. Brandwein assisted in the preparation of the section on the accelerated public-works program, and Miss Patricia DeYoung and Mr. Robert Hanson, II, served as research assistants and prepared the statistical tables. Professors Halsey R. Jones, Garth Mangum, and Richard C. Wilcock prepared summaries of ARA activities in Pennsylvania, Utah, and southern Illinois respectively, supplying insights for evaluating the program.

The study was also improved as a result of critical comments offered by Roger S. Adkins (U.S. Budget Bureau), Murray D. Dessell (U.S. Census Bureau), Victor R. Fuchs (National Bureau of Economic Research), Marvin P. Gordon (Maryland University), Peter E. de Janosi (Ford Foundation), Herbert J. Lahne (U.S. Department of Labor), Jonathan Lindley (Senate Committee on Banking and Currency), Herman Miller (U.S. Census Bureau), John M. Peterson (Arkansas University), Herbert E. Steiner (Upjohn Institute), and Murray Wernick (Federal Reserve Board). In addition, ARA officials gave incisive criticism to an earlier version of the manuscript. Mrs. Ivis B. Steele worked cheerfully and efficiently on the various stages of the manuscript.

The study was prepared under a Ford Foundation grant. In accordance with the practice of The Ford Foundation, I was permitted full freedom in pursuing my own course in the preparation of the volume.

The George Washington University   Sᴀʀ A. Lᴇᴠɪᴛᴀɴ
Washington, D.C.

September 30, 1963

Preface to the Second Printing

◆◆◆◆◆◆◆◆◆◆◆◆◆◆◆◆◆◆◆◆◆◆◆◆◆◆

Five years of additional experience with federal depressed area legislation provides no basis for changing the tentative conclusions and theme of this study. Congress has continued to provide only limited resources to the program and its administrators have continued to disperse rather than concentrate these meager funds. There is no evidence that the tools provided in the Area Redevelopment Act and the Economic Development Act are adequate to deal with the intractable forces that cause economic stagnation and depression in certain economic areas.

Washington, D.C.   SAR A. LEVITAN
September 15, 1968

Contents

++++++++++++++++++++++++++++

LIST OF TABLES

Federal Aid to Depressed Areas

✦✦✦✦✦✦✦✦✦✦✦✦✦✦✦✦✦✦✦✦✦✦✦✦✦✦

Chapter 1

The Politics and Economics of Depressed Area Legislation

++

In 1954 Senator Paul H. Douglas was campaigning for re-election. His travels took him throughout his state and gave him an opportunity to observe firsthand the depressed conditions in southern Illinois. The country and the state were emerging from the second post-World War II recession, but southern Illinois had gained little from the upward economic trend. Even throughout the peak of the previous business cycle, when national unemployment dropped below the 3 per cent level, southern Illinois remained a depressed area.

The results of the election were most gratifying to Senator Douglas —he won by a majority of 241,000. But, besides giving him a decisive victory, the campaign in southern Illinois also impressed upon the Senator, who is a distinguished economist and past president of the American Economic Association, the acute economic needs of this region. As a result of the campaign, Douglas gained the conviction that the federal government has the responsibility for assisting depressed areas in rehabilitating themselves. The depressed economic conditions in southern Illinois convinced him that indigenous resources were inadequate in many cases to put these areas on the road to prosperity and that national economic growth and prosperity too frequently tend to by-pass depressed areas. He concluded that specially tailored programs were necessary for rehabilitating the chronically depressed areas and that the persistence of labor surpluses in these areas serves as a drag upon the total economy. Douglas also reasoned that it would make poor economic sense to permit the abandonment of such areas— the communities of southern Illinois and depressed communities in

other parts of the country represented investments of considerable social capital. Moreover, as an economist, he knew that human resources
are relatively immobile and that middle-aged and older persons, in
particular, tend to develop strong economic and social roots which
militate against mobility. The solution was to devise methods for
bringing jobs to the labor-surplus areas.

ANTECEDENTS OF THE FIRST DOUGLAS BILL

With the opening of the Eighty-fourth Congress in January, 1955,
Senator Douglas obtained the opportunity of voicing his ideas publicly.
The Democrats had won control of the Senate in the 1954 election,
and it was their turn to appoint a chairman of the Joint Committee
on the Economic Report. The senior Democratic senator on this committee was John Sparkman, but since he was already the chairman of
another committee, Douglas was next in line for the chairmanship
of the Joint Economic Committee.[1]

In 1955 President Eisenhower's Council of Economic Advisers
touched upon the problem of depressed areas but viewed the adjustment problem of these areas as one that "should be carried out by the
local citizens themselves." According to the council, the federal government's contribution to the depressed areas should be limited to a
sound, over-all, national economic policy which would assure a generally high level of employment and income.[5]

In reviewing the Economic Report of the President, Senator
Douglas and the majority of his Democratic colleagues on the Joint
Economic Committee took strong exception to the Administration's
position and recommended a "positive program" to aid depressed
areas. But at this stage Senator Douglas had not yet fully developed a
comprehensive program; the majority's recommendations were general in nature and included:

1. A broad public-works program for slum clearance, construction
of schools, hospitals, highways, and other public facilities to aid areas
where unemployment exceeded 12 per cent.

2. The establishment of an industrial development corporation,
with federal support, which would extend long-term credit to businesses locating or expanding in depressed areas—the report, however,
did not supply a definition of depressed areas.

[1]The name of the Joint Committee on the Economic Report was changed under
Douglas' chairmanship to the Joint Economic Committee.

3. Provision for federal technical assistance "designed to help depressed localities solve their own problems."

4. Expansion of unemployment insurance to a minimum of twenty-six weeks, with a provision that unemployed workers in distressed areas who were willing to undertake training for new jobs would become eligible for an additional thirteen weeks of unemployment insurance benefits.[11]

Immediately after the publication of the 1955 JEC report, Senator Douglas instructed the Legislative Reference Service of the Library of Congress to develop a comprehensive program to aid depressed areas based upon the general principles developed by the Joint Committee on the Economic Report.[2]

Senator Douglas made a number of modifications in the draft bill presented by the Legislative Reference Service and circulated it among liberal Democratic colleagues. He then introduced the bill for himself and six co-sponsors on July 23, 1955, a few days before the close of the first session of the Eighty-fourth Congress.[3]

Originally it was intended that the draft of the bill would be held over until the 1956 session, which would have given the Senator, his staff, and other technicians sufficient time to improve and perfect it. As introduced, the bill had a number of technical flaws.[4] There are two interpretations for the apparent haste. The obvious reason might have been that Douglas was anxious to publicize his concern for a program to aid depressed areas and to solicit comments from interested parties during the interim before the opening of the 1956 session.

[2]Senator Douglas was not satisfied with the general recommendations made by the Joint Committee on the Economic Report and desired a specific legislative program which he could introduce as a bill. Howard Shuman, his legislative assistant, supplied the Legislative Reference Service with additional details which the Senator wanted included in the bill. The "Douglas man" for depressed areas was Harold Brown, who later became the top SBA official dealing with the ARA program.

[3]Many of the provisions of the bill (S. 2663) were "borrowed" from S. 751, Eighty-fourth Congress, introduced by Senators John F. Kennedy and Hubert H. Humphrey, which was an early version of the Trade Adjustment Act and which, in turn, was based upon some of the views developed by the Randall Commission. One major modification made by Senator Douglas included the deletion of the provision which would have subsidized mobility of labor from depressed areas.

[4]For example, the bill contained a provision which would have called for the establishment of a consultative advisory committee at a subcabinet level. Due to typographical error, the Department of Commerce was omitted from membership on the committee. This was interpreted as a slight to the then Secretary of Commerce, Sinclair Weeks. This error occurred in the original draft and was not caught in the hasty review given to the bill prior to its publication.

4   Federal Aid to Depressed Areas

There was also some pressure from labor lobbies, particularly from the
CIO, for a bill to aid depressed areas, and Douglas was committed to introduce such a bill. However, there was another reason, more political in nature, which might have motivated the Senator to hasten the
introduction of his bill.

Though the Administration had taken the official position that
depressed areas were a local problem, it was known that as early as
March, 1954, the Council of Economic Advisers had established a
task force to study the problems of depressed areas.[5] During 1954–55
the task force prepared a number of "administratively restricted"
papers which were basically in agreement with the position the council took in January, 1955. But this position became politically untenable, and it was known that Arthur F. Burns, chairman of the
council, was considering recommending some legislation to aid depressed areas. Within a week after Douglas introduced his bill, the
Budget Bureau submitted to the White House a paper on depressed
areas which had been drafted prior to the Douglas bill. It is possible
that the hasty introduction by Senator Douglas of his bill was intended
to prevent the "opposition" from jumping the gun on him. There is
some basis for this hypothesis because in January, 1956, the Council
of Economic Advisers reversed itself and found that "the fate of distressed communities is a matter of national as well as local concern."
The council also concluded that the existing programs were inadequate to cope with the problems of depressed areas and suggested
"that other measures are needed."[6] These views were embodied in
an Administration-backed bill introduced at the opening of the 1956
session.

THE FIRST ROUND—EIGHTY-FOURTH CONGRESS

The purpose of the Douglas bill (S. 2663) was to aid depressed industrial areas which had been subjected to high levels of chronic unemployment. Urban areas with average unemployment of 6 per cent
for a period of three years or 9 per cent for a period of eighteen
months were eligible for assistance. Underlying Douglas' approach was
the assumption that there was inadequate venture capital in such

[5]This was a task force on local unemployment consisting of top technicians from
the Council of Economic Advisers (Collis Stocking, chairman, Clarence D. Long,
and Irving H. Siegel), the Department of Commerce (Louis Paradiso and Victor
Roterus), the Department of Labor (Louis Levine), the Office of Defense Mobilization (John F. Hilliard), and the Small Business Administration (Jules Abels).

areas for new or expanding industry. He therefore called for the establishment of a $100 million revolving fund from which new or expanding industries in depressed areas could borrow funds, at low rates of interest, to cover as much as two-thirds of their capital needs for land, building, and equipment. Another revolving fund of $100 million was to be established for construction of the public facilities needed to improve the infrastructure and public services offered by these communities. To help train unemployed workers in the depressed areas, the bill provided that the Secretary of Labor develop training facilities and authorized the extension of unemployment compensation to thirteen weeks for workers undergoing training. No limit was placed on the funds that might be expended for the training of workers and the payment of subsistence benefits. In addition, the bill provided for the extension of rapid tax-amortization privileges to firms locating in the depressed areas and urged federal agencies to procure "to the maximum practicable extent" supplies and services from depressed areas.

The Administration bill (S. 2892) provided only for the establishment of a $50 million revolving fund from which loans could be made to new or expanding firms in depressed areas. These included, according to the definition of the bill, labor markets with an average unemployment of 8 per cent for the major portion of each of the preceding three years.

With the opening of the 1956 session of the Eighty-fourth Congress, Senator Douglas lost little time in advancing the cause of his bill and took immediate steps to "process" it through the legislative mill. S. 2663 was referred to the Subcommittee on Labor of the Senate Labor and Public Welfare Committee. Douglas was the chairman of this subcommittee and on the second day of the session started hearings on his bill. Hearings were held intermittently over a period of nearly four months, and on July 12, 1956, the Senate Committee on Labor and Public Welfare reported the bill out with a number of changes. Douglas, as will be shown later, had second thoughts about the desirability of the rapid tax-amortization provision. This provision permitted firms in depressed areas to write off in five years, instead of the longer, normal depreciation period, the cost of new plants, including equipment and machinery.

As a result of the hearings, the provisions for eligibility were relaxed to qualify more areas for assistance under the Act. A major change made in the committee report on the bill was the extension of aid to low-income rural areas. During November, 1955, after the original

Douglas bill had been introduced, a subcommittee of the Joint Economic Committee, under the chairmanship of Senator John Sparkman, held hearings on the economic conditions of low-income rural areas and emphasized the economic needs of these areas.[12] Congressman Brooks Hays, of Arkansas, and other liberal congressmen from southern districts where underemployment in rural areas was a major economic problem urged Senator Douglas to include provisions in his bill which would also aid low-income rural areas. Such a provision had considerable political appeal since it was hoped that it would attract the support of congressmen from rural areas who had little to gain from Douglas' original bill. Also, the Sparkman report argued persuasively for including special provisions to aid rural areas.[13] Douglas therefore added a provision establishing a $50 million revolving fund to grant loans to firms locating in low-income rural areas. Assistance for public facilities was raised to $125 million, of which $75 million was to be allotted for loans and $50 million for grants.

By the time the Senate Committee on Labor and Public Welfare reported the bill out, Senator Douglas had left the committee to fill a spot vacated on the Senate Finance Committee and Senator John F. Kennedy had assumed the chairmanship of the Subcommittee on Labor. It became his responsibility to get the bill through the Senate.

Jurisdictional Snag

At this time, Senator J. William Fulbright, chairman of the Senate Committee on Banking and Currency, interposed a jurisdictional objection to the Senate's considering the bill reported by the Senate Committee on Labor and Public Welfare. Since the major provisions of the bill dealt with the extension of credit, Senator Fulbright claimed that it was properly within the jurisdiction of his committee and that the Senate could not take up the bill until the Senate Committee on Banking and Currency had held hearings and had reported it out to the Senate. However, Senator Fulbright did not insist upon interposing jurisdictional objections if the sponsors of S. 2663 would

[6]The negotiations for the introduction of the Fulbright amendments were carried out at the staff level: Jack Yingling represented Senator Fulbright, Lee White and Theodore Sorensen represented Senator Kennedy, and Frank McCulloch represented Senator Douglas. White and Sorensen later moved on to become top White House aides under President Kennedy, and McCulloch became the chairman of the NLRB.

accede to a number of amendments which he favored.[6] Fulbright's price for relinquishing jurisdiction centered on two provisions:

1. The bill as reported out by the Senate Committee on Labor and Public Welfare provided for the establishment of two separate revolving funds to extend loans to expanding or new firms in depressed areas: $100 million for urban areas and $50 million for rural areas. In addition, the bill limited assistance to the 300 poorest rural counties. Fulbright, coming from Arkansas, a low-income rural state, insisted that urban and rural areas receive equal treatment under the bill. He proposed that the bill impose no restrictions on the number of rural counties which might qualify for assistance—just as there were no limitations on the number of urban areas. Similarly, he demanded that the revolving fund for loans to urban and rural areas be equalized by raising the latter to $100 million.

2. Senator Fulbright insisted on the termination of the procurement provisions that gave areas which were eligible for assistance preferential treatment under federal procurement. This was a perennial controversy between New England and older industrial sections which favored preferential treatment for labor-surplus areas as against the growing industrial interests in the South and other areas.

Senator Kennedy stated that he would readily accept the first Fulbright amendment, but he was reluctant to accept the second. However, in order to expedite the passage of the bill through the Senate—this was July 25, 1956, and Congress was close to adjournment—he also agreed to the procurement amendment.[1]

There was little additional debate on the floor of the Senate with regard to introduction of the bill. The whole discussion on the controversial measure took only half an hour. It started about 10:30 in the evening, with only a handful of senators on the floor. The Senate adopted the bill formally on the next day by a 60–30 vote. Only three Democratic senators joined twenty-seven Republicans in voting against the bill, while a third of the Republicans voted for it.[2]

House Rules Committee Blocks S. 2663

In the House, the Committee on Banking and Currency meanwhile approved S. 2663 with only slight modifications. But further progress was stymied by the Rules Committee, which refused to clear it for House consideration. Two Democrats, including Chairman Howard Smith, and all four Republicans on the committee were opposed to the bill and bottled it up in their committee. This political alliance was a common occurrence during the fifties, and many liberal proposals were killed by the Rules Committee. On July 27, one day after the Senate approved the bill and the last day of the Eighty-fourth Congress, Congressman Daniel J. Flood declared on the floor of the House that he had tried to prevail upon Administration spokesmen to help clear its bill for House consideration, but his entreaties and those of his Republican colleagues were of no avail. According to Congressman Flood, the Republican leadership in the House and the representatives of the Department of Commerce who spoke for the Administration on matters relating to depressed areas "refused even to agree to consider the Administration bill as proposed by their President."[3] A few days later, President Eisenhower denied that he knew anything about the attempt to bring his bill up for House consideration, but Congressman Flood's allegations were never denied.[7]

The Battle Lines Are Formed

The refusal of the Republican Administration to consider any bill to aid depressed areas killed the chances for any legislation during the Eighty-fourth Congress. The bill became a legislative bone of contention during the next five years and a major political issue in the 1958 congressional elections and in the 1960 presidential primaries and election. But despite the prolonged legislative skirmishes, Senator Douglas' approach to aiding depressed areas changed little over the years. The same was basically true of the Administration's approach. As the position of the parties hardened, some of Douglas' support faded. A number of Republican senators and some southern Democrats who voted for S. 2663 withdrew their support. Even in 1961, with the change of administrations and with a Democratic two-to-one majority, the Douglas bill mustered only three more Senate votes than in the Eighty-fourth Congress.

When Douglas introduced his bill in 1955, there was very little interest in the program. The country was generally prosperous, unemployment hovered nationally around the 4 per cent level, and there was little national awareness of depressed-area problems. The two-to-one support that the bill gained in the Senate in 1956 was not a result of wide recognition of the problem; it was rather due to the fact that arguments against the legislation had not been sufficiently developed and that the opposition had not coalesced. Numerous representatives of local chambers of commerce testified in favor of the bill before the Douglas subcommittee while the opposition was scattered and unorganized.[7] Under the circumstances, many senators found it rather difficult to vote against a modest measure to combat chronic unemployment in depressed areas.

The failure of the House to act in 1956 gave the opposition a chance to organize and to muster its forces. The Administration succeeded in gathering support for its own measure, thus offering an alternative to the Republicans who wished to vote against the Douglas program. The U.S. Chamber of Commerce, which opposed any legislation to aid depressed areas, organized an educational campaign against the legislation and exerted influence upon local chapters in depressed areas to withdraw their support from the Douglas bill.[8] On the other hand, the AFL-CIO supported the Douglas bill but never placed it on the top of its legislative priority list.[9] To organize support for the Douglas bill, proponents formed the Area Employment Expansion Committee, which was financed by modest union contributions.[10]

ROUND TWO—EIGHTY-FIFTH CONGRESS

Shortly after the opening of the Eighty-fifth Congress in 1957, Senator Douglas introduced another bill to aid depressed areas (S. 964). It differed little from the bill which was approved by the Senate the previous year. An Administration bill (S. 1433), introduced by Senator Martin, of Pennsylvania, was also very similar to its 1956 predecessor. This time both bills were referred to the Senate Commit-

[7]For an excellent and detailed account of the lobbying organizations and pressures that dealt with the depressed-area legislation, see Roger Davidson, "The Depressed Areas Controversy: A Case of American Business Politics" (Unpublished Ph.D. dissertation, Columbia University, 1963). The original plans of the present study called for an examination of the lobby operations, but Dr. Davidson's study makes such a discussion superfluous.

[8]While the chamber leadership would normally oppose legislation which would interfere with free-market mechanisms, as was implied in the Douglas and the Administration proposals, the credit or blame, depending upon one's view, for supplying the intellectual arguments against the legislation is due to Guy Waterman, a brilliant young economist who was then on the staff of the U.S. Chamber of Commerce.

[9]The AFL-CIO staff economist charged with the responsibility of working on depressed-area legislation was Frank Fernbach, assistant director of research.

[10]While a number of people worked on this committee, Solomon Barkin, who was the research director of the Textile Workers Union of America, provided the intellectual leadership and guidance for the committee. The AFL-CIO Industrial Union Department was the major financial angel of the AEEC and contributed the bulk of the $10,000 raised by the committee to defray its expenses during its five years of activity.

tee on Banking and Currency. Meanwhile, Senator Fulbright, chairman of the committee, expanded the number of the Senate Banking and Currency subcommittees in order to give each of the Democratic members on the committee the chairmanship of a subcommittee. Senator Douglas was assigned the chairmanship of the Subcommittee on Production and Stabilization, and the bills on depressed areas were referred to his subcommittee. But Douglas found that his influence as the chairman of the subcommittee was considerably restricted, at least in so far as depressed-area legislation was concerned. In addition to Douglas, there was only one senator on the subcommittee who favored the legislation, while the other five members opposed the Douglas bill and, possibly, any other proposed legislation to aid depressed areas.[11]

The Subcommittee on Production and Stabilization held hearings on the Douglas and Administration bills during March, April, and May of 1957. These were largely repetitive of the 1956 hearings, with the notable exception that opponents of the legislation were better organized and more vocal in expressing their opposition. The number of local chambers of commerce that supported the bill was reduced because of increasing U.S. Chamber of Commerce pressure against it. Once the hearings were completed, Douglas found himself faced with a majority of the subcommittee clearly opposed to his bill. The legislation might have died at this stage, but the recession which started in the summer of 1957 and the increased unemployment during 1958 revived interest in measures to combat unemployment. Ironically, Douglas never viewed his program as an antirecession program. On the contrary, as an economist he realized that a successful program to aid depressed areas would be most effective during a generally prosperous period when the special inducement offered for the expansion of depressed, local economies would benefit from the general prosperity and labor shortages existing in other communities.

On the House side, bills to aid depressed areas lay dormant during 1957 and were resurrected in 1958 as part of hearings devoted to "legislation to relieve unemployment." The House Committee on Banking and Currency did not have a special subcommittee devoted to depressed-area problems, and none of the members of the committee in 1957 showed any particular zeal in behalf of the legislation, though

[11]The sole supporters of the Douglas bill on the subcommittee were Senator Sparkman and, of course, Douglas himself. The other members of the subcommittee were Senators Fulbright and Frear (Democrats) and Capehart, Bricker, and Bush (Republicans). Douglas charged that the composition of his subcommittee was stacked to prevent favorable consideration of depressed-area legislation.

a majority of the committee was in favor of aiding depressed areas. Brent Spence, the venerable chairman of the committee—who retired in 1962 at the age of eighty-eight and was at that time the senior member of Congress—did not place the Douglas program at the top of his priority list and seemed to view the bill with skepticism, in spite of the fact that he represented a depressed area.

On February 24, 1958, Senator Douglas took steps to revive his bill by holding a one-day hearing in Washington, concentrating on that portion of his program which would aid rural depressed areas. The only witnesses at this session were five professors of agricultural economics. But Douglas still did not have the votes to report his bill out from the subcommittee, and a nose count of the fifteen-member parent committee indicated that the bill would be defeated by an 8–7 vote. Douglas needed just one "convert" on the Banking and Currency Committee to gain a majority.

The break came when Senator Frederick G. Payne, of Maine, indicated interest in the passage of legislation to aid depressed areas. On March 11, 1958, he introduced for himself and six other Republican senators a bill (S. 3447) similar to the Douglas proposal. Senators Douglas and Payne found it relatively easy to compromise their differences and joined forces. Since Senator Payne was a member of the Banking and Currency Committee, Douglas now could count on a majority of the committee supporting the Douglas-Payne bill. His plan called for the full committee to take up the bill rather than having it first voted on by the subcommittee, where he faced certain defeat. It is not an unusual situation for a senator to place a bill before a parent committee if he expects his proposal to receive better treatment from the whole committee than from a subcommittee. However, Chairman Fulbright had by now expressed opposition to the Douglas approach; he favored instead a $2 billion community facilities bill as a means to combat the national recession, rather than assistance to selected depressed areas. It was evident that if Congress approved the Fulbright community facilities bill, the depressed-area program might be shoved aside.

On March 18, 1958, the Senate Committee on Banking and Currency met in public hearings to consider Fulbright's community facilities bill. Before the chairman had a chance to call any witnesses, Senator Payne moved that the committee go into executive session to consider the depressed-area bill. Senator Fulbright was apparently taken by surprise and objected to the unusual procedure of the proponents of depressed-area legislation. An acrimonious public discussion followed. But Douglas had the votes on his side, and Fulbright, while he opposed the legislation, was not disposed to frustrate the will of the majority, a goal he could easily have achieved given the broad powers which the chairman of a committee possesses. A majority of the committee voted to make the depressed-area bill the business of the committee. Within five weeks the Senate Committee on Banking and Currency reported out the Douglas-Payne bill (S. 3683).[14] A few weeks later the Senate approved a bill very similar to the one that had passed two years earlier. Instead of the two-to-one majority in favor of the bill in 1956, the vote in 1958 was forty-six in favor and thirty-six opposed. However, the bill still retained considerable bipartisan support; twenty-nine Democrats and seventeen Republicans voted for it, while twelve Democrats and twenty-four Republicans opposed it. Substantively, there was little difference between the 1956 and 1958 Senate bills. A major difference was that instead of establishing a new independent agency to administer the bill, as was planned in 1956, the 1958 bill placed the administration of the program under the Housing and Home Finance Agency. This was one of the compromises between Douglas and Payne. The Administration had insisted that the program be administered by the Commerce Department and had opposed the establishment of a new, independent agency. Douglas feared that conservative influences within the Commerce Department would tend to distort the purposes of the program and compromised with Payne by placing the administration of their bill in the HHFA.

The House also showed little inclination to blaze new trails and adopted with only minor changes the Senate-approved bill by a 216–159 majority. As in the Senate, there was considerable bipartisan support for the bill in the House: 159 Democrats were joined by 57 Republicans in support, while 46 Democrats and 113 Republicans voted against the program. Forty-five of the Democratic votes in favor of the bill came from the South, exclusive of the border states of Kentucky and West Virginia. As might be expected, the congressmen in these two states voted unanimously for the legislation.

The Eighty-fifth Congress adjourned shortly after it approved the depressed-area bill, and President Eisenhower nullified it with a pocket veto. The President's opposition to the program, as stated in his veto message, was based on the following points:

1. The bill allowed 100 per cent grants for public facilities.
2. The criteria for eligibility to qualify for assistance were loosely drawn.
3. The bill made rural areas eligible for assistance.

4. The bill failed to require adequate local participation for industrial and commercial loans.

5. The administration of the bill was placed in the HHFA rather than in the Department of Commerce.[8]

These were the basic differences between the Douglas-Payne bill and the Administration program, and the veto message apparently indicated that the President was not going to approve a bill which exceeded or departed from the Administration program to aid depressed areas.

ROUND THREE—EIGHTY-SIXTH CONGRESS

The presidential veto gave the Democrats a major issue in the 1958 congressional campaign, which was held during the height of the recession. The rate of unemployment during the summer and fall of 1958 exceeded 7 per cent and marked a new post-World War II high. Unemployment started to taper off in the fall, but by that time the campaign was over. Democratic candidates tended to make excessive claims for the impact which the legislation would have had and suggested, particularly in depressed areas, that the problem of unemployment would not have been as acute if the President had not vetoed the bill.

The 1958 congressional campaign centered on bread-and-butter issues, with unemployment playing a paramount role. It is therefore probably no accident that congressional districts with depressed areas, which would have been eligible for assistance under the vetoed Douglas bill, accounted for the bulk of the Democratic sweep—Democrats won forty-eight seats held by Republicans and lost only one seat to a Republican. About four out of five congressional districts where Democrats won Republican seats were located in depressed areas.

Most of the sophisticated senators and congressmen, particularly Senator Douglas, recognized that the possible benefits of the bill were emphasized beyond any realistic proportions. Nevertheless, with the opening of the Eighty-sixth Congress in 1959, a plethora of bills to aid depressed areas was introduced. The major ones included warmed-over versions of the Douglas bill (S. 722) and the Administration bill (S. 1064), and a new compromise bill by Senator Hugh Scott, of Pennsylvania (S. 268). The newly reconstituted Senate Committee on Banking and Currency, consisting of ten Democrats and five Republicans, gave Douglas a 9–6 vote in favor of his bill (seven Democrats and two Republicans for, three Democrats and three Republicans opposed). Douglas introduced his new bill with thirty-eight co-sponsors on January 27, 1959, and the Senate Committee on Banking and Currency approved it in less than two months.[15]

But the economic recovery during the spring of 1959 took the steam out of the legislative drive to aid depressed areas. By the time the bill came up before the Senate two months later, unemployment had dropped to 4.9 per cent, and economists predicted that it would continue to drop. (It turned out to be the lowest unemployment level during that and the next business cycle.) But despite the recovery, federal deficit financing continued to mount, and fiscal 1959 had the highest peacetime deficit ($12.4 billion) in U.S. history. The Administration blamed Congress for the high deficit and attacked the Democrats as being the party of "fiscal irresponsibility."

In this atmosphere, aid to depressed areas became a political football. The Administration continued to attack the Douglas bill, and the Democrats refused to accept the Scott bill or any other compromise measure. As a result, when the Douglas bill came up for a vote before the Senate on March 23, 1959, it only won by a 49–46 majority. Conservative Democrats withdrew their support of the bill, and a number of liberal Republicans who in previous Congresses voted in favor of the Douglas bill supported the Scott compromise. But when the Scott bill came up for a vote, it was rejected overwhelmingly (74–20) by a coalition of liberal Democrats who insisted upon the approval of their own bill, Administration stalwarts who supported the Republican bill, and conservatives who opposed all legislation to aid depressed areas. The Administration bill could muster only a few Democratic supporters and was defeated by a 52–43 vote. Since it contained no provisions to help rural depressed areas, it had little to offer the southern Democrats, and, of course, the liberals considered it completely inadequate.

One day after the Senate approved S. 722, the House Committee on Banking and Currency voted out a similar bill.[9] But the House committee was strongly influenced by the charges of "fiscal irresponsibility" and cut the authorization appreciably, presumably without initially impairing the program. This was an attempt by the Democratic majority of the House Committee on Banking and Currency to have their cake and eat it too.[12] The plan was to cut the initial au-

---

[12]The bill was reportedly worked out by John Barriere, majority staff member of the committee, who acted as the unofficial committee co-ordinator and tactician on matters pertaining to depressed-area legislation.

thorization without sacrificing any part of the program: the revolving funds for industrial and commercial loans were cut from the $200 million provided by the Douglas bill to $150 million, loans for public facilities were cut from $100 million to $50 million, and grants for public facilities were reduced from $75 million to $35 million. The annual authorizations of $19 million for vocational training, subsistence payments, and technical assistance were left unchanged. Thus the House strategists reduced the initial "cost" of the bill from the $389.5 million authorized by the Senate to $251 million. Presumably, the thought behind this strategy was that the reduced authorization would make it more difficult for the President to veto the bill; meanwhile the program would remain initially unaffected, since it would take some time to spend the funds authorized by the House. Hoping to retain southern rural support and possibly attract new converts, the House committee listed 662 rural counties which would be eligible for assistance under the bill. This, in part, later proved to be the undoing of the bill, since the eligibility requirements were based on rather flimsy information and opened the bill to attack by its opponents.[13]

The maneuver was of no avail. Howard Smith, chairman of the Rules Committee, remained adamant and refused to let the bill out of his committee for a vote. One Democrat and the four Republicans on the twelve-member committee supported the chairman. Since a majority vote of the Rules Committee is required to report a bill out to the House, this might have been the undoing of the bill had not hard economic facts operated to keep the issue alive. The decline in unemployment during the last few months of 1958 and the early months of 1959 was soon arrested, and the unemployment rate continued to fluctuate between 5 and 6 per cent during the next year. In September, 1959, before Congress adjourned, the Senate appointed a committee to study the causes of unemployment and to recommend

[13]The report from which the list was drawn was prepared by the Legislative Reference Service, Library of Congress, and stated: "In case legislation is enacted to aid low-income areas, techniques for measurement of the unemployment in such areas will obviously be necessary. Meanwhile, some *tentative and preliminary estimates* can be obtained as to the counties which might be aided by the proposed bills." (Italics in original.) U.S. House of Representatives, Committee on Banking and Currency. *Federal Assistance to Labor Surplus Areas,* 85th Cong., 1st Sess., 1957, p. 30. The 662 counties were selected from Department of Agriculture lists of the 500 counties which had the lowest levels of living for farm-operating families and the 500 counties having the highest percentage of commercial farms producing less than $2,500 worth of products for sale in 1954. The majority of the counties appeared on both lists and consequently the total number of counties declared eligible for assistance was 662.

appropriate cures. The committee made its report to the Senate in March, 1960, and while the Democrats and Republicans filed separate reports, both emphasized the need for legislation to aid depressed areas.[21] In addition, labor and other liberal groups continued to press for the legislation, and the Area Employment Expansion Committee, under the leadership of Solomon Barkin, continued its effective lobbying in favor of the program.

The crucial factor in favor of reviving the legislation was the promise given by Speaker Sam Rayburn to the proponents of the legislation that they would get a chance to present their bill in the House before the Eighty-sixth Congress adjourned. When Howard Smith and his supporters on the Rules Committee proved intransigent, the House Democratic leadership resorted on May 4, 1960, to the seldom-used Calendar Wednesday device to bring S. 722 before the House. The House rules provide that each Wednesday the chairmen of standing committees may bring up bills approved by their committees which they desire to present before the House. House action on such bills must be completed the same day. This procedure is seldom resorted to in the House, and prior to May 4, 1960, it was last used over a decade earlier. When Chairman Brent Spence called up S. 722 on May 4, 1960, the opposition resorted to a variety of parliamentary tactics to prevent a vote on the bill. But the coalition between the Republicans and southern Democrats broke down that day, and after protracted parliamentary delays, the House approved the bill by a vote of 202 (179 Democrats and 23 Republicans) to 184 (69 Democrats and 115 Republicans). A motion to substitute the Administration bill was rejected by a two-to-one standing vote.[14]

The Senate approved the House version of the bill two days later and sent it on to the President, who vetoed it on May 13, 1960. It was reported that Vice-President Nixon favored approval of the bill in order to remove aid to depressed areas as an issue in the forthcoming presidential election. This rumor, while widely circulated in the newspapers, was never confirmed. The presidential message accompanying the veto was largely a repeat of the arguments used two years earlier when the President rejected an earlier version of the legislation. An attempt on May 18 by the Senate to override the veto failed by a 45–39 vote in favor of the bill, short of the two-thirds majority required to override a veto. Southern Democratic support for the

[14]Unconfirmed reports suggested that White House pressure was exerted on Republican House leaders not to participate actively in the obstructionist delay tactics, which would have prevented the House from "voting its will."

depressed-area bill had almost disappeared: only four southeastern Democrats voted in favor of overriding the veto.

An attempt to revive the legislation during the closing days of the Eighty-sixth Congress proved futile. The Eighty-sixth Congress had adjourned during July to permit the members to attend the national conventions of their respective parties. The nomination of John F. Kennedy, who made aid to depressed areas a major issue in his crucial primary campaign in West Virginia, assured that the controversy would remain an issue in the 1960 presidential election. In a compromise attempt, the Administration announced it would be ready to support a bill which would authorize $75 million in loans to aid depressed industrial areas (S. 3569), but otherwise the new proposal differed little from the Administration's earlier bills. This gave Douglas the opportunity of charging that the Administration would only allow Congress to rubber-stamp its own bill and was not willing to compromise with congressional proposals.[18] Douglas, for his part, refused to compromise with the Administration position. He anticipated that his bill would have a better chance under the Democratic administration which he hoped would be elected later in the year.

THE FINAL ROUND—EIGHTY-SEVENTH CONGRESS

President John F. Kennedy, when he assumed office on January 20, 1961, was well acquainted with the problems of depressed areas. The problem was a familiar one in his native state of Massachusetts, and in 1956 he had led the floor debate which resulted in the first passage of the bill in the Senate. In the course of his campaign for the Presidency in 1960, he was further exposed to the problems of the most depressed areas in the United States.

The primary contest in West Virginia was crucial for Kennedy if he was to receive the presidential nomination, and he campaigned intensively in the state.[22] The campaign aroused the conscience of the American people about the economic plight of depressed areas and made the problems of these areas an important issue in the 1960 campaign. As a candidate, Kennedy promised that if he were elected, aid to depressed areas would receive top legislative and administrative priority.[15]

President Kennedy kept his promise and immediately after his elec-

---

[15]A compilation of Kennedy's campaign speeches revealed sixty-one separate references to the depressed-area issue. Roger Davidson, "The Depressed Areas Controversy," p. 163.

tion appointed a number of task forces to investigate the major issues which his administration would face. These task forces were to make policy recommendations in their respective areas. The importance President Kennedy attached to the problems of depressed areas is shown by his singling out this task force for special publicity and by his appointing the top expert on depressed areas, Senator Douglas, as chairman of the group. The report prepared by the task force was submitted to the President-elect on New Year's Day; it recommended a comprehensive, multibillion-dollar aid program for aid to depressed areas. Moreover, it designated the Douglas program as an immediate first step in this program.

The Senate leadership indicated the priority it gave to the depressed-area program by assigning the Douglas bill the coveted S.1. Thirty-eight Democrats and five Republicans joined Senator Douglas as co-sponsors of his bill.

The Douglas bill's designation proved to be a mixed blessing. It meant that the bill had to be ready by the time the Senate opened for business. The election of a new administration made it possible, for the first time, for the technicians in the Labor and other departments to assist actively in improving the draft of the bill. During the Eisenhower Administration, Douglas received very limited aid from technical experts in the executive departments, and frequently such assistance had to come "unofficially." The Administration was not going to extend any aid either to improve or to perfect a bill which it strongly opposed. It was known that during the years when the bill was under consideration, technicians in the various executive agencies had offered technical as well as substantive recommendations to their respective chiefs for improving Douglas' depressed-area program. However, this advice was not made available to the Senator. After the 1960 election, the technicians felt free to offer the fruits of their labor. But Douglas was away from Washington during most of December, resting from his arduous campaign (he had won by 437,000 votes, double his 1954 majority), and the staff member he left in charge of the bill did not feel free to incorporate the substantive recommendations made by the executive agencies.[16]

The President-elect designated his Senate legislative assistant, Myer Feldman, to represent the new Administration on redrafting the depressed-area bill.[17] But Feldman became involved with problems

[16]Milton Semer, later general counsel for the Housing and Home Finance Administration.

[17]Feldman was later appointed deputy special counsel to the President.

surrounding the presidential transition and left the redrafting of the bill to Douglas' representative.

As a result, S. 1 as introduced was very similar to S. 722, which Douglas had introduced in the previous Congress. Of course, additional changes could have been made in the committee, and some were actually included before the bill was reported out by the Senate Banking and Currency Committee. An evaluation of the "lost" recommendations prepared by the technicians in the Department of Labor amply supports the conclusion that the final legislation would have been much improved if these recommendations had received the consideration due them. The major effect of the proposed technical amendments would have been to clarify and tighten the eligibility requirements of areas qualifying for assistance. If these amendments had been adopted, they would have saved the Area Redevelopment Administration considerable difficulties.[18]

Douglas started hearings on S. 1 two days before the inauguration of the new President, his idea being to combine some business with the inaugural festivities. Democratic luminaries from all over the country converged on Washington, and Douglas used the occasion to bring them before his subcommittee to endorse the bill. According to an unconfirmed rumor, he intended to hold hearings for just the two days prior to the inauguration and then to get the bill to the Senate immediately after President Kennedy took office. But the Republican members of the subcommittee insisted on hearing spokesmen from the newly appointed Administration on the proposed legislation. These were merely delaying tactics, since Douglas knew that, with strong Administration backing, he had the votes to push his program through the Senate.

Interestingly enough, the only fly in the ointment came from the Administration. Five days after he took office, President Kennedy sent Congress his own depressed-area bill; it paralleled S. 1 but contained some significant differences. The most important clash came from the Administration's desire to place the administration of the program within the Department of Commerce, rather than in an independent agency. The new White House spokesman on depressed-area legislation, Myer Feldman, an assistant counsel, was well aware of Senator Douglas' opposition to having the program placed within the Department of Commerce. Douglas was quite adamant on this point.

[18]Most of these amendments were prepared under the guidance of Mrs. Aryness Wickens, at that time economic adviser to Secretary of Labor James P. Mitchell, Robert Goodwin and Louis Levine, the two top officials of the Bureau of Employment Security.

The reasons that led the Administration to oppose Douglas on this point are not quite clear. The normal good-management opposition to "proliferation of new agencies" propounded by the Budget Bureau does not appear as an adequate reason for the Administration to oppose Douglas. Another reason may therefore be more appropriate. It was known that the newly appointed Secretary of Commerce, Luther Hodges, wanted the depressed-area program under his wing and the Administration may have been favorably disposed to "beef up" the Department of Commerce. The new Secretary of Commerce was one of the major southern supporters of President Kennedy, and the Administration may have found it more difficult to oppose his views. Anyway, Douglas was about to have the rest of the bill for which he had fought for six continuous years.

Douglas had to acquiesce to Administration desires by agreeing to have his program placed in the camp of the "enemy," the Department of Commerce. But the rest was easy. On March 15, 1961, the Senate approved the Douglas program to aid depressed areas by a 63–27 vote. Ten southern Democrats and Senator Frank J. Lausche, of Ohio, who normally votes with southern conservatives on welfare legislation, remained steadfast in their opposition to the program. Surprisingly, the Republicans were almost evenly divided on the final vote: fifteen Republicans voted in favor of S. 1, while sixteen opposed the bill to the end.

The House acted two weeks later, on March 29, 1961. Here, too, the changed sentiment in favor of the bill was clear-cut, and the enlarged Rules Committee was no longer an obstacle in getting the bill before the House. In 1960 the bill won in the House by only a score of votes. Yet, despite the fact that the Democrats lost double that number of votes in the Eighty-seventh Congress, most of whom had supported the bill in 1960, the House approved S. 1 by the comfortable margin of 251–167. Forty-three Republicans, almost a quarter of all those voting, deserted the reservation on this occasion to vote for the bill, while 125 Republicans and 42 Democrats remained opposed.

The President signed the Area Redevelopment Act (P.L. 87–27) on May 1, 1961, almost six years after Douglas had originally introduced the legislation.

ISSUES RAISED BY THE AREA REDEVELOPMENT LEGISLATION

The survival of the program to aid depressed areas through protracted legislative conflict is easily explainable. When Senator Douglas originally introduced the program in July, 1955, his bill evoked little attention either in Congress or outside. The public was little concerned with problems of unemployment during a period of economic prosperity and expansion. "In the beginning," a Douglas staff man said, "P.H.D. was all alone." Douglas recognized that over-all economic growth was uneven and that high levels of chronic unemployment in selected areas served as a drag on the total economy. Moreover, concern for the lot of the unemployed in the depressed areas was sufficient reason for him to inaugurate a program which he thought would help the unemployed in the area.

The creeping unemployment which prevailed in the country throughout most of the six years following the introduction of the Douglas bill stimulated increased interest in his program. When the Senate approved the Douglas bill in 1956, 21 of the nation's 149 major labor-market areas averaged an unemployment rate in excess of 6 per cent, which the Department of Labor classifies as "substantial labor surplus." In 1958 the average number of substantial labor-surplus areas rose to 69. While the number of such areas declined from 1958 to 1960, there still remained almost twice as many labor-surplus areas in 1960 as in 1956. When Congress finally approved the bill, during the recession of 1961, two out of every three major labor-market areas had unemployment above 6 per cent. This disturbingly high level of unemployment, which prevailed during the years while the Douglas bill was being debated in Congress, helped gain support for the program. There is little chance that the bill would have survived in a high-employment economy, although a prosperous and growing economy would have been best suited for its successful administration. An ambitious program introduced in 1949 to help labor-surplus areas died a-borning with the economic recovery in 1950 and the full employment which prevailed during the subsequent years.[19]

[19]The "Economic Expansion Act of 1949" (S. 281, 81st Congress) was introduced by Senator James Murray and co-sponsored by fourteen other Democrats and two Republicans. Title V of the bill was concerned with the "treatment of serious unemployment whenever it arises in any geographic or industrial area." The bill provided for a $2.2 billion fund to aid depressed areas, $100 million annual ex-

A program to help depressed areas would appear to have been good politics during the late fifties, and the cost of the program does not adequately explain the opposition it experienced. To be sure, one should not take lightly the authorization of nearly $400 million of new expenditures, which still remains a respectable chunk of money. But Congress annually approves several times that amount for pork barrel legislation, and certainly enough senators and congressmen were sufficiently interested in the program to assure its enactment as part of a legislative deal. Moreover, the total authorization advocated by Douglas amounted to less than 0.5 per cent of the total federal budget in 1961, and more than three-quarters of that amount was earmarked for the establishment of revolving funds to be used for the disbursement of loans, presumably to be repaid eventually to the federal treasury. The actual expenditures contemplated by the advocates of the program would have constituted, therefore, only about one-thousandth of the annual federal expenditures.

Obviously, money expenditures do not adequately explain the protracted debate over the bill and the willingness on the part of the Eisenhower Administration to give the Democrats a political issue in two successive campaigns, particularly after the debacle of the 1958 congressional elections. The explanation for the controversy that arose over the program must therefore be found elsewhere. It involved deep issues concerning the proper role which the federal government should play in the economic life of the nation, in long-standing regional conflicts over national economic policies, and in congressional procedures, which may leave the public cold, but are dear just the same to the hearts of many congressmen.

Higher Level Debate: The Philosophic Issue

In its most elementary form, the debate about aid to depressed areas centered around the question of whether this was an appropriate field of action for the federal government. Proponents of the legislation were fond of insisting that such a debate was fruitless and would serve only to turn the clock back. They suggested that this issue had already been settled in the post-World War II period when Congress adopted the Employment Act of 1946. This Act made it the responsibility of the federal government to create an economic climate which stimulates

penditures for retraining and relocating the unemployed, and preferential treatment to depressed areas in government procurement. Douglas, a freshman senator at that time, was not among the seventeen sponsors of the bill, and there is no evidence that it in any way influenced his more modest program of 1955.

maximum employment and production. The very existence of chronically depressed areas, according to Senator Douglas and his associates, indicated the failure of the federal government in meeting its responsibility. The phenomenon had to be overcome by a special federal program designed to aid the depressed areas.

Senator Kennedy, who acted in 1956 as floor manager for the Douglas bill, stated:

> The responsibility of the Federal Government to aid such areas is commonly acknowledged. The responsibility is in the interest of the areas which are subject to chronic unemployment and underemployment, and coincides also with the interests of the Nation. The fact is that these less fortunate areas exert a general drag upon the economy, and the Federal Government, in order to assure full prosperity for the Nation as a whole, should do all it can to eliminate pockets of unemployment and underemployment.[1]

And, again, on the same occasion: "It is more than a decade since Congress declared it to be the policy of this Government to utilize its resources in order to establish conditions which would assure maximum employment throughout the United States."[1]

Not surprisingly, Senator Barry Goldwater, of Arizona, remained unimpressed. He acknowledged the existence of depressed areas but found the situation neither alarming nor new, however unfortunate. To the Senator from Arizona this was a normal application of economic Darwinism and part of the cost of change.[20] Throughout our history, according to Goldwater, the nation has "experienced the boom development of certain areas, only to realize, at some later date when the economic sources were dissipated, the collapse of whole communities, which exist today only as ghost towns."[20]

In the past, such developments, Goldwater explained, were taken for granted, and the people in such communities did not turn to the federal government for a handout. Victims of declining communities accepted their tribulations "with stout hearts and strong backs." Senator Goldwater did not think that the clamor for federal legislation to

---

[20]"The ARA signifies a rejection of economic Darwinism. This is not taken to mean that every area has a potential that can be exploited for the purpose of economic growth. What it does mean is that we do not know the potentials of any area until an exhaustive program of action research has been undertaken by the community itself, and steps taken to implement the suggested solutions emanating from such an analysis." Address by Dr. Harold L. Sheppard, assistant administrator, ARA, before the National University Extension Association Annual Meeting, April 29, 1962, Lincoln, Nebraska.

aid depressed areas was necessarily an indication of the deterioration of the moral fiber of the American people, but rather "a phobia afflicting certain politicians and pseudo-liberal left-wing theorizers, who would substitute for our free enterprise system the awful spectre of the planned superstate."[20] The problems of depressed areas would disappear, concluded Goldwater, if the central planners in Washington would not continue to insist upon thwarting the free enterprise system.

The Eisenhower Administration, as we have seen, at first seemed to have been in sympathy with the Goldwater viewpoint, though it never spoke with such strong words. In 1955 the Council of Economic Advisers viewed the problem of depressed areas as one that "should be carried out by the local citizens themselves."[5] But a year later the council seemed to have had a change of heart and found that "the fate of distressed communities is a matter of national as well as local concern."[6]

Is Federal Financing Necessary?

Setting principles aside, Douglas' opponents questioned whether the tools offered by the depressed-area program would provide adequate medicine for correcting the ailments of these areas. They rejected the assertion that lack of adequate venture capital is the cause of depressed conditions in selected labor-market areas. The Republican minority on the House Committee on Banking and Currency in 1959 based its opposition to the committee-approved bill basically on the position that lack of capital is not a major factor impeding the rehabilitation or economic growth of the depressed areas.[9] The opponents assumed that a promising venture would attract private capital and that government financing would be channeled to unsound projects. The opponents of the Douglas program insisted that local interests are normally adequate for meeting the needs of communities and that the financing necessary for attracting new industry can be raised at the local level without federal financing. In short, the opponents of the program insisted that private capital is sufficiently mobile and would take advantage of any promising opportunities, and that optimum national production would result if the government did not interfere with the operations of the "unseen hand."

In the same vein, Senator Wallace F. Bennett, of Utah, argued that ample resources are available in numerous depressed areas to attract industry and that many of these communities have constructed shell buildings which have failed to attract new industry.[16] The moral of this argument was obvious: obstacles to the economic rehabilitation of depressed areas do not lie in the absence of venture capital but rather in inherent weaknesses of the local economies which cannot be corrected by the federal government throwing good money after bad. Similarly, the opponents of the Douglas program suggested that so-called depressed areas do not have any problems in raising money for the construction of public facilities.[10]

These arguments were, of course, denied by Senator Douglas and his supporters. They noted that witnesses from numerous communities throughout the United States, testifying before the Senate and House Committees on Banking and Currency on depressed areas, had asserted that lack of venture capital and inadequate public facilities hindered the economic development of their communities. As in most such arguments, neither side convinced the other, and it is likely that both sides were right. Since hundreds of communities were involved, obviously it was easy to find instances supporting the contentions of either side. One can only conclude that the antagonists looked at different parts of the elephant and came up with different pictures.

The Camel's Nose

It was unavoidable that the opponents of the program should look into the future and see the sinister possibilities of the program. They feared that the Douglas program represented only the proverbial camel's nose and that once adopted it would commit the federal government to continued interference with private decision-making and substitute government financing for the free enterprise system. They pointed to the billions of dollars of private capital already invested in those areas which the Douglas program was designed to assist, and they asserted that, even under the most favorable conditions, the $200 million which Senator Douglas proposed to loan to businesses expanding or locating in depressed areas would just constitute "a drop in the bucket."

In reply to critics who asserted that the proposed legislation was too skimpy, Douglas never denied that additional authorizations might be necessary if the program proved successful. But he was willing to start with a modest program, though he was ready to favor a larger, initial authorization if that would win additional support. He chided his conservative opponents who criticized the bill on the basis that it was too limited to have any impact.

MR. DOUGLAS: Does the Senator from Indiana wish to offer an amendment to double the sum of money available under the bill, since he thinks the sum is not adequate in amount?

MR. CAPEHART: I would be happy to double the amount provided in the bill if the Senator would accept my amendment.

MR. DOUGLAS: No. If the Senator will double the amount, then we can do more for the areas for which his heart is bleeding.[4]

On one occasion, Douglas ended this type of argument with a Chinese proverb, "A thousand mile journey begins with a single step." To which Senator Bennett replied, "I am neither Chinese nor a philosopher, but I know that if that first step starts out in the wrong direction, we must travel more than the original thousand miles. . . ."[18]

Regional Conflicts

The battle was by no means fought on lofty philosophical grounds. More immediate practical factors played an important role. By its very nature the legislation was aimed at extending help only to selected areas; but during most of the period while the bill was debated in Congress, the nation experienced economic slack and rising unemployment, and not a single major labor market throughout this period experienced general labor shortages. Under these circumstances, some congressmen simply refused to vote for legislation that might encourage potential employers to locate in areas other than their own.

Moreover, some congressmen who indicated a general sympathy for the Douglas program feared that established industry in more prosperous communities would relocate in areas favored by the legislation, in order to benefit from federal aid. This is the runaway-shop argument. The proponents of this argument sought guarantees that the legislation would not assist the relocation of industry, which they finally succeeded in getting into the bill.[9] Nevertheless, the nature of the legislation made it impossible to extend ironclad guarantees that relocation would be completely avoided. An employer could still establish a branch plant in a depressed area and then transfer his activities slowly to the new community. Such transfers would be difficult to police, particularly if the employer could show that production costs in the new branch were more profitable and economical. It is hard to evaluate the effectiveness of the whole program on the basis of this possibility. Nevertheless, those who had reservations about the program solely on the basis of the runaway-shop argument were satisfied by the prohibition of relocation and voted for the program.

However, the opposition of southern congressmen who voted against the area redevelopment bill appears on the surface more puzzling, since many of their districts would have benefited by the legislation. No doubt many of them voted against the legislation because of general hostility to federal welfare legislation. Regional economic interests also played a role in their animosity. For example, Senator Fulbright stated in 1958 that he opposed the Douglas program because he considered it as "special legislation for a few spots in Illinois, Pennsylvania and a few other places. I am interested in national legislation."[19]

Senator Fulbright was not opposed to additional federal expenditures, for instead of the depressed-area legislation, he favored a $2 billion community facilities program. From a regional point of view this approach was obviously sound. Given the construction of public facilities with federal money, the lower wages, ample labor supply, and rich natural resources, many areas in the South would obviously have a distinct relative advantage in competition with older industrial areas in the North. Fulbright and other sophisticated southern members may have therefore felt that the Douglas legislation would not necessarily benefit the South in the long run, since industry of its own account chose the low-wage southern areas for new plants. Others who were even opposed to the public-facilities program may have believed that the comparative advantages of the South would have worked in favor of the region without any federal assistance. In addition, southern spokesmen thought that the region had already organized financial subsidy programs and therefore had an advantage over other areas in attracting new industry. Theirs was an attitude of "God save us from our friends and we'll take care of the enemies."

CONCLUSION

The controversy over depressed-area legislation involved much more than an authorization of some $389 million. It was concerned with the basic philosophic issue of the role of the federal government in the economic development of local economies. The Employment Act of 1946 provided that the federal government would be responsible for the creation of an appropriate economic climate to foster maximum production and employment. The depressed-area legislation committed the federal government to provide the funds for generating new economic activity and employment. Therefore, it goes considerably beyond the apparent, original intent of the 1946 Employment Act.

The Area Redevelopment Act also touched upon deep, regional economic conflicts and called for active federal participation in the development of private as well as public sectors of local economies. The fears of the opponents that the original Area Redevelopment Act would constitute a new welfare program and stimulate additional federal aid to depressed areas had materialized by 1963. Within less than two years after the Area Redevelopment Act was approved, the Kennedy Administration requested Congress to more than double the original authorization. This legislation was pending before Congress in mid-1963. The advocates of the legislation have claimed that the accomplishments of the ARA during its first two years of existence justify continued support.

The achievement of the ARA mission to combat unemployment and underemployment in the nation's economically distressed areas would have been a difficult task under the best of circumstances. With the high level of unemployment that has prevailed nationally during the past two years, this task has been even more formidable. It will take years before the ARA's impact on the economy can be fully measured. Meanwhile, the debate for a federal program to aid depressed areas will continue and the protagonists will find ammunition in ARA activities to support their respective positions.

REFERENCES

1. *Congressional Record.* July 25, 1956, p. 13313. All references are to daily editions.
2. *Congressional Record.* July 26, 1956, p. 13355.
3. *Congressional Record.* July 28, 1956, p. A5984.
4. *Congressional Record.* March 15, 1961, p. 3765.
5. *Economic Report of the President.* Washington: Government Printing Office, 1955, p. 57.
6. *Economic Report of the President.* Washington: Government Printing Office, 1956, p. 61.
7. *New York Times.* August 2, 1956.
8. *New York Times.* September 7, 1958.
9. U.S. House of Representatives, Committee on Banking and Currency. *Area Redevelopment Act.* Report 360, 86th Cong., 1st Sess. Washington: Government Printing Office, May 14, 1959, pp. 29–43, 40–42.
10. ———. Report 186, 87th Cong., 1st Sess., March 22, 1961, pp. 37–39.

11. U.S. Congress, Joint Committee on the Economic Report. *Joint Economic Report.* Report 60, 84th Cong., 1st Sess., March 14, 1955, pp. 38–40.
12. ———. *Hearings on Low Income Families.* 84th Cong., 1st Sess., 1955.
13. ———. *A Program for the Low Income Population.* 84th Cong., 1st Sess., 1955, pp. 8–11.
14. U.S. Senate, Committee on Banking and Currency. *Area Redevelopment Act.* Report 1494, 85th Cong., 2d Sess., April 28, 1958.
15. ———. Report 110, 86th Cong., 1st Sess., March 18, 1959.
16. ———. Report 61, 87th Cong., 1st Sess., March 8, 1961, pp. 50–59.
17. ———. *Hearings on Area Redevelopment Legislation.* 86th Cong., 1st Sess., August 18, 1960, p. 6.
18. ———. *Hearings on Area Redevelopment Act Amendments of 1963.* 88th Cong., 1st Sess., 1963, p. 292.
19. ———. *Hearings on Community Facilities Act of 1958.* 85th Cong., 2d Sess., 1958, p. 2.
20. U.S. Senate, Committee on Labor and Public Welfare. *Area Redevelopment Act.* Report 2555, 84th Cong., 2d Sess., July 12, 1956, p. 54.
21. U.S. Senate, Special Committee on Unemployment Problems. Report 1206, 86th Cong., 2d Sess., March 30, 1960.
22. White, Theodore H. *The Making of the President 1960.* New York: Atheneum, 1961, pp. 123–37.

Chapter 2

✦✦✦✦✦✦✦✦✦✦✦✦✦✦✦✦✦✦✦✦✦✦

The ARA Sets Up Shop

✦✦✦

On May 1, 1961, President John F. Kennedy put his signature to the Area Redevelopment Act (P.L. 87–27), the first major legislative product of the New Frontier. In signing the bill, he observed that there was "no piece of legislation . . . which gives me greater satisfaction to sign." The President also voiced great hopes for the long-range impact of the new law. "In this free society," he stated, "we want to make it possible for everyone to find a job who wants to work . . . and this bill is an important step in that direction."[5]

A less propitious moment could hardly have been selected for inauguration of the area redevelopment program. The nation was just emerging from the trough of its fourth post-World War II recession, and unemployment hovered around the five-million mark—or 7 per cent of the civilian labor force. Moreover, this disturbingly high rate of unemployment was relatively widespread: about two of every three major labor markets reported at least 6 per cent jobless. Despite general economic recovery during the next two years, large-scale unemployment persisted. While unemployment averaged 6.7 per cent of the labor force in 1961, it declined only gradually to 5.6 per cent the following year and remained at that level during the first half of 1963.

This was an unfavorable environment for the infant program. Depressed-area assistance would be most effective in a tight national labor market, when the affected areas would enjoy the distinct advantage of surplus manpower in attracting new industry. The depressed-area program inaugurated by West Germany a decade earlier, for example, owed its success in large measure to the existence of sustained full-employment conditions which prevailed in the country after the passage of the legislation. With the loose labor market which prevailed following the enactment of P.L. 87–27, however, most communities throughout the United States were forced to compete intensively for available industries and jobs. Under such conditions, the disadvantageous position of the labor-surplus areas was only heightened. It was under such a handicap that the new Area Redevelopment Administration set up operations in mid-1961.

THE ORGANIZATIONAL FRAMEWORK

Recruitment of Personnel

Upon signing S. 1 into law, President Kennedy appointed William L. Batt, Jr., as administrator of the Area Redevelopment Administration.[1] Batt had long experience with depressed-area programs. During the Truman and Eisenhower Administrations he had served as a special assistant to the Secretary of Labor; and in this capacity he had helped to draft Defense Manpower Policy No. 4 (1953), a directive designed to give preference to depressed areas in government procurement policies. Later, as secretary of labor and industry in Pennsylvania, a position he held under two governors, Batt was active in the implementation of the Pennsylvania Industrial Development Authority (PIDA).

Batt was also a key participant in the six-year struggle leading to passage of the Area Redevelopment Act. As a cabinet member in his home state of Pennsylvania, he testified repeatedly before congressional committees concerning the Pennsylvania experience. With Solomon Barkin, he was a co-organizer of the Area Employment Expansion Committee, a lobbying group established in 1956 to encourage passage of the legislation. In late 1960 Batt was named to President-elect Kennedy's special Task Force on Area Redevelopment. As a chief aide, Batt brought along his capable associate in the Pennsylvania Department of Labor and Industry, Harold W. Williams, who later became deputy administrator of the ARA.

Batt's most pressing initial problem was the recruitment of competent staff personnel for the new agency. Though unemployment in the early nineteen-sixties was geographically widespread, it was heavily

[1]According to P.L. 87–27, the Secretary of Commerce is technically responsible for administering the program. However, the entire congressional debate was in terms of a separate administrator, and in practice, the Secretary of Commerce has delegated actual direction of the program to the Area Redevelopment Administrator. Hence, the term "Administrator" is used in this study to refer to the latter official.

concentrated among certain demographic groupings—blue-collar workers, ethnic and racial minorities, and young people. For the white-collar, professional worker sought by the ARA, there were plenty of jobs to be found. And during the postwar period, governmental salaries—at least at the higher professional levels—tended to lag behind salaries in private industry and were even lower than in the better-financed universities and colleges from which the ARA particularly hoped to attract talented manpower.

Another source of high-level personnel for a new agency, the "raiding" of established federal agencies, was foreclosed by the bill's primary sponsor, Senator Douglas. The Illinois senator was opposed on principle to high civil service salaries. During congressional consideration of his bill, Douglas insisted upon limiting the number of "supergrade" civil service positions allotted to the new agency. ("Supergrades" refer to the highest three civil service grades.) In fact, the Senate version of the 1961 bill authorized only one supergrade for the ARA; the House bill, which originally provided for fifteen, was pared down on the floor to five, and this number went into the final wording.[2]

This limitation proved to be something of a burden in the ARA's early recruitment efforts. Civil servants are, quite naturally, reluctant to leave their jobs in established federal agencies in order to join a unit whose future is at best uncertain. To overcome this handicap, a new agency often uses the inducement of "supergrade" jobs in luring top personnel away from posts of greater security. Moreover, the ARA's relatively small allotment of supergrades tended to lower the civil service ratings of those who could be recruited up and down the organizational hierarchy. This resulted from the fact that a civil servant's rank determines the rank of those who can be hired to serve under him. With only five supergrade personnel, the ARA had to assign lower grades to supervisory posts, thus in turn lowering the ranks of subordinates.

Despite these two hurdles, the ARA did have an initial personnel cadre. This was in existence, even before P.L. 87–27 was signed, in the experienced corps of personnel in the Commerce Department's Office of Area Development (OAD). Virtually all of the OAD's staff of approximately fifty persons were retained by Batt, though some were reassigned to different jobs within the agency. The ARA was thus overlaid upon the old OAD, an operation which was carried off with surprisingly little friction.

At a relatively early date, it was determined that the ARA would be a small, co-ordinating unit of no more than three hundred persons.

This decision was reached by Secretary Hodges in the spring of 1961 and was agreed to readily by Batt and his advisers. Once the Act was signed, the hiring began in earnest, and by the end of September about one hundred people had been signed up. Congressional failure to appropriate funds for the ARA until October apparently was not a serious problem, since Congress authorized the obligation of funds in the interim period. Moreover, the ARA could not possibly have obtained its full complement of personnel within that time.

It should be noted parenthetically that the ARA divisions concerned with field operations and the processing of applications filled up their staff rosters somewhat faster than the research division. The ARA's preoccupation with short-term "results" at the expense of basic research—a phenomenon to be discussed presently—was probably the primary cause. Another may have been the fact that those in charge of operations were more aggressive and more imbued with a sense of urgency in getting the program underway than was true of the research people. The type of personnel skills required for operations was no less scarce than those needed for research. The operations men had to combine technical knowledge of economic development and community finances with the political skills required to work with various community interests involved in ARA activities.

Table 2-1: ARA Personnel, Fiscal 1961–64

	1961 Actual	1962 Actual	1963 Estimate	1964 Estimate
Total number (permanent)	44	296	388	466
Other (full-time equivalent)	2	33	28	26
Average number, all employees	39	214	376	466
Number of employees, end of FY	44	347	444	522

SOURCE: U.S. House of Representatives, Committee on Appropriations, *1963 and 1964 Budget Hearings.*

Given the executive decision to limit the ARA's mission to that of a co-ordinator-supervisor, congressional authorizations for personnel were most generous; for fiscal 1962 and 1963, Congress approved all ARA requests for personnel. Yet the agency has labored constantly under the handicap of manpower shortages. Basic research on unemployment problems probably suffered the greatest from an early lack of personnel. Inadequate staff was also a basic culprit in the continuing crisis over slowness in processing aid applications. Appearing before an Appropriations subcommittee in February, 1963, Batt explained the consequences:

> Our existing staff simply cannot get around to provide adequate staff services to all the communities active in the program. It has become increasingly clear that one of the primary reasons for delay in the handling of communities' requests for financial, technical, and other assistance is lack of completeness and clarity which results in time-consuming correspondence, redoing, frustration, and deferment of final action.[7]

Staff deficiencies also helped to deter further delegation of responsibility to the field, making interagency co-operation at that level more difficult.

Whatever the staff inadequacies for performing the ARA's original mission, however, the agency was totally swamped when new responsibilities were added. In September, 1962, Congress passed the Accelerated Public Works Act, and the President designated the Commerce Department to administer it. Secretary Luther Hodges in turn delegated responsibilities of the Commerce Department relating to the accelerated public-works program to the ARA. It is not clear whether the ARA sought the additional duties or whether these duties were thrust upon the agency. The choice of the ARA to administer the new program was a logical one, since the bulk of the proposed public works affected the same communities served by the ARA.

Regardless of the merits of selecting the ARA to administer the new program, there is no doubt that it had an unfortunate impact upon an agency already struggling to get on its feet. In anticipation of the new responsibilities, plans and reports had to be generated quickly, while the legislation was still grinding in the legislative mills, and the ARA had no personnel designated for this task. Hence, the regular ARA staff was deterred from its original responsibilities throughout mid-1962: Planning and Research was hit first, then the Operations staff. Ultimately, the ARA's staff was increased to meet some of the responsibilities connected with the new mission; by June, 1963, about sixty employees had been added for this purpose. But during the crucial year of 1962, the work on accelerated public works impeded the ARA's effectiveness.

Organization of the ARA

Given the legislative history of the depressed-area program, undoubtedly the most important attribute of the new ARA was that it was placed within the Department of Commerce. Ever since his initial involvement with the issue in 1955, Senator Douglas had insisted that the aid program be placed in a newly created, independent agency. Douglas assumed that his "kit of tools" should be administered by a single body of personnel oriented to the unique problems of chronic labor-surplus areas. Though the Eisenhower Administration, echoed by conservative interest groups, maintained that such a program belonged in Commerce, the Illinois senator remained firmly committed to his position. He feared that the Commerce Department was controlled by business interests, personified by the Business Advisory Council.[2] Moreover, he expressed suspicions that top Commerce officials, and even technicians in the Office of Area Development, were hostile to the program he proposed. In short, he feared that, in the unfavorable climate of the Department of Commerce, his program would be the victim of slow strangulation.

President Kennedy had hardly been sworn in when Douglas discovered, much to his surprise, that the new Administration was in agreement with its predecessor in advocating Commerce Department administration.[3] The newly appointed Secretary of Commerce, Luther Hodges, apparently wanted the program under his jurisdiction and persuaded President Kennedy to agree. Even then, the White House refrained from insisting upon its position and, in fact, made it clear that it was ready to accept the decision of Congress.[3]

The Administration's expressed preference for the Commerce Department, however, served to undermine Douglas' drive for an independent agency. The advent of a Democratic Administration obviously blunted the Senator's argument that the Commerce Department would be hostile to his program. Thus, after holding on as long as possible to maximize his bargaining power on other issues, Douglas reluctantly acquiesced.

Douglas' position was more than a politically based suspicion of Republican businessmen whom he saw influencing Commerce Department policies. Supporters of the Douglas approach argued that the depressed-area program would cross traditional jurisdictional lines and involve many established departments and agencies—including the Departments of Agriculture, Interior, Commerce, Labor, Health, Education and Welfare, the Small Business Administration, and the

[2]This council was later called the Business Council and lost its official connection with the Commerce Department.
[3]This development was not without irony because one of the most effective speeches in favor of the independent-agency approach was delivered by Senator Kennedy on the Senate floor in 1956.[1]

Housing and Home Finance Agency. It would thus be inappropriate, they argued, to fix the administration upon any single agency. Only a newly created, co-ordinating agency, it was concluded, would achieve the necessary autonomy and unity of approach for the program.

Douglas' supporters were apparently not impressed by the standard, textbook maxims of public administration which militated against "the proliferation of agencies." This textbook position was advocated by the much-discussed reports of the Hoover Commissions of 1949 and 1955; within the executive branch, the position is usually upheld by the Budget Bureau. It is rather doubtful whether there is real substance to this argument. Proponents of an independent agency argued that the federal government has long passed the stage where it can be organized conveniently under a conventional organization chart. In actual practice, control over the activities of a federal agency is exercised through the Bureau of the Budget within the executive branch as well as through the appropriation process in the congressional committees on appropriations. Each program is reviewed separately, and it appears to make little difference whether a given program is part of a department whose head is a member of the cabinet or part of an independent agency. Each program is subject to the same scrutiny.

Most of the cabinet-level departments are conglomerations of slightly related or completely unrelated programs, of which the Department of Commerce is an excellent example. This department has long been run as a sprawling empire with a multitude of semi-independent fiefdoms. There is little affinity of purpose between the Business and Defense Services Administration, the Maritime Administration, the Patent Office, and the Weather Bureau, to mention just a few of the many agencies which are included in the Department of Commerce. The fact that each of the bureaus is part of a larger department does not produce any discernible economy of size.

Proponents of placing the new program in Commerce also contended that a new agency would necessarily duplicate depressed-area programs already operative in established agencies. An independent agency thus raised the specter of a burgeoning bureaucracy. Finally, the theory was advanced that the depressed-area program would gain prestige by being in an old-line department headed by a cabinet member who "has the ear of the President."

The experience of the Area Redevelopment Administration has offered mixed evidence on these points, though on balance it seems that an independent agency would have been preferable. Secretary

Hodges and the established Commerce Department bureaucracy imposed certain limitations on the ARA during the new agency's first two years. The decision on the ARA's size, as has been seen, was supported by Hodges. Departmental procedures also served to put brakes on the ARA's enthusiasm with regard to such matters as personnel recruitment. And although ARA officials reported that these restrictions helped to keep them "out of trouble," the tangible assets of affiliation with Commerce were hard to verify. Some feeling existed that the ARA was a kind of "stepchild" within the department. For example, the ARA did not receive a single one of the supergrade positions redistributed within Commerce during the two-year period. Only one official in the Secretary's office, Hyman Bookbinder, maintained a continuing interest in the ARA, and in the summer of 1962 he left the department. However, when Franklin D. Roosevelt was appointed undersecretary in 1963, he took an active interest in the ARA.

Commerce also failed to allocate adequate space to the ARA, which literally had a cramping effect upon the new program. Recruitment of personnel was delayed because there was no room for new people.

Secretary Hodges' personal role is equally difficult to assess. Though he consulted with President Kennedy on several occasions concerning ARA business, such communications were relatively rare. Indeed, the President took the initiative in several instances and dealt directly with Batt. On top of this was Hodges' curious public ambivalence toward area redevelopment. Even before the Act was passed he had voiced misgivings that, unless administered properly, depressed-area assistance could become a "boondoggle."[10] And his much-publicized observation during an October, 1961, press conference that the ARA was moving too slowly was an unwarranted blow to the morale of the infant agency.[6]

But the evidence in favor of an independent agency is not conclusive. Though in the ARA's case this is an "iffy" question, the debate is a familiar one to students of public administration. From the agency's point of view, the question is: Can the program's goals be best realized if the agency is an independent actor, or if it enjoys the protections (and restraints) of an established department? In light of the fact that there are both "rich" and "poor" agencies in each category, the answer to the question probably varies from case to case.

From the public's point of view, the question may in a sense be the opposite one: In which form—independent agency or old-line department—are administrative and policy controls best effected? Again the answer is fuzzy, if not impossible. In theory at least, the controls at the disposal of Congress and executive instruments such as the Budget Bureau can be exercised with equal vigor (or torpor) upon both departments and independent agencies.

Structure of the ARA

Along with personnel recruitment, another initial problem facing Batt and his colleagues was that of evolving an organizational instrument to put into operation the provisions of the Area Redevelopment Act. Even before the law was passed, Batt was meeting informally with OAD technicians and a Budget Bureau representative who had been detailed to Commerce to chart the ARA's organization. The final plan was drafted by Messrs. Batt, Williams, and Bozman, the Budget Bureau man who retained a top position in the ARA. The organizational make-up of the ARA remained substantially intact during its first two years (Figure 2–1).

With the exception of the Office of Public Works Acceleration, which was added in 1962 to handle the accelerated public-works program, the organization shown in Figure 2–1 has remained relatively stable during the lifetime of ARA. Based on the assumption that field activities constituted the ARA's main thrust, the Office of Operations was viewed as the very heart of the agency. In this unit, both field and Washington personnel were to act essentially as "promoters" of the ARA's "kit of tools." The Office of Planning and Research, on the other hand, was designed to develop the ARA's long-range program. The "promoters" and the "thinkers" were to be balanced by a third unit, the Office of Administration and Finance. An independent appraisal of proposed projects was to emanate from its Financial Assistance Division. Other divisions of this office performed housekeeping functions for the entire agency.

This arrangement was not without its difficulties. First, there was clearly no reason for the Office of Administration and Finance to be involved in program review. Second, the pressures of designating areas eligible for assistance and of processing local economic plans and project proposals were so overwhelming that project rather than program review became the dominant preoccupation of almost every ARA division. The Office of Planning and Research was assigned diverse operational responsibilities. As a result, during the ARA's

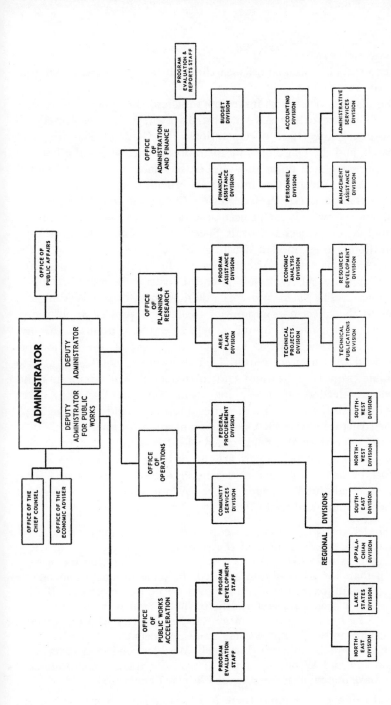

Figure 2–1: U.S. Department of Commerce: Area Redevelopment Administration

first two years Planning and Research had little time to plan, and even less to do research.

The dispersion of program-review functions was especially troublesome. Guidance of the ARA's substantive programs was loosely divided among the Office of Operations, the Office of Planning and Research, and the Office of Administration and Finance—the last two being primarily staff units. In addition, the Office of the Chief Counsel and the Project Review Committee were brought into the program-and-policy-making act. The Project Review Committee constituted the penultimate review unit for project proposals; Batt reserved for himself the final say on project approvals. Specific responsibility for processing applications was retained in Washington.

The ARA has never confronted the implications of a field organization. Originally, ARA officials intended to base their entire staff in Washington. The "field" workers would actually live in Washington, travel to the affected communities to develop project applications, and then return to the capital to help steer these proposals through the lengthy review process. This plan never got off the ground because field workers were required on the scene almost constantly to stimulate project applications and to co-operate with applicants and community leaders in developing them. Yet the ARA has never delegated substantive responsibilities to these "field co-ordinators."

The structure of the ARA's field organization is rather unorthodox. The line officers in the field, called "field co-ordinators," cover one or more states; sometimes there are two or three for a single state. The number of field co-ordinators has never exceeded three score. This number is admittedly inadequate, as Administrator Batt explained to a Senate subcommittee in 1962:

> Under our present plan we provide about a man per state. In the states where most of the state is eligible for help in the program, a state like Kentucky, we are finding the need for more help than we originally anticipated. In some instances two men per state, in some instances three men. In no case more than that. We find a need for secretarial help, that a man is far more effective if he has a base of operations and a secretary who can cover that base and help him become more productive.
>
> I was out in Colorado last week. We have one man covering Colorado and Wyoming. The distances out there are enormous. We have one man in the state of Florida, I believe.[8]

For each of the six regions there is a "senior field co-ordinator," but the dimensions of this job vary greatly among individuals. Some of these men actually supervise their field co-ordinators, while others function primarily as a liaison among state agencies, delegate agencies, and the ARA Washington staff. The senior field co-ordinator usually reports directly to one of the six "regional division chiefs" in Washington. Again, the supervision exercised by these division chiefs varies greatly. Assisting the division chiefs are "area co-ordinators" in Washington who work directly with the field co-ordinators in preparing the project proposals and following them through ARA processing. As if this cumbersome field arrangement were not enough, there has also been a severe shortage of clerical and technical personnel backing up the field and area co-ordinators.

An organization and manpower survey completed in mid-1963 by a private management consultant included the following recommendations: (1) More attention should be paid by ARA top staff to the agency's over-all objectives; (2) the ARA's field staff should be expanded and organized along more conventional lines; (3) more authority should be delegated to the field staff; and (4) direction of the ARA's substantive programs should be consolidated in a new office of program administration.

The ARA's organization during its initial two years was particularly conditioned by the perceived necessity of "getting project approvals." This preoccupation with immediate, tangible results, a product of overwhelming pressure brought to bear upon the ARA from diverse quarters, put the mechanism of project-generation and project-processing at the very apex of the ARA's organization. Overall program and policy development, not to mention basic research and data compilation, suffered as a result of this preoccupation. And, as we have seen, the processing of project applications was plagued by insufficient staffing, poor organization, and inadequately trained personnel.

RELATIONS WITH DELEGATE AGENCIES AND OTHER ORGANIZATIONS

The "Delegate-Agency" Concept

A crucial decision made in the ARA's early days was the determination to rely largely upon other government agencies. This determination stemmed in part, though not exclusively, from the wording and legislative background of the Act and was in line with Hodges' testi-

mony before the Senate Committee on Banking and Currency following his appointment as Secretary of Commerce.

Opponents of depressed-area assistance had repeatedly charged that
such a program would involve the creation of a "vast bureaucracy"
which would duplicate the work of existing agencies.[4] Senator Douglas
and his colleagues responded that a "one-stop" agency was needed to
co-ordinate the various existing programs which related to chronic
unemployment. Douglas, himself no friend of "vast bureaucracies,"
anticipated that the ARA would utilize the facilities and expertise of
existing agencies. The 1961 House bill went so far as to require the
agency to use these facilities "whenever possible." This wording was
regarded as somewhat extreme, and the final bill was amended to read
"to the extent practicable."[2]

This legislative history formed the background for the decision to
organize the ARA as a relatively small, co-ordinating agency of about
three hundred people. The decision, made in the spring of 1961 by
Batt and the Commerce Department, has already been discussed. It
was assumed that the technical and detailed work of the ARA would
be done by other agencies. An analogy to government contracting procedures will illustrate the ARA's intended relation to these agencies:
as the "prime contractor" for federal depressed-area assistance, the
ARA would delegate specific programs to "subcontractors" as needed.
Though such delegation is not wholly unknown in the federal government, the ARA's case was unique in the extent and magnitude of the
delegations.

No sooner had the enabling act been signed than Batt and his associates were confronted with the delegate-agencies problem. Simply
stated, the dilemma concerned the extent to which the ARA could
"farm out" its functions without surrendering its autonomy. During
May and June of 1961 the Department of Agriculture—which seems
to prosper in inverse relation to the number of farmers in the nation—made a bid to obtain complete authority for the rural program
(i.e., 5[b] areas, which included many smaller urban areas and was
by no means a "rural" program). Supporting this move were the
major farm lobbyists, including the influential National Rural Electric Cooperatives Association. ARA officials argued that such a dele-

----

[4]See, for example, the minority views of the Senate Committee on Banking and
Currency in 1959 and 1961, and the statements of Senators Thurmond and Mc-
Clellan, and of Representative Meader, in the *Congressional Record*, 1961, pp.
3660, 3743, and 4925 respectively.

gation would constitute a denial of their responsibilities under the law. Instead, they proposed to retain final authority for designations of areas and granting of loans, while allowing the Agriculture Department to have considerable working responsibilities. The ARA-Agriculture controversy remained unresolved until Budget Director David Bell, acting upon the advice of his staff, sided with the ARA and persuaded Secretary Freeman to capitulate.

The Agriculture Department's delegation pattern was followed with other agencies. Loans and grants for community facilities were processed and administered by the Housing and Home Finance Agency's Community Facilities Administration. Industrial loans were handled by the Small Business Administration. In addition to these three major delegations, manpower retraining was jointly administered by the Department of Labor and the Department of Health, Education and Welfare as provided in the Act. Labor also advised the ARA on area designation. And projects involving Indian reservations were handled by the Interior Department's Office of Indian Affairs. Each delegation, needless to say, carried its own unique problems of communication and co-ordination.

One important, though somewhat technical, issue revolved about the method of funding the ARA money that was being channeled to the delegate agencies. It was finally agreed that the ARA should reimburse, rather than allocate, money which these agencies spent on ARA projects. This had two fortunate consequences for the ARA: (1) Personnel in the delegate agencies who were assigned ARA tasks appeared on the rolls of the delegate agencies. If the money were allocated, they would appear on the ARA's rolls, thus officially doubling ARA personnel. (2) The ARA reimbursed the delegate agencies each quarter for money obligated during the preceding three months. This allowed the ARA to make continuous, minor adjustments in the rate of money flowing to the delegate agencies. Under the allocation system, the ARA would have had little control of the funds once they had been allocated for the fiscal year.

An even more significant variable was the method of hiring personnel in the delegate agencies. Two patterns prevailed during the ARA's first two years. In one instance the delegate agency simply instructed its technicians to add ARA matters to their normal duties. As the system operates in the Community Facilities Administration, a technician works on a whole series of projects—of which the ARA's public-facilities program is but one. Even though the staff is enlarged to handle the new work load, relatively few workers are exclusively concerned with ARA programs.

The second pattern called for specific technicians to be designated for ARA work only. This was essentially the method employed by the Small Business Administration. Though much preferable to the CFA scheme, this practice also had its difficulties. First, the work load on ARA programs fluctuates so greatly that it is not always feasible to set aside a given number of staff members to handle it. Second, though these workers are specifically designated to work on ARA matters, they retain ties to their divisions within the SBA. Given the uncertainties of the ARA's future, these technicians are understandably reluctant to overcommit themselves to the new programs. In the SBA, this means that they are reluctant to work exclusively on a program outside the mainstream of SBA activities and that they are overcautious in approving loans: should the ARA be discontinued, they do not wish to develop bad reputations within the SBA by recommending what might later turn out to be unsound loans.[5]

In many cases the SBA's local teams of experts have worked out exceptionally well; in other cases, the results have been mixed. However, the fact that each technician retains loyalty to his own SBA division sometimes makes co-ordination difficult. If the delegate system is to be continued, special ARA divisions should probably be created within each agency and charged with virtually complete responsibility for the delegated programs.

The fundamental debate over the delegate system itself did not subside after two years of operation. Indeed, it was probably more acrimonious in 1963 than at the agency's birth. One manifestation of the problem has been the lengthy time required to process ARA applications. The average time from submission of an application to final approval for commercial and industrial loans was 162 days for the first eight months of fiscal 1963; during the same period an average of 188 days was required for public-facility projects.[9] ARA officials repeatedly complained that the SBA and the CFA were taking excessive time to process applications before turning them back to the ARA. This may well have been the case, but it was hardly a defensible charge by mid-1963, when ARA processing times were increasing even faster than those of the delegate agencies. In comparing fiscal 1962 averages with the first eight months of fiscal 1963, it

[5]This distinction becomes more meaningful when it is recalled that many, if not most, ARA loans are by nature more marginal in character than those financed by the SBA.

was discovered that the SBA's average processing period rose from 75 to 98 days; the CFA's from 97 to 103 days; and the ARA's from 35 to 64 days!

The excessive processing time was an external manifestation of serious, fundamental problems. Communications between the ARA and its co-operating agencies were so poor that in some cases field officers were issued conflicting instructions from their parent agencies. Suspicions and resentments were widespread among officials both in Washington and in the field. One of the results of such attitudes was the ARA's reluctance to delegate authority to the other agencies.

One potential instrument of co-ordination, the Policy Advisory Board (PAB), failed to provide adequate liaison between the agencies. This group, composed of the top echelons from all departments and agencies involved in ARA programs, met only three times during the first two years, and their meetings were dominated by formal progress reports. At the staff level, the group meets once a month and apparently has served as a safety valve for interagency tensions. But the staff representatives have not been authorized to resolve the issues and thus have been unable to remove the causes of the tensions.

The disenchantment of ARA officialdom with the delegate system reached the point, early in 1963, of precipitating overt efforts to change the system. In late summer of 1962 a full-dress meeting of the PAB was staged and the problem of processing delays was discussed. Each agency head resolved to do his part to improve the situation, but in fact the agencies felt that they were already doing their utmost and the situation remained unchanged. In the fall of 1962 the ARA began an intensive program of checking weekly on the status of applications and projects in each regional SBA and CFA office. In February, 1963, the ARA asked the Budget Bureau to review the CFA-SBA delegate-agency question. In light of the Budget Bureau's known commitment to, and fondness for, the delegate system, this last move was futile from the ARA's point of view.

The delegate-agency question is thus probably the major problem surrounding the ARA's operations. Though the initial conflict with the Department of Agriculture has apparently been settled by the ARA designating more rural areas than Agriculture expected and by the ARA consulting with Agriculture on all proposed projects in rural areas, the controversy between the ARA, the CFA, and the SBA had reached a stalemate in 1963. ARA officials were asking by mid-1963 for a reconsideration of the delegate system. In the ARA view, the delegations should be recalled and the central agency empowered to administer all of its various programs. Another viewpoint held that the cure for the controversy was not less but real delegation. Whether either of these views would prevail, or whether some compromise would be reached between these positions, was not at all clear in mid-1963.

External Pressures

No account of the ARA's first two years would be complete without mention of the external pressures which impinged upon its operations. It is unfortunate but perhaps inevitable that any program involving subsidies to local areas takes on the aspects of a "pork barrel." This is not to negate the economic rationale of depressed-area assistance, but merely to observe that it is prone to be the victim of political pressures.

ARA officials were continually besieged to approve certain projects or, at least, to "expedite" their processing. Members of Congress, local officialdom, and the White House office all get into the act at one time or another. In view of such a multitude of competing pressures, it is no wonder that the ARA failed to please everybody.

Some observers noted that the ARA was not above playing politics with its programs when the occasion arose. It was observed, for example, that the ARA's two major projects went to states having key representatives on the House or Senate public-works committees. In two publicized instances, the ARA's political machinations got the agency into hot water. In 1962, for example, incumbent Congressman Arch Moore (Republican) and Cleveland Bailey (Democrat) were pitted against one another in a newly consolidated West Virginia district. The ARA reportedly allowed Bailey to announce new redevelopment projects in *Moore's* part of the district before the election. It turned out that the ARA had bet on the wrong horse, and when Representative Moore returned to Washington, he brought uncharitable thoughts toward the ARA, which he proclaimed whenever the opportunity to criticize arose. In 1963 he voted against additional authorizations for the agency.

A similar incident involved veteran Republican Congressman Clarence Kilburn, ranking minority member of the House Banking and Currency Committee—to which the ARA must turn for additional authorizations. The ARA had apparently assured Kilburn that no projects would be announced for his district in northern New York State before the 1962 election. Therefore, when his Democratic challenger announced the approval of an ARA project in the district one day prior to the 1962 congressional election, Kilburn began to denounce the agency publicly. Kilburn was re-elected by his constituents (a not-too-difficult prediction for the ARA to have made, since he had won previous elections by comfortable margins and since the district had been represented by a Republican for decades), and he vowed to trim the ARA's sails. Kilburn's earlier behavior made the ARA's miscalculation even more glaring. Though he had always opposed area redevelopment, Kilburn had never before assumed leadership of the opposition in committee. The ARA had not made a new enemy, but it had certainly activated a previously dormant one. The Bailey-Moore incident might be justified on the basis of partisan politics, but ARA meddling in the Kilburn election, which was a foregone conclusion, is difficult to understand.

Another set of external pressures were those institutionalized in the National Public Advisory Committee on Area Redevelopment (NPAC). This group, provided for in Section 4(b) of the Act, was composed of local and state officials, economists, professional people, and interest-group spokesmen involved in area redevelopment. The NPAC included representatives from AFL-CIO, the Committee for Economic Development, the National Rural Electric Cooperatives Association, the National Farmers' Union, the National Grange, the Council of Mayors, and other representatives of the loose coalition which had supported the Douglas bill during the six years preceding the passage of the legislation. LeRoy Collins, chief executive of the National Association of Broadcasters and former governor of Florida, was the group's first chairman. In 1963 Frank Graham, former U.S. senator, took over the position. The NPAC met quarterly with top-echelon representatives of the ARA and its delegate agencies.

The NPAC conceived its task as including the following: (1) hearing and evaluating reports from the Secretary of Commerce concerning ARA progress and plans; (2) submitting to the Secretary periodic evaluations of ARA programs and recommendations for changes; (3) preparing an annual report including "a broad conceptual appraisal of overall national need and performance"; and (4) reporting to the Secretary concerning "public understanding and acceptance of the program."[4]

The NPAC, working largely through four subcommittees which meet with relevant ARA officials, makes periodic policy statements.[6]

---

[6]The subcommittees are: National and International Economy; ARA Operations; Manpower Development; and Technical Assistance and Research.

The activities of the subcommittees have varied widely, depending upon the interest of the chairmen, and it is hard to generalize about their effectiveness. Some activists, including labor union representatives, urged the NPAC to expand its supervision of the ARA's administration, but Chairman Collins insisted that the group was empowered to play only an advisory role. The NPAC's task would seem to be the difficult one of injecting perspective into ARA operations without meddling in day-to-day administration.

ARA FINANCES

The method of financing the ARA's loan programs generated a particularly interesting series of parliamentary maneuvers during the 1961 congressional consideration of the bill. Senator Douglas had asked for Treasury financing rather than the customary annual appropriations in order to permit the ARA to make long-range financial commitments and to cope with a highly fluctuating financial work load. Douglas also feared that ARA appropriations might be cut during prosperous times, when the program might be able to perform most effectively. By so-called "backdoor financing," the funds allotted in the authorizing legislation may be spent by administrators without going through the appropriations committees. Douglas won this point over the traditional sensitivity of the House conferees to encroachments upon the appropriations process.

Douglas' strategy was later frustrated by the House. In the final bill of the 1961 session, a supplemental appropriation bill, House Appropriations Committee Chairman Clarence Cannon and his colleagues wiped out "backdoor financing" for the ARA by appropriating it $170,750,000 for fiscal 1962. The House passed the bill (P.L. 87–332) and then adjourned for the year. The "other body" was engaged in debating the bill when the senators learned that the House had presented them with a *fait accompli*. Though the Senate sullenly approved the bill, it was indicated that the interhouse dispute had not ended.

On the other hand, the House Appropriations Committee granted the ARA virtually everything it asked for during fiscal 1962 and fiscal 1963 and more than the agency could spend. During its first year, ARA-approved loans and grants amounted to only a sixth of the total appropriations. As the program picked up momentum, the ARA spent nearly all the grant money that was appropriated for fiscal

1963, but only $91 million out of the $115 million appropriated for loans.

Table 2-2: ARA Financial and Technical Assistance, Fiscal Years 1962 and 1963

($'s in thousands)

	1962 [a]		1963	
	Appropriated	Committed	Appropriated	Committed
Total	$165,875	$29,915	$153,600	$128,415
Industrial and commercial loans [b]		7,959		61,361
	122,500		115,000	
Public-facility loans [b]		12,733		29,497
Public-facility grants	40,000	6,046	35,000	33,995
Technical assistance	3,375	3,177	3,600	3,562

[a] For fiscal 1962 Congress appropriated a lump sum for ARA, but specified maximum amounts that could be spent on loans, grants, and technical assistance.

[b] Loan appropriations were made in one lump sum.

SOURCE: ARA Financial Assistance Report, July 31, 1963.

It would, therefore, be erroneous to conclude that Douglas' battle for "backdoor financing" was in vain. It apparently induced Cannon and his committee colleagues to exercise caution in overruling the authority given the ARA to resort to Treasury borrowing. When ARA officials appealed in 1962 to the Senate Appropriations Committee to reinstate Treasury financing, Senator Spessard Holland, of Florida, attempted to smooth over the situation:

SENATOR HOLLAND: Are the funds any more there when they exist as a matter of backdoor authorization for the year than as a matter of appropriation. . . ?

. . . .

When the House has granted your full estimate, which they certainly haven't done as to other agencies . . . I don't see any great validity in your protesting.

. . . .

In the House report . . . they add these words: "In the event that the amount allowed proves insufficient"—and they have allowed the full amount of your estimate—"a supplemental request may be submitted for consideration by the Congress." Which I think is a rather generous attitude as manifested by the House committee. . . .

SENATOR KEFAUVER: Yes, they usually fuss at us for increasing the amounts of the supplemental appropriation.[8]

It was clear that the House was retaining its prerogatives in direct violation of the provision of the Act; but, apparently thinking that principle was more important than a few dollars, it was careful to give the ARA little cause for complaint.

Yet there remained an unanswerable case for direct Treasury financing—especially where a revolving loan fund was concerned. William Bozman, the ARA's chief financial officer, summarized the argument during the same Senate hearings:

> This is a lending operation, and in a lending operation it is difficult to forecast your workload precisely. That is, the number of valid requests for loans you will receive during a year. In addition, at the end of the fiscal year you are in effect reviewing applications for projects which will not be finally approved at the end of the fiscal year. Under the terms that we are operating today, our loan funds lapse at the end of each fiscal year and this we find a rather awkward problem administratively.[8]

EVALUATION OF THE ARA ORGANIZATION

Passing judgment upon a newborn agency is a risky enterprise. And in the ARA's case the task is rendered even more hazardous by the experimental character of both the program and the organizational instrument. The program itself falls outside the traditional federal economic programs, and even its loan aspects are hardly conventional. The ARA's structure, too, is unique. The "delegate-agency" arrangement, which became the source of so much controversy, is a new approach to administration.

Underlying the intent of Congress in urging the ARA to use other agencies "to the fullest extent practicable . . . to avoid the duplication of existing staff and facilities" (Section 24[a]) was the suspicion that every agency has some "fat" and that it could absorb additional duties without further expansion. Congress thus hoped that the work of the ARA which cut across the responsibilities of existing agencies would be absorbed with a minimum of additional outlays.

But the ARA found that existing agencies do not believe in any "free lunches" and that they were going to charge for any and all work performed. Roughly two of every five dollars appropriated for ARA operations were used to reimburse "co-operating agencies" for the services performed for ARA activities. It is quite obvious that no self-respecting bureaucracy will accept additional duties without receiving adequate reimbursement for the work performed. An agency which is already overloaded with work obviously cannot absorb additional chores with existing personnel, and one which has enough "fat" is not going to admit it publicly. An analysis of ARA operations leads to the conclusion that the agency has been forced to rely too heavily upon other agencies to do its work. Contrary to congressional hopes, this has led neither to budgetary savings nor to efficiency.

The futility of relying upon other agencies to do the ARA's job was possibly best illustrated by responses to a letter sent by the President to fourteen federal agencies on February 27, 1962. In this letter, the President expressed his deep concern "about the continuing chronic area unemployment and underemployment in certain communities . . . where unemployment remains far too high despite the general improvement in the national economy." He then requested the heads of the agencies to report to him on the activities that their agencies had undertaken to aid the ARA and requested appraisals for further action that might be undertaken administratively.

The responses of the agencies must have been disheartening to the ARA, though some of the reports looked impressive. Since the designated redevelopment areas cover a considerable amount of real estate with close to 35 million people, some agencies had no difficulty in pointing to massive programs which they had undertaken in these areas. For example, the Federal Highway Administration reported that it spent $666 million to build 7,100 miles of roads in depressed areas between January 1, 1961, and February 28, 1962. But it could not point to a single mile of road which was constructed as a result of priorities accorded to depressed areas. The Defense Department reported that $6.3 billion in prime military contracts was awarded in areas of substantial unemployment during fiscal 1961—about half of the major labor-market areas were so classified—but only $50 million of this, or less than 1 per cent, resulted from the preferential treatment accorded to those areas under Defense Manpower Policy No. 4 (discussed in Chapter 8).

A few agencies indicated that they had hired extra help to assist in various phases of the economic development of depressed areas. But an examination of the source of funds under which the new hands were hired disclosed that this was done with ARA funds. Several other agencies candidly admitted that they had not done anything for depressed areas outside of their regular program, but they also indicated a willingness and readiness to make the old college try. There is no evidence that the presidential effort to stimulate action to aid the ARA resulted in the creation of any jobs in depressed areas.

The delegate-agency question is a fundamental one, and here there is unfortunately little federal experience to suggest a solution. At this writing, the situation is a stalemate. From the ARA's point of view, it would be advantageous for most if not all of its programs to be administered directly by its own staff. This alternative seems unlikely from a political standpoint. It is doubtful that the Budget Bureau, not to mention Congress, would tolerate the substantial enlargement of the ARA which would be necessitated by such a step. The Budget Bureau also appears committed to continue with the delegate-agency experiment. Moreover, the delegate agencies now have a stake in keeping their piece of the pie and are not likely to give it up without a fight.

In light of the overwhelming power arrayed in favor of the delegate arrangement, it seems reasonable to assume that it will be retained. The realistic course of action for ARA policy-shapers would be to exert greater effort to improve the system and to remove existing frictions among the top echelons of the ARA and the delegate agencies. This will require the creation of workable lines of liaison and the delegation of more operating responsibility to the delegate agencies. This solution may not be the most satisfactory to establish a smoothly operating program, but it is far better than the present system.

The ARA's preoccupation with the processing of applications has been understandable, but basic research and policy formulation have suffered severely as a result. A new agency is naturally concerned with immediate, tangible results in order to justify its existence; yet the long-run attack upon hard-core unemployment requires basic research regarding its characteristics and the available alternatives to combat chronic unemployment. And the ARA's experience with congressional probers suggests that even short-term interests would be served by more attention to program formulation, policy direction, and the development of basic operational statistics. After asking technical questions for the second year in a row and receiving no response from Batt, John Rooney, chairman of the House Appropriations subcommittee, exclaimed: "You people do not seem to be very well prepared in connection with this budget. Every time we get to a real pertinent question that might lead to something else we find you do not have the information with you."[7] The slighting of basic research has been partially a consequence of generalized staff deficiencies; but inefficient use of existing personnel has also been a factor.

Given the unfavorable environment in which the ARA operated during its first two years, and given the unique quality of its structure and mission, the most surprising fact is that the agency is operating as smoothly as it is. The perils of a new and untried agency are too numerous to permit glib criticisms at this early date. Yet critical problems remain, and upon their solution the ARA's future may depend.

REFERENCES

1. *Congressional Record.* July 25, 1956, p. 13313.
2. *Congressional Record.* March 29, 1961, pp. 4947, 4946.
3. Kennedy, President John F. Letter to U.S. Senate Committee on Banking and Currency. *Hearings on Area Redevelopment.* 87th Cong., 1st Sess., 1961, p. 330.
4. National Public Advisory Committee resolution. Meeting No. 2, September 14, 1961.
5. *New York Times.* May 2, 1961.
6. *New York Times.* October 4, 1961.
7. U.S. House of Representatives, Committee on Appropriations. *1964 Commerce Department Budget Hearings.* 88th Cong., 1st Sess. Washington: Government Printing Office, 1963, pp. 163, 206.
8. U.S. Senate, Committee on Appropriations. *1963 Commerce Department Budget Hearings.* 87th Cong., 2d Sess., 1962, pp. 562, 587–88.
9. U.S. Department of Commerce, Area Redevelopment Administration. "Processing Times Schedule for Approved Financial Assistance Projects." February, 1963. (Mimeographed.)
10. *Wall Street Journal.* December 5, 1960.

++++++++++++++++++++++

Chapter 3

Area Designation
and Characteristics

++

The first job that the ARA Administrator had to face was the designation of areas which would be eligible for assistance. Though Congress did not appropriate funds for the new agency until five months after the President had signed the bill, pressure from the various communities wishing to qualify for assistance started as soon as the legislation was enacted. The prolonged legislative battles over the legislation and the frequently exaggerated claims for the ARA on the part of proponents of the bill led many communities to seek a portion of the promised benefits. But the Act provided that before an area could become eligible for assistance it had to be so designated by the Area Redevelopment Administrator. This first job of the ARA turned out to be complicated, arduous, and laden with controversy.

LEGISLATIVE ISSUES AND PROVISIONS

The congressional debate over the determination of areas eligible for benefits under the Act was both extended and crucial to the enactment of the legislation. Basically, the debate centered about how thinly the benefits of the program were to be spread. Starting with the assumption that the resources allocated to the program would be rather limited, the bill's supporters realized that an effective program would have to limit the areas eligible to benefit from the legislation.

Industrial Areas (Section 5[a])

Political facts of life made it difficult to restrict eligibility. Douglas originally designed his program to aid only urban areas suffering from chronic unemployment. He proposed that eligibility for assistance be restricted to labor-market areas with unemployment of 6 per cent for three consecutive years, but he permitted a shorter period if unemployment in the areas averaged 9 per cent or higher. By the standards of 1955, when Douglas introduced the bill, 6 per cent unemployment was high (about 50 per cent above the national average): in 1955 and 1956 the average, national unemployment hovered around the 4 per cent level. These original criteria would have restricted eligibility to forty or fifty labor-market areas. But the 1956 hearings on the bill indicated that a number of the advocates of the legislation favored more relaxed standards. For whatever reasons, the supporters of loose criteria apparently succeeded in persuading Douglas that the original criteria were too rigid. His revised bill, which passed the Senate in the Eighty-fourth Congress (1956), made it easier for areas to qualify for benefits. The new criteria were as follows: (1) 12 per cent unemployment for twelve months preceding the application for aid; (2) 8 per cent during at least fifteen months of the eighteen-month period preceding the application; or (3) 6 per cent during at least eight months in each of the two years preceding the application.

The advent of the 1958 recession and the increase in the national level of unemployment made it more difficult to determine eligibility on the basis of 6 per cent unemployment, since total national unemployment averaged almost 6 per cent between 1958 and 1960. Consequently, Douglas dropped his original criteria, which had been based upon absolute ratios of unemployment, and instead accepted the Administration approach, with some modifications. The new criteria based eligibility upon a sliding scale of excess unemployment above the national average in a given area as follows: (1) unemployment in the area had to average at least 6 per cent during the qualifying period; and (2a) 50 per cent above the national average for three of the preceding four calendar years, or (b) 75 per cent above the national average for two of the three preceding calendar years, or (c) 100 per cent above the national average for one of the preceding two calendar years.

At the same time, the supporters of the legislation did not want to tie the hands of the Administrator. Thus they vested him with discretionary authority to designate areas based upon other criteria that he might devise in addition to the mandatory tests inserted in the Act. The case of the one-industry, one-plant town was frequently cited in congressional hearings and debates. It was felt that where a plant closed down in an area which was in large measure dependent upon it for employment, that area should not have to wait for at least a year until it became eligible for assistance. The proponents of the legislation believed that in such instances remedial action should be taken immediately after economic disaster struck. However, a proposed provision which would have explicitly granted the Administrator discretionary power to designate such areas as eligible for assistance was attacked on the basis that it would authorize the Administrator to designate any area and was deleted from the bill. The intent of Congress in rejecting this amendment was apparently to deny ARA authority to take any preventive measures.

Another problem surrounding the designation of urban areas related to boundaries. Labor-market statistics are collected by the federally financed but state-administered employment services. The geographic boundaries of these areas are established by the federal Bureau of Employment Security with the co-operation of the state agencies primarily on the basis of the commuting pattern of the labor force in the area. A considerable amount of evidence was presented during the hearings suggesting that occasionally such boundaries are arbitrary. Moreover, the employment-security statistics were limited to labor-market areas with a labor force of 15,000, including 8,000 engaged in non-agricultural occupations. Not wanting to preclude smaller areas from receiving benefits just because statistics were not available for them, Congress provided the ARA Administrator with discretionary power to designate smaller areas which might be eligible if appropriate statistics were available. These discretionary powers were not written into the Act, but were supplied in the report of the Senate and House conferees which resolved the differences between the House and Senate versions of S. 1, the bill finally approved as the Area Redevelopment Act.[3]

Rural and Smaller Urban Areas (Section 5[b])

The designation of rural and smaller urban areas was even more troublesome from a technical point of view. The problem of rural areas is normally not one of complete unemployment, but rather one of underemployment. Criteria of eligibility for industrial areas could be easily based upon the relationship of the number of unemployed to the total labor force. An individual would be classified as unemployed if, during the survey week, he was not engaged in gainful activity and was looking for work. (Gainful activity is defined as any work for pay or profit, or fifteen hours or more work performed during a week as an unpaid family worker on a family farm or in a family business.)

These criteria could not be effectively applied to low-income rural areas. The nature of farming, with its variety of chores, does not generally afford much opportunity for complete idleness, even on small or marginal farming units. Consequently, there is little complete "unemployment" in the farm population. Data on unemployment consistently show a lower percentage of unemployment even in the lowest-income rural areas than in the urban labor market.

The problem in rural areas is, therefore, one of underemployment rather than of total idleness. (Underemployment has been defined as "employment in jobs which [occupy] only a part of the workers' available time or permit only partial utilization of their capacities.")[7] Criteria other than unemployment were therefore necessary to determine the eligibility of rural areas. At first, Douglas tried to limit designation of rural areas to the three hundred counties with the largest number and percentage of low-income farm families; he further limited to fifteen the number of rural counties that might be designated in any state. These restrictions were removed on the floor of the Senate by the 1956 Fulbright amendments which charged the Administrator of the program with designation of rural areas eligible for assistance.

But the vagueness of rural-area eligibility criteria left some proponents of the legislation unsatisfied. In order to get votes for the bill, these strategists reasoned that they needed definite evidence to show waivering solons that their respective areas would benefit by the proposed legislation. To make a list of specific areas which would be eligible for assistance they relied upon two criteria: gross income of commercial farms, and the levels of living for farm-operating families.

A brief explanation of the above two criteria might be in order. The economic classification of farms developed by the Bureau of the Census and the Department of Agriculture separates farms into two major categories—commercial farms and other farms. The categories are based on the value of farm products sold and the off-farm work and other income of the farm-operating family.

Commercial farms are those operated as farm businesses which provide the major source of income and employment for the farm family. Other farms include mainly part-time and residential farms. The families operating these farms are dependent primarily upon off-farm sources of income.

The farm level-of-living index is a measure designed to reflect the average level of current consumption or utilization of goods and services. The index was based on four items drawn from the Census of Agriculture data for each county in the United States. These are the following: (1) percentage of farms with electricity; (2) percentage of farms with telephones; (3) percentage of farms with automobiles; and (4) average value of products sold or traded, in the year preceding the Census, per farm reporting, adjusted for changes in purchasing power of the farmer's dollar.[1]

It should be stressed that these level-of-living indexes only measure relative changes among different geographic areas and among different periods of time. They do not cover all the goods, services, and other factors that make up the level of living of farming families. However, many studies have shown that the various items are closely associated. Farmhouses with telephones are more likely to have other household facilities and conveniences than those without telephones. Farm families with automobiles are more likely to be able to take advantage of various services located away from the farm—such as health facilities, libraries, and recreation—than those without automobiles.

In 1959 the House Committee on Banking and Currency selected the 500 counties in the United States which, according to the 1954 Census of Agriculture, ranked lowest in terms of level of living for farm-operating families and the 500 counties in the United States with the highest proportion of commercial farms having gross sales of farm products of less than $2,500. A total of 662 counties—or more than a fifth of the total counties in the United States—appeared on these lists, and about two-thirds of these appeared on both lists. These were to be designated as eligible for assistance. The bulk of these counties was located in the southeast: five states—Alabama, Arkansas, Georgia, Mississippi, and Tennessee—accounted for more than half of the total counties.[9]

In 1960 the Senate adopted the House bill which included the mandatory designation of 662 rural counties. It represented an obvious attempt to persuade southern congressmen to vote for the legislation

[1] This index was revised in 1962.[13]

and to make it uncomfortable for those who would not get in on the "pork barrel." But the strategy misfired. Data based on specially selected but isolated criteria in some cases did not represent the true economic conditions of the designated counties. Opponents of the legislation could point to horrendous examples of relatively rich agricultural counties or of counties with a substantial industrial base where the farmers were not necessarily dependent upon farm income for their livelihood. President Eisenhower used this argument as a persuasive basis for his veto of the 1960 bill:

> The most striking defect of S. 722 is that it would make eligible for Federal assistance areas that don't need it—thus providing less help for communities in genuine need. . . . The dissipation of Federal help . . . would deprive communities afflicted with truly chronic unemployment of the full measure of assistance they so desperately desire. . . .[11]

In 1961 Congress despaired of an attempt to specify the rural areas which would be eligible for assistance under the depressed-area program and left this task to the Administrator. The Administrator was directed to consider the following criteria in designating rural areas:

> . . . the number of low income farm families in the various rural areas . . . the relationship of the income levels of the families in each such area to the general levels of income in the United States, . . . the availability of manpower in each such area for supplemental employment, . . . the extent of migration out of the area, . . . and the extent to which "rural development" projects have previously been located in any such area under programs administered by the Department of Agriculture. . . . (Section 5[b].)

The final criterion refers to a program inaugurated in 1956 by Secretary of Agriculture Ezra Taft Benson to aid the economic development of rural areas. The program was by no means restricted to the poorest or neediest rural counties; rather, areas were selected on the basis of the apparent feasibility of industrial or commercial development, and some prosperous counties were included. The amendment to include the rural areas as eligible for designation under the provisions of the Act was introduced by Senator Bush, of Connecticut. Senator Douglas accepted the amendment without debate.[2] Inserted into the Act at the urging of the National Rural Electric Cooperative Association, this provision later proved to be very troublesome.

Senator Proxmire, who supported Douglas' depressed-area program, believed that the bill discriminated against his own State of Wisconsin in the allocation of rural areas. The 662 rural counties which were listed as eligible for assistance under the 1960 approved bill contained only 13 counties north of the Mason-Dixon line, and not a single Wisconsin county was included. (These criteria were based solely upon the level of commercial farm income and level of living.) Senator Proxmire argued that the benefits of the legislation should be distributed more widely on a geographic basis.[10] A provision was therefore inserted into Section 5(b) urging the Administrator of the Act to "distribute the projects widely among the several States . . . in order that actual experience with this program may be had in as many States and in as many areas and under as many different circumstances as possible."

A final group which received special attention under the Area Redevelopment Act was the Indians. But this group offered few problems. It was generally agreed that Indians living on reservations were an economically distressed group and that any program to aid depressed areas should include them.

THE ARA STAKES CLAIM TO A THOUSAND COUNTIES

The discussion of the legislative history and provisions of the Act dealing with the criteria for designation clearly indicates that Congress intended to give the Administrator considerable latitude in selecting eligible areas. Congress lacked the necessary data to define clear criteria; moreover, it was apparently not inclined to tie the hands of the Administrator in future designations of eligible areas. Rigid provisions, unless they were broad enough to include all those who had any claims to benefit from the provisions of the bill, might have alienated some supporters. In brief, Congress passed the buck for designating areas to the administrators of the program.

Major labor-market areas, as well as smaller ones with a labor force in excess of 15,000, including 8,000 non-agricultural workers, did not present any particular problems. The Bureau of Employment Security in the Department of Labor had, for many years, accumulated data on most of these labor markets and for a number of smaller labor markets, and the congressional criteria were sufficiently specific to determine the areas which would qualify for assistance. No comparable data were available either for rural counties or for many smaller labor-market areas. The Bureau of the Census, of course, prepares the decennial county-income data; but at the time the ARA was designating counties eligible for assistance, the latest available data were for 1949, since the data for the 1960 Census had not yet been processed.

Left apparently in a no-man's land were hundreds of smaller towns with a labor force of less than 15,000 for which the Bureau of Employment Security did not collect data and for which designation as rural redevelopment areas would be inappropriate. These smaller urban areas did not, as a rule, qualify for assistance under the low-income criteria, nor were sufficient data available to qualify labor markets with less than 15,000 persons under the unemployment criteria.

A proper refinement of the loose criteria drawn up by Congress would have required, at the very least, months of work by an experienced staff. The new Administrator did not have such a staff at his disposal, nor did he have the necessary time to prepare in advance carefully drawn criteria which could be used to evaluate areas. The ARA therefore had to depend upon other departments, particularly the Departments of Agriculture and Labor, for assistance in determining areas eligible for assistance. It soon became quite clear that wholehearted co-operation was not forthcoming from these departments. Technicians from Agriculture and Labor could not agree upon the criteria for the designation of smaller urban areas. The Labor Department felt that such areas were really urban communities and that the designation should be left to criteria worked out by technicians in their department. The Agriculture technicians disagreed vehemently. They contended that in most cases these smaller towns were located in the midst of agricultural areas and that the appropriate authority for establishing criteria should be the Department of Agriculture.

The Agriculture Department also had another ax to grind. Having failed in Congress to get legislation delegating it the authority for administering the part of the program dealing with rural areas, it exerted pressure to receive this authority administratively. When Administrator Batt refused to break up his program, the Department of Agriculture refused to play ball. It was therefore left to the ARA to designate smaller urban and rural areas without the direct help of the Department of Agriculture, though the latter continued to exert pressure to designate rural areas and participated in the final decisions.

Meanwhile, pressures were mounting on the ARA to release a list of areas eligible for assistance. Hastily devised criteria were drawn up to qualify areas with a work force of less than 15,000. It was decided,

upon Agriculture's recommendations, that counties would qualify
for assistance where the median family income was one-third or less
of the national median or where the median farm-family income was
one-quarter of the U.S. median. But the latest available county-income
data were for 1949. Obviously, many changes had occurred in the
twelve years since the Census Bureau collected these data. Some hastily
improvised adjustments were made to bring county data in line with
1960 income levels. The technique used was to adjust 1949 county
median family-income data by the extent per capita income rose in
the state between 1949 and 1960.

Low farm income and the extent of low-production farming were
the other two criteria listed in the Act and are closely associated with
low-income levels, but not necessarily so. In many counties only a
small percentage of the work force is engaged in farming, and a few
low-production farms in a non-agricultural area were not intended to
qualify a county for ARA assistance. But the ARA failed to establish criteria as to minimum number of low-production farms
which would qualify a county as eligible for assistance. As a result,
some non-agricultural counties were designated as eligible on the basis
of the above criterion. Two counties, Clear Creek and Gilpin, Colorado, qualified for assistance as being low farming-production areas,
though each of the counties had, according to the 1960 Census, only
one commercial farm. Altogether, more than three hundred counties
qualified as eligible for ARA assistance on the basis of low income or
low level of farm production.

In addition, as a sop to farm lobbies and to placate the Department
of Agriculture, all the 230 counties selected by the Department of
Agriculture under its rural redevelopment program were added to the
list of eligible areas, without reference to the level of income or unemployment that prevailed in these areas. The equity of including all
the rural redevelopment areas is certainly open to question. ARA authorities never justified their action, and it is doubtful if they had a
good explanation. For example, the Texas Agricultural Extension
Service chose to designate 43 counties in east Texas for participation
in the Rural Redevelopment Program, while the Tennessee Agricultural Extension Service selected only 5. But the ARA was indiscriminate in designating rural redevelopment areas. Even a cursory evaluation of the relative economic conditions of the 43 Texas counties
would have disclosed that many of them had no claim on ARA assistance and some even resented the designation. Less than a third of
the designated 230 rural redevelopment areas would have qualified

for assistance under the other criteria of either low income or high unemployment.

Since no historical data were available upon which designation of smaller urban areas with a labor force of less than 15,000 could be based, the Bureau of Employment Security agreed that these areas should be designated on the basis of unemployment compensation information. Such data are not a good measure of total unemployment in any area, and they are especially inaccurate for agricultural areas where farm employment is an important factor. Since agricultural laborers are not covered by state unemployment compensation laws, in rural areas this program covers only a part—and frequently less than a majority—of the total labor force. Nevertheless, the political situation demanded that the ARA designate smaller urban areas regardless of the unavailability of adequate statistical data. So, the fragmentary unemployment compensation data were utilized to designate more than three hundred counties. More careful scrutiny disclosed later that several score of these areas were by no means eligible to receive assistance from the ARA. But once designated, these areas retained their eligibility status. Of course, many areas qualified for ARA assistance on more than one basis. A rural redevelopment area might have also qualified on the basis of low income or high unemployment, and a low farm-production area was normally also a low-income area with high unemployment or underemployment.

Some counties failed to qualify for assistance even under the broadly interpreted, loose criteria contained in the Act. But congressmen who had voted for the legislation and who had promised constituents that their areas would benefit from the law exerted pressure on the ARA to designate counties in their states or districts. To accommodate these pressures, new "rounding-out" concepts were devised. Under the new scheme, a county, or a series of counties, could be designated as eligible for assistance if it was contiguous to counties which were already eligible for assistance. The rationale for designating contiguous counties was that the group of counties constituted a single economic unit and that ARA assistance to a "rounded-out" county would benefit the unemployed and underemployed in the contiguous areas. A total of twenty-four counties qualified for ARA assistance on the basis of the "rounding-out" criterion.

Another device, used in only two cases, was to break up the boundaries of labor-market areas established by the Bureau of Employment Security in order to qualify areas for aid. Passaic and Paterson Counties, New Jersey, were classified by the Bureau of Employment Security as a single labor-market area. The total area did not qualify for assistance under the criterion of unemployment spelled out in Section 5(a) of the Act. But by splitting the labor-market area into two parts, the unemployment situation qualified Passaic County for assistance. A similar situation prevailed in the Troy-Schenectady-Albany labor-market area, and Schenectady County qualified for ARA assistance when it split from the Albany-Troy area.

This was perfectly permissible under the provisions of the Act. The Administrator is not bound to adhere to employment service labor-market boundaries, and he is authorized to determine the geographic boundaries for the purposes of designating an area. The legislative history, however, specifically prohibits the Administrator from dividing up a single municipality or from designating part of a town as a redevelopment area.

Within eight months after the Area Redevelopment Act was approved, the Administrator had designated 129 industrial urban areas as 5(a) and 657 rural and smaller urban areas as 5(b), including close to 900 counties eligible for assistance. More than a sixth of the total U.S. population lived in these presumably depressed areas.[2]

Still pressures continued for further designations, and once the loose criteria had been established, spokesmen for areas claimed eligibility for ARA assistance on the basis of flimsy data; in many cases, the ARA could not deny the requests. Most of the 170 areas that were designated during 1962 and early 1963 qualified on the basis of unemployment insurance data. As stated earlier, these data offered the least reliable basis upon which areas should have been designated.

Termination of Designation

It became quite apparent to ARA officials that the agency had over-extended itself in designating too many areas. The ARA's extremely limited resources were inadequate to assist many of the designated areas in any way. Moreover, a number of areas had been erroneously designated under the broad criteria used by the ARA. Some forty smaller areas (with a labor force of less than 15,000) that had been designated on the basis of unemployment insurance data did not actually have sufficiently high levels of unemployment to qualify as redevelopment areas. In addition, scores of counties designated on the

[2]On the first anniversary of the ARA, May 1, 1962, a wag suggested that the ARA adopt the slogan: "Today a thousand counties, tomorrow the world."

basis of low median family income or other broad criteria in Section 5(b) of the Act had, according to the 1960 Census, a much higher level of income than the earlier estimates indicated. This was particularly true of counties which qualified because they were designated earlier by the Department of Agriculture as rural development areas.

By early 1962 the ARA was ready to reduce the number of eligible areas. Once the original mistake had been committed, however, the agency found it difficult to retrace its steps. There were usually interests in any given area that saw in the designation such possible benefits as lower interest rates on SBA loans or preferential treatment in government procurement.

Meanwhile, the Administration came out in the spring of 1962 in favor of a program of accelerated public facilities. Designated communities qualified automatically under the newly approved legislation for a minimum grant of 50 per cent for the construction of public facilities which otherwise had to be undertaken completely at local expense. If they lost their designation, they would have been disqualified from partaking in this new federal program (Chapter 5). Under these circumstances, it became politically unfeasible to terminate the designation of areas, and the original designations remained in effect, except for twenty-four areas. Nine of these areas were designated under the criteria spelled out in Section 5(a) of the Act. The unemployment in these areas had dropped below the 6 per cent level and the ARA was required to terminate their designation. The remaining fifteen areas were designated under the criteria of Section 5(b), and the ARA has not devised techniques for dedesignating rural areas originally designated on the basis of low income. The only data relating to median family income in counties on a national basis are based on the decennial census, and new data will not become available until 1971. However, a few counties did not care to wait for the development of new data, and two counties insisted, for whatever reasons, in "getting off" the government's depressed-area list; their requests were granted. Several areas were originally designated due to clerical errors, and their eligibility was terminated. In the balance of the cases, more up-to-date unemployment data clearly indicated that the areas were not entitled to government assistance. The total population in the dedesignated areas was 1.4 million.

The ARA has been fully cognizant of the inadequacy of data relating to the designation and dedesignation of rural and small urban areas. In 1963 its research staff was exploring the feasibility of developing a new series of county-income and other economic data which would aid the agency in determining changes in the economic conditions of areas on a current basis.

Two years after the ARA opened for business, its total clientele, including the areas whose eligibility was terminated, exceeded 37 million persons. They lived in 1,061 separately designated areas in every state—at least one county in each state made the ARA list—and in American Samoa, Guam, the Virgin Islands, and Puerto Rico. (See Map.)

Table 3–1: Population and Number of ARA-Designated Areas by Region as of April 30, 1963 ª

	Population (Thousands)					
		ARA Areas			Population in Designated Areas as Per Cent of Total in Region	Per Cent of Total Population in Designated Areas
			Work Force			
Region	Total Region	Total	15,000 and Higher 5(a)	Less than 15,000 5(b)		
Total U.S.	179,323	34,788	20,370	14,416	19.4	100.0
New England	10,509	2,753	2,455	297	26.2	7.9
Middle Atlantic	34,168	7,918	7,049	869	23.2	22.8
East North Central	36,225	7,820	5,882	1,938	21.6	22.5
West North Central	15,394	1,112	515	597	7.2	3.2
South Atlantic	25,972	5,136	2,013	3,123	19.8	14.8
East South Central	12,050	4,687	1,385	3,301	38.9	13.5
West South Central	16,951	3,182	339	2,843	18.8	9.1
Mountain	6,855	914	92	822	13.3	2.6
Pacific	21,198	1,266	640	626	6.0	3.6

ª Excludes Indian reservations, Puerto Rico, Guam, the Virgin Islands, American Samoa, areas whose designation has been terminated, and areas in New England where parts of counties were designated and for which population statistics are not available. The total population in the above designated areas exceeds 2 million.

SOURCE: Computed from special Bureau of the Census tabulations.

While the ARA has been widely criticized for designating too many areas, it appears that a majority of Congress approved of the ARA action and refused to tighten the eligibility criteria. In 1963, when Congress considered the authorization of additional funds for the ARA, amendments were introduced in the House and Senate which would have restricted eligibility criteria based only on unemployment in an area and would have eliminated the loose criteria of Section 5(b) used to designate labor markets with a work force of less than 15,000.

The amendment was defeated in the House on a teller vote, 130–94.[4] (On a teller tally there is no record as to the vote of individual members.) In the Senate, the amendment was defeated by a 60–28 vote. But three of every four Senators who voted for restricting eligibility also voted later against the whole bill.[5] Most Senators who favored the legislation opposed tightening the criteria to restrict area eligibility.

Opposition to Designation

The clamor for designation for the benefits of the ARA was by no means universal. A few communities, or at least some groups in designated communities, objected to being labeled redevelopment or depressed areas. When San Benito County, California, was designated as a redevelopment area, the editor of the local paper protested the designation. He suggested that any unemployment problems in the county could be solved only by free-market forces and that the government program would be a waste of the taxpayers' money.[8] The duly constituted authorities, the county board of supervisors and the city councils of the two cities in the county, as well as some private groups in the area, also objected to the classification of San Benito as a redevelopment area. Similarly, some of the citizens of Walker County, Texas, objected vehemently to their classification as a redevelopment area and demanded that the ARA withdraw such designation.

A closer examination of the opposition to designation as redevelopment areas indicates that the objections may not have been based solely on lofty principles. For example, the Growers Farm Labor Association, of San Benito County, opposed designation on the grounds that, as a redevelopment area, the county would not be allowed to import Mexican labor; presumably a depressed area should have an ample, unutilized labor force. On the other hand, some businessmen seeking Small Business Administration loans favored the designation; otherwise the interest rate charged by the SBA would have been 5.5 per cent rather than the 4 per cent charged in a designated area. When last heard from, San Benito County had applied for federal assistance under the urban redevelopment program. Part of the funds of the federal grant was to be used for the development of an over-all economic development program.[12] But Walker County and neighboring Greer County had their wish and were removed from the ARA list of designated areas.[1]

The experience of Greer County, Oklahoma (population 8,000), illustrates the internal community conflicts over ARA designation. A meeting held under the auspices of the Mangum (the county seat) Chamber of Commerce protested the designation and wanted to have nothing to do with area redevelopment. The leader of the movement, a local rancher and a retired brigadier general, wrote Secretary Hodges that: "Greer County is enjoying a period of great prosperity, and there is no such thing as substantial and persistent unemployment. Actually, there is a shortage of labor in Greer County, and we have a great growth potential." But another meeting of some six hundred towns-people, concluding that federal aid for the economic development of their county would be desirable, endorsed the designation by a four-to-one vote and authorized the county commissioners to name a committee to work up redevelopment plans. Obviously, different groups in the community appraised their economic situation in different lights.

The ARA position of designating areas, contrary to the desires of the constituted authority in the areas, became untenable, even if objections were raised only in a few isolated cases. Opponents of federal aid to depressed areas used such designations most effectively, creating the impression that the federal government was foisting its largess upon communities which spurned federal handouts. Typical of such attacks upon the ARA was the story in a national weekly head-lined: "U.S. Aid Wanted or Not: Rice County, Kansas, citizens ask why a county enjoying good times can't handle its own problems."[15] The story went on to quote an editorial which appeared in a local newspaper: "A strong, prosperous and economically sound county, once proud to stand on its own two feet and meet its own problems as they came, has been shockingly prostituted under the ever-extending wing of the Welfare State. . . ."

In response to such attacks, the ARA adopted a policy of serving notice to areas prior to their designation and thus allowing the authorities in the area the opportunity of rejecting the benefits of the ARA.

Some areas remained completely apathetic to designation. As will be shown later, the mere act of designation does not qualify an area for assistance. The initiative for assistance must come from the area itself; before an area receives any assistance, it must establish a redevelopment corporation representing the various interest groups in the community. This group must submit to the ARA an over-all economic development plan before applying for assistance. During the ARA's first year, less than half of the designated areas took the necessary steps to qualify for assistance. Another 20 per cent filled this requirement during the second year.

It might be argued that the designation by the ARA did not harm any community and therefore was of little consequence. In practice, however, it would appear that the overextension in designating areas might have harmed both the ARA and the designated communities. The designation may have fostered hopes in communities that they would receive assistance for economic development, and since in most cases it was not forthcoming, disillusionment and disappointment in the ARA program resulted. Such indiscriminate designation also tended to spread the meager resources of the ARA too thinly—a year after it was established the ARA had only about fifty field people throughout the country—which made it impossible to concentrate on the neediest areas and left most of the benefits to the better-organized designated areas. Certainly the image of the ARA suffered through its failure to extend any meaningful help to the vast majority of areas it had designated.

WHAT IS A DEPRESSED AREA?

A high rate of chronic unemployment is only one of many socioeconomic characteristics signaling distress in an area. A stagnating population, deterioration in the quality of available labor resources, declining labor-force participation rates, low wages and income, inadequate investment in capital outlays, and substandard housing are associated with chronic labor-surplus areas.

In order to indicate the magnitude and evaluate the significance of these factors, the following discussion compares socioeconomic characteristics in non-designated areas with the redevelopment areas eligible for ARA assistance. Since the impact of these structural factors depends upon an area's size, industrial composition, geographical location, and length of time it has suffered economic hardship, the designated areas were further separated into seven groups in an attempt to better reflect such influences. The seven groups of ARA-designated areas discussed in this section are: [3]

1. all designated areas—129 5(a) and 657 5(b) areas (Table 3–2); [4]
2. all 129 5(a) areas;
3. one hundred and twenty 5(a) areas;

[3]See Note on the Seven Groups of Designated Areas at end of this chapter.
[4]Tables 3–2 through 3–19 will be found at the end of the chapter.

4. thirty 5(a) areas (Table 3–3);
5. five 5(a) depressed areas;
6. all 657 5(b) areas; and
7. thirty-four 5(b) areas (Table 3–4).

Population and Labor Force

Population in the ARA areas barely held its own between 1950–60, with the natural increase in population only slightly offsetting losses due to outmigration. The thirty 5(a) areas and thirty-four 5(b) areas suffered even more severely from outmigration and population decline in the decade. In contrast, in the more prosperous non-designated areas of the country, population increased by almost one-fourth.

Net civilian migration alone accounted for a loss of more than one-tenth of the 1950 population in all designated areas and was much higher in the selected 5(a) and 5(b) areas. At the same time, the more prosperous areas were increasing their population—a rise of 5 per cent —because of the inmigration of civilians (Table 3–5).

Outmigration in designated areas is highly selective and is heavily concentrated among males in the primary working ages and among those with the highest educational attainments. The impact of outmigration among the prime working-age groups is very striking in the selected areas: in the thirty 5(a) areas, the proportion of the population eighteen to forty-four years of age drops to 31.1 per cent, and in the thirty-four 5(b) areas to 28.8 per cent. Among those in the oldest age group, migration has an opposite effect; 8.5 per cent of the U.S. male population was sixty-five years and over in 1960, but 10.6 per cent in the thirty 5(a) areas was in this age group. Much the same age pattern is found in the female population and would seem to imply that outmigration consists largely of married families under forty-five years of age and tends to be permanent as long as economic activity is declining (Table 3–6).

In non-designated areas, the pull of expanding economic activity and low unemployment rates tends to increase the relative proportion of the important, prime working-age groups in the population. In these more prosperous areas, 35.2 per cent of the male population is in the eighteen-to-forty-four-year-old group. In contrast, in all ARA areas it is only 32.3 per cent. The magnitude of this drain on manpower resources is perhaps more readily understood if the age distribution in the ARA areas is applied to the population of the prosperous areas. Under such conditions, there would be over two million fewer males eighteen to forty-four years old in the non-designated areas. At the same time, an increase would take place among males who are primarily non-producing or dependents—under eighteen or over sixty-five years of age.

A significant feature about the labor force in chronic labor-surplus areas is that the lack of job opportunities delays the entry of youths into the labor force, drives older persons out of the labor force at an earlier age, and discourages women from entering the labor force. Exactly half of the persons aged fourteen and over in the 120 5(a) areas were in the labor force when the 1960 Census was taken. In non-designated areas, fifty-six of every one hundred persons fourteen and over were in the labor force. The low participation rate is more pronounced in 5(b) areas than in the 5(a) areas (Table 3–7).

The lack of job opportunities in designated areas seems to affect women relatively more than men as far as participation in the labor force is concerned. According to the 1960 Census, women constituted exactly one-third of the total labor force in non-designated areas, compared with 30.8 per cent in all depressed areas. In the selected 5(a) areas, females constituted 31.1 per cent of total civilian labor force (Table 3–9).

The total labor force in the non-designated areas, according to the 1960 Census, would have been reduced by 2.8 million—1.8 million males and 1 million females—if the participation rates in those areas were as low as in all designated areas. The impact of high unemployment on labor-force participation rates is even more severe in the chronic labor-surplus areas. If the labor-force participation rates had dropped in the non-designated areas to the rate in the thirty 5(a) areas, then the total labor force would have been reduced by 3.6 million, a decline of over 6 per cent.

A positive correlation exists between outmigration and decline in labor-force participation. The 129 areas designated 5(a) include 240 counties, and the population in 62 of these counties declined by 10 per cent or more between 1950 and 1960. In all of these 62 counties, labor-force participation for males was below the average rate of 78.2 per cent in non-designated areas; and in two-thirds of these counties, the male labor-force participation was below 65 per cent. Similarly, the population in 285 of the 657 counties designated 5(b) declined by 10 per cent or more, and in only 9 counties did the male labor-force participation rate exceed the national average.

The sharp difference in labor-force participation rates therefore suggests that the reported unemployment rates in expanding economies and depressed areas are not entirely comparable. A significant proportion of the potential manpower resources in the latter areas is not counted in the labor force, and this tends to understate the rate of unemployment in depressed areas. Thus, unemployment rates in depressed areas cannot present the full implication of the lack of job opportunities, and they fail to measure the full impact of wasted human resources. If this hypothesis is correct, and the data seem to justify it, comparisons of unemployment rates for periods of full employment and high unemployment for the country as a whole lose some of their validity. During bad times many persons do not enter, or withdraw from, the labor force because jobs are not available and they are not counted as unemployed.

Unemployment and Employment

The rate of unemployment for all designated areas during April, 1960, the date for the 1960 Census, was 7 per cent, barely half again as much as the 4.8 per cent in other areas. However, Census data do not measure underemployment, and the unemployment rate of 6.2 per cent for 5(b) areas is misleading, since the major economic problem in rural areas is underemployment. A more valid comparison of unemployment rates can be made between 5(a) areas and national averages. Unemployment in 5(a) areas was 46 per cent higher than the national average during the Census month (Table 3–9). In addition, preliminary, unpublished data collected by the Census Bureau indicate that the average annual rate of unemployment in the 5(a) areas exceeded the national average by 44 per cent in 1960 and 50 per cent in 1961.

The 1960 Census and the preliminary data for 1960 and 1961 indicate that some areas which were certified for designation by the Bureau of Employment Security would not have qualified to receive ARA assistance on the basis of Census data. In order to qualify for assistance, unemployment in an area must exceed the national average by at least 50 per cent during three of the preceding four years. The fact that during the two years unemployment in all the 5(a) areas did not exceed the national average by more than 50 per cent would suggest that some areas must have had, according to Census data, a rate of unemployment less than 50 per cent above the national average.

An examination of shifts in employment distribution by industry between 1950 and 1960 reveals some of the major causes which have contributed to economic stagnation or decline in chronic labor-surplus areas. These data were prepared only for the group of thirty areas. In 1950 one of every nine employed persons in these areas was engaged in mining, but a decade later almost two-thirds of the mining jobs were gone. This accounted for a loss of 67,300 jobs out of a total of 1,019,000 that existed in these areas when the 1950 Census was taken. The decline of agricultural employment contributed to the loss of an additional 50,000 jobs, while employment in manufacturing remained virtually unchanged. As a result of stagnation or decline in primary industry, growth in services, trade, finances, and government employment, which accounted for the bulk of growth in U.S. employment during the fifties, was also arrested, and the relative employment gain in each of these sectors was less than half the gains made in the U.S. Total employment in these areas declined by 10 per cent between 1950 and 1960, compared with a gain of 12 per cent for the U.S. (Tables 3–10 and 3–11).

A breakdown of the shifts in occupational distribution between 1950 and 1960 also shows wide variations in employment patterns for the United States and the sample of thirty areas. Employment in professional, clerical, and service occupations, which experienced the greatest expansion in the country during the fifties, increased in the thirty 5(a) areas but at a much slower rate than for the U.S. as a whole. This is the result of the stagnation of secondary industries where the bulk of persons in the above occupations are employed. The five depressed areas experienced a decline in all major occupational groups except services (Table 3–12).

Unemployment in almost every occupation in the sample areas was higher than the national pattern.[5] In the thirty 5(a) areas, the occupations which had the highest unemployment relative to those for the nation were craftsmen and semiskilled workers. Unemployment in these occupations in the thirty areas was more than two-thirds higher than in the United States. A notable variation involved laborers whose rate of unemployment in 5(b) areas was lower than nationally. One possible explanation of this phenomenon is that the sharp decline in demand for workers in this group had caused many unskilled workers to withdraw from the labor market, which reduced the number of "statistically" unemployed in this category (Table 3–13).

[5]Unemployment data by occupation differ from total unemployment data discussed earlier because the former includes only persons who have had previous job experience.

Education

Data on educational attainment in designated areas support the frequently stated assertion that the better educated are more prone to migrate from depressed areas than those with lesser educational achievements. For those in the school ages, the pattern of education does not differ in designated and more prosperous areas. Almost the same proportion of teenagers attend school in both types of areas. But the proportion of high school graduates was significantly lower in ARA areas than in other areas of the country (Table 3–14). This holds true nationally and in each of the nine Census regions. The highest differential existed in the east-south-central states where ARA areas accounted for more than a third of the population. The proportion of net civilian outmigration from ARA areas in this region between 1950 and 1960 also exceeded that of any other region. This adds further support to the contention that the incidence of outmigration is more prevalent among those who graduated from high school than among those who did not.

As will be shown later, depressed areas allocate a higher proportion, but less per capita, of the total local expenditures to education than non-designated areas. Apparently, the more prosperous areas are the beneficiaries of the depressed-area investment in the development of human resources. Whatever the cause, the educational attainment of adults remaining in depressed areas is below that of adults in non-designated areas. In 1960 half of the adults in the United States had completed 10.6 years of formal school; in the thirty larger areas, the comparable figure was 9.5 and for the thirty-four smaller areas the median years of school completed by adults was barely above the elementary school level, 8.3 years. Eight per cent of the nation's adults had completed less than five years of school; for the thirty-four counties, the comparable figure was 18 per cent. At the other extreme of the educational spectrum, the proportion of college graduates among heads of families in designated areas was half that found in the more prosperous areas, 7 and 14 per cent respectively.[6]

Income

Declining employment opportunities and the associated economic influences of outmigration, the lower level of educational attainment, lack of jobs for potential, secondary family wage earners, differences of industry-mix, higher rates of unemployment, larger proportions of farm population, and the generally undeveloped state of some designated areas account for a lower level of income in these areas than in non-designated areas. As shown in Table 3–15, per capita income in the latter areas was more than a fourth higher than in ARA areas. In each region, except New England, the per capita income in 5(a) areas was significantly lower than in the rest of the region. The largest differential existed in the west-south-central states where per capita income in 5(a) areas ($1,065) was only two-thirds of that in non-designated areas. The lowest per capita income of 5(b) areas prevailed in the east-south-central states ($841), which account for more than a quarter of the total 5(b) population. In this region, the per capita income in 5(b) areas was less than half of the national average.

By any standards, an annual family income of less than $3,000 in the United States connotes poverty. Based on this criterion, more than one of every five families in the United States was impoverished during 1959; but in designated areas, the comparable ratio was three of every ten families, and in the thirty-four 5(b) areas, the income of more than half of the families was below the poverty line. It is significant to note that if the proportion of families in designated areas with an annual income of less than $3,000 were reduced to the same rate as in the total U.S., this would hardly affect the elimination of poverty in the country: it would reduce the proportion of impoverished families from 21 to 20 per cent. Poverty is still widespread in the U.S. outside of chronic labor-surplus areas.

At the top end of the income distribution curve we find, according to the previously mentioned study of the Michigan Survey Center, one of every six families outside of designated areas enjoying in 1962 an income of $10,000 or higher compared with one of ten families residing in 5(a) areas. Such affluent families were rare in 5(b) areas and constituted only 3 per cent of the total.[6]

As a result of lower labor-force participation and higher unemployment rates, there are more dependents per gainfully employed person in chronic labor-surplus areas than in the balance of the country. Low income level accounts for the larger number of families in designated areas depending upon public assistance for a livelihood. Three per cent of the population depended in 1961 on public assistance for support in non-designated areas, compared with 4.6 per cent in this category in all ARA areas and 6.4 per cent in 5(b) areas.

Wages

Wages are lower in chronic labor-surplus areas than in other parts of the U.S. However, the extent to which the differentials are due to industry-mix or to the lower level of earnings that prevail in these areas is unknown and cannot be judged from the limited data prepared for this study.

In manufacturing, the differentials in average annual earnings might be explained by variations in value added. The differences in average annual wages in the selected areas and in the country as a whole were almost identical to the spread in value added per employee, as follows:

	Thirty *5(a) Areas*	*Thirty-four* *5(b) Areas*
Per cent of U.S. annual wage	87.5	62.2
Per cent of U.S. value added per full-time employee	85.5	62.6

Between 1947 and 1958 annual manufacturing wages rose less in the chronic labor-surplus areas than in the rest of the nation. This lag may have been due to a surplus supply of labor or to the fact that the incidence of relatively long layoffs and a shorter work week was concentrated in these areas during 1958. However, in retail and wholesale trade, although the wage levels were lower, the percentage increase in annual wages was more rapid in chronic labor-surplus areas. This phenomenon might have been due to a greater expansion in the nation as a whole of part-time employment of women. In chronic labor-surplus areas the ample labor supply might have made it unnecessary for employers to require part-time help (Table 3–16).

Housing

Housing conditions also reflect the economic stagnation that prevails in chronic labor-surplus areas. The proportion of dwellings built within the decade prior to the 1960 Census accounted for almost 28 per cent of the total housing units; the comparable proportion of newer housing units in chronic labor-surplus areas was about 17 per cent.

Home ownership is somewhat more prevalent in the chronic labor-surplus areas than in the balance of the United States; more than three of every five U.S. families reside in their own homes. However, there is a considerable difference in the condition of the occupied housing units; less than a seventh of the 1960 housing units in the country were classified as substandard; in the sample of 5(a) areas, three of every ten houses were so classified, compared with more than half of the housing units in the thirty-four rural and smaller urban areas.[6]

Since there are relatively more substandard housing units in depressed areas than in the rest of the country, the median cost of housing and rental are appreciably lower in such areas than for the country as a whole. However, the ratio of the value of the housing units in depressed areas to the United States median is somewhat lower than the comparable cost of rent: this may be due to the fact that depressed economic conditions may tend to reduce the value of houses more than the cost of rent because of the difficulty in selling homes due to the high rate of outmigration. But the statistics do not support the claim that outmigration leaves many housing units in depressed areas vacant. The proportion of vacant housing was lower in the chronic labor-surplus areas than for the country as a whole; even in the five most-depressed areas, the proportion of vacant units hardly exceeded the national average. Depressed economic conditions and outmigration tend to discourage the construction of new homes, but older structures, though in poor condition, apparently continue to be utilized longer in depressed areas (Table 3–17).

Local Government Finances

A 1957 Bureau of the Census survey of local finances disclosed that the tax bite of local governments differs little in redevelopment areas from the balance of the country. The per capita general revenue for local governments for that year amounted to $131 in 5(a) areas, $105 in 5(b) areas, and $146 in the balance of the country. In redevelopment areas, local revenue amounted to 8 per cent of personal income, compared with 7.6 per cent in other areas.[7] But chronic labor-surplus areas seem to go less into debt relative to income than non-designated areas. For the United States, total personal income in 1957 was 8.3 times the outstanding debt of local government, while in the thirty 5(a) areas the ratio of personal income to local-government debt was

---

[6]The Public Housing Administration classifies a housing unit as substandard if it lacks hot and cold piped water, a flush toilet, and bathtub or shower for the exclusive use of the occupants of the unit.

[7]In both cases, local revenue is for 1957 and personal income is for 1959.

thirteen to one; in the thirty-four smaller areas, the comparable ratio was eleven to one.

Once the economic base of a community deteriorates, real estate values decline—property taxes account for half of local-government revenue—and the whole tax base is impaired. This limits the ability of declining communities to invest new funds in capital outlays and to enter into further debt. In the United States, capital outlays accounted for 28 per cent of total local-government general expenditures in 1957, compared with 18.5 per cent in the sixty-four chronic labor-surplus areas and 11 per cent in the five depressed areas. The deteriorated tax base tends to make chronic labor-surplus areas a poor credit risk and may either increase the cost of borrowing money by depressed communities or prevent them altogether from increasing debt by borrowing in the open market.

The relatively meager expenditures allocated by chronic labor-surplus areas for capital outlays has raised demands for federal aid to improve the infrastructure of these areas (Chapter 5). Those in favor of federal aid for the construction of public facilities in depressed areas argue that such facilities have never been developed or that they are permitted to deteriorate since depressed areas presumably cannot afford to allocate adequate funds to capital outlays. But others suggest that if these areas would borrow to the same extent as more prosperous areas, they would have the funds needed for the construction of public facilities. Whether it is feasible for local governments in depressed areas to incur heavier debts remains questionable.

Chronic labor-surplus areas devote a larger share of their resources to education than more affluent areas. In 1957 local governments allocated 44 per cent of their general expenditures to education, but in the thirty urban areas and thirty-four smaller selected areas, education accounted for 56 and 58 per cent of total expenditures, while the five depressed areas spent 71 per cent of their total expenditures on education. The fact that depressed areas spend such a large proportion of their resources on education has been used as an argument for federal aid to education. This argument is further buttressed by the earlier discussion which showed that an appreciable proportion of the resources allocated to education in depressed areas actually benefits expanding areas, which absorb youth who were educated in depressed areas.

Persons in depressed areas are more apt to receive public assistance than persons residing in other areas. Per capita expenditures for public welfare by all local governments amounted to $7.00 in 1957; the comparable figure for the group of thirty chronic labor-surplus areas was $8.00, less than $3.00 for the thirty-four smaller areas, and only $1.00 in the five depressed areas. These funds cover a small part of public assistance expenditures, and the brunt of public assistance costs in chronic labor-surplus and depressed areas is borne by the federal government. This further supports the argument that depressed areas are a national problem (Table 3–18).

Farm Level of Living

Farming in 1960 was the source of livelihood for every tenth employed person in all designated areas (Table 3–10). In 5(b) areas a fifth of the gainfully employed were in agriculture and three of every ten were so engaged in the thirty-four 5(b) areas. Probably the best relative measure of the economic well-being of the farming population in the United States can be secured from the 1959 level-of-living index published by the U.S. Department of Agriculture. This index is based on five items: (1) average value of sales per farm; (2) average value of land and buildings per farm; (3) percentage of farms with telephones; (4) percentage of farms with home freezers; and (5) percentage of farms with automobiles.[13] Based on an average index of 100 for the country, the unweighted level-of-living index of the farm operator for the thirty-four counties was 74. In only six of the counties was the index above the national average, while in five counties the index was below 50. These data indicate that the level of living of farm operators in the majority of thirty-four counties was appreciably below the national average (Table 3–19).

COMMENT ON DESIGNATION POLICY

The federal area redevelopment program was conceived as a modest proposal to aid a few score depressed communities. As it went through the legislative mill, the resources allocated to help stagnating areas remained virtually unchanged, but more areas qualified for assistance. It is reported that when President Kennedy signed the bill he thought that assistance under the program should be limited to some two hundred areas. But Secretary of Commerce Luther Hodges and others convinced the President that, in light of the legislative history of the Area Redevelopment Act, more areas than the President suggested must be designated. During the first two years, the ARA designated even more areas than Congress apparently expected. Under the circumstances, the meager resources of the agency are being spread ever more thinly. And still the clamor for designation continues.

An analysis of the socioeconomic characteristics of designated areas indicates that social capital invested in depressed areas is deteriorating and is frequently wasted because of the high rate of outmigration. Impoverished and depressed communities educate their young only to benefit richer and growing communities which then absorb some of the surplus manpower from the declining communities. But outmigration is no solution for many unemployed and underemployed in depressed areas who fail to raise stakes for a variety of complex reasons. Many of these remain unemployed, depending upon public assistance and relief for a source of livelihood. And a significant proportion of those who are forced into idleness withdraw from the labor force.

A closer examination of individual area profiles indicates that some do not display the usual pattern of characteristics associated with areas with chronic labor surplus. This may be due to a combination of factors. Unemployment in some areas may have been high for only a relatively short period of time, and therefore structural changes were not yet obvious. It is not improbable that errors of classification on the part of the Labor Department have resulted in the designation of some areas which should not have got into the program.

The policy implications are fairly obvious. As the program has expanded and an increased number of areas has been designated, the additional areas, although they may even meet the minimum criteria for designation, are much more marginal in their requirements for assistance than the hard-core areas. Given the limited resources available, the attempt to include marginal areas in the program can only result in inadequate assistance for those areas with greater distress. At the same time, available funds are too meager to make any appreciable dent in unemployment in the large number of marginal designated districts.

The area redevelopment program was enacted to alleviate the misery of the unemployed and underemployed in depressed areas and to help rehabilitate their communities. But as the problems of unemployment and chronic labor-surplus areas have become increasingly pressing, Congress and ARA policy-shapers have extended the program to areas with nearly a third of total U.S. unemployment. This raises the crucial question whether a meaningful program can be developed to aid depressed areas with the limited resources allocated by Congress when the program is so thinly spread.

NOTE ON THE SEVEN GROUPS OF DESIGNATED AREAS

The discussion of the socioeconomic characteristics of ARA-designated areas is based on statistical profiles prepared by the Census Bureau under an ARA contract for each area.[14] These profiles contain information on age distribution of the population and the labor force, distribution of the labor force by major industry and occupational groups, educational attainment and housing conditions, level of income, number of persons receiving public assistance, and financial data on revenue and expenditures of local governments. For a number of items the area statistical profiles also contain comparable historical information. But most of the information in the profiles is limited to the 1960 Census.

The Census Bureau has prepared a composite profile of the 786 areas designated by January, 1962, as eligible to receive ARA assistance. These 786 areas are divided into two groups:

1. A total of 129 labor-market areas, most of which had a minimum labor force of 15,000 in 1960 that included at least 8,000 non-agricultural workers. These 129 areas cover 240 counties and are termed 5(a) areas because they were designated as eligible to receive ARA assistance under Section 5(a) of the Area Redevelopment Act.

2. A total of 657 counties, most of which had a labor force of less than 15,000 in 1960. These 657 counties contained either small urban centers or were predominantly rural.

An examination of the 129 5(a) areas disclosed that the characteristics of some of the designated areas hardly differed from over-all U.S. averages. Three groups of areas offered special problems:

1. It was found that the unemployment rate in the six New England areas was lower than the comparable rate for the balance of the same region—4.3 and 4.6 per cent respectively. This was in part due to the unavailability of separate data for some designated areas in New England, and the areas included in the Census tabulation for such areas were combined with larger geographic areas.

2. Detroit and Pittsburgh—the two largest designated areas—accounted for 30 per cent of the population in the 5(a) areas.

3. The ARA terminated the designation of several areas shortly after the composite profile was prepared. Presumably the above national level of unemployment in the dedesignated areas was of short duration and not chronic. The largest of the dedesignated areas was Flint, Michigan.

A separate tabulation was therefore prepared for 120 5(a) areas, excluding the six New England areas, Detroit, Pittsburgh, and Flint. The total 1960 population of the nine areas was nearly 9 million, or 43 per cent of the total population in the 129 areas.

The Census Bureau summary is restricted to only a few selected characteristics of designated areas. Except for changes in size of total population and labor force between 1950 and 1960, it contained no other historical data. Regrettably, the Census composite profile was prepared manually, and, to save labor costs, many of the characteristics included in the profiles of individual areas were not tabulated for the composite profile.

Aside from the incompleteness of the summary, it could hardly be claimed that the characteristics of all designated areas are descriptive of "depressed areas." The Census Bureau summary covered 897 counties with nearly a fifth of the total U.S. population. To obtain a less diluted and a more meaningful profile of the socioeconomic characteristics of chronic labor-surplus areas than could be found in the Census summary, additional tabulations were prepared for this study covering thirty areas with a labor force in excess of 15,000 (5[a]) areas and thirty-four smaller (5[b]) areas.

The selection of these areas, especially the group of thirty larger areas, was somewhat arbitrary. Two major considerations were given in the selection of the thirty chronic labor-surplus areas. It was desired to include areas from all geographic regions and also to take account of the variety of factors which have contributed to economic stagnation and high unemployment in many designated urban areas. No simple formula was found upon which to base the selection. Twenty-three of the 129 areas experienced, between 1950 and 1960, a population growth higher than the national average of 18.5 per cent. None of the twenty-three areas was included in the group of thirty areas on the assumption that rapid population growth is not representative of chronic depressed economic conditions. At the other extreme, an equal number of areas had experienced a population decline of more than 10 per cent during the decade; only five of these twenty-three areas were included in the group of thirty areas. The average labor force in the thirty areas was 34,000, compared with 41,000 in all designated areas, excluding Detroit, Pittsburgh, and Providence, the three largest areas. The population of the thirty areas ranged, according to the 1960 Census, from 42,000 to 235,000 and averaged 96,000, compared with an average of 112,000 for all the designated areas, excluding the three largest areas.

The 129 areas designated 5(a) were located in twenty-nine states, while the thirty selected areas represented twenty-two states. The designated areas from the other seven states either experienced a population growth of more than the national average or were represented by areas whose high unemployment was due to a decline of employment in bituminous coal or agriculture. There were already ten areas in the sample whose economic difficulties were due to the decline in employment of bituminous coal or agriculture.

The causes for the high level of unemployment could be easily pinpointed in the majority of the thirty selected areas. In seventeen areas the employment decline in a single industry group between 1950 and 1960 accounted for more than 10 per cent of total 1950 employment in the area, as follows: agriculture, five areas; bituminous coal mining, five; other mining, two; manufacturing, four; and transportation, one. In the thirteen other areas the causes of economic decline were more widespread and could not be attributed to a single factor.

Five of the thirty areas were selected for special tabulation. Each of these five labor-market areas—Mt. Vernon, Illinois, Uniontown-Connellsville, Pennsylvania, Beckley and Welch, West Virginia, and Pikeville-Williamson, West Virginia-Kentucky—lost more than 10 per cent of its population between 1950 and 1960. It is assumed that the characteristics of these areas are representative of our most depressed areas and that the composite of the thirty areas represents a profile of the socioeconomic characteristics of chronic labor-surplus areas. Selected characteristics of the thirty areas are presented in Table 3–3.

The 657 smaller areas designated 5(b) also included many areas which hardly reflected the characteristics of depressed areas. To select a manageable sample of these counties, it was decided to include only areas with a labor force in excess of 6,000 which met at least one of the following criteria:

1. median family income for 1959 of $1,887 or below, i.e., one-third or less of the national median;

2. average unemployment in 1958 and 1959 three times greater than the national average; and

3. average unemployment in 1958 and 1959 of twice the national average and a median family income in 1959 which did not exceed 80 per cent of the comparable national figure.

The combination of income and unemployment criteria was designed to allow for a broad geographic presentation of the areas to be included in the sample. If the selection were made exclusively on the basis of low income, regardless of the population size, the sample would have been limited to southern counties. Conversely, exclusive use of unemployment data would have eliminated southern counties because of the relatively low unemployment, despite the high under-employment, in this region.

The above criteria yielded a sample of thirty-five counties. But one county, Lapeer, Michigan, was arbitrarily excluded. The BES data indicated that for 1958 and 1959 Lapeer had an unemployment rate of triple the national average. But all other available data indicated that the county showed none of the symptoms of a stagnating economy. Following Henry Clay's admonition that "statistics are no substitute for judgment," Lapeer was excluded from the sample. Some of the other thirty-four counties might have been excluded on the same basis. But the data in the other instances were not as obvious as in the case of Lapeer, Michigan, and since the purpose of the sample was to find characteristics of depressed areas and not the most-depressed areas, further tampering with the sample was avoided. The average population of the thirty-four counties exceeded 27,000, com-pared with nearly 18,000 for all the 657 areas from which the sample was drawn, and the thirty-four counties accounted for 8.1 per cent of the total population residing in 5(b) areas. Selected characteristics of the thirty-four areas are presented in Table 3–4.

REFERENCES

1. ARA Press Release. May 1, 1963, pp. 63–163.
2. *Congressional Record.* March 15, 1961, p. 3777.
3. *Congressional Record.* April 20, 1961, p. 6013.
4. *Congressional Record.* June 12, 1963, p. 10118.
5. *Congressional Record.* June 26, 1963, p. 11039.
6. Institute for Social Research, Survey Research Center. "The Geographic Mobility of Labor." Ann Arbor, Mich.: The Institute, 1963, p. 229. (Mimeographed.)
7. National Bureau of Economic Research. *The Measurement and Behavior of Unemployment.* Princeton, New Jersey: Princeton University Press, 1957, p. 156.
8. *San Juan Bautista Mission News.* April 27, 1962.
9. U.S. House of Representatives, Committee on Banking and Currency. *Report on Area Redevelopment Act.* House Report 360, May 14, 1959, pp. 23–28.
10. U.S. Senate, Committee on Banking and Currency. *Hearings on the 1961 Area Redevelopment Act.* 87th Cong., 1st Sess., pp. 463, 633.

11. ———. *Hearings on Area Redevelopment Legislation.* 87th Cong., 2d Sess., August 18, 1960, p. 100.
12. ———. *Hearings on Area Redevelopment Act Amendments, 1963.* 88th Cong., 1st Sess., p. 295.
13. U.S. Department of Agriculture, Economic Research Service. *Farm Operator Level-of-Living Indexes.* Statistical Bulletin No. 321. Washington: The Department, 1962.
14. U.S. Department of Commerce, Bureau of the Census. *Statistical Profiles, Redevelopment Areas.* Washington: Government Printing Office. (Series SP.)
15. *U.S. News and World Report.* April 11, 1963, pp. 40–41.

CHAPTER 3: STATISTICAL APPENDIX

Table 3–2: Population and Number of ARA-Designated Areas by Region as of December 31, 1962

	Population			5 (a) and 5(b) Per Cent of Total Population	Number of Areas	
	Total	5(a) Areas	5(b) Areas		5(a)	5(b)
Total	32,820,960	21,073,650	11,747,310	18.3	129	657
New England	2,539,866	2,455,175	84,691	24.2	5	4
Middle Atlantic	7,902,288	7,121,152	781,136	23.1	35	22
East North Central	7,715,272	6,184,434	1,530,838	21.3	22	78
West North Central	1,003,484	514,872	488,612	6.5	6	42
South Atlantic	4,906,592	2,308,839	2,597,753	18.9	28	149
East South Atlantic	4,246,778	1,418,728	2,828,050	35.2	17	155
West South Atlantic	2,542,297	338,889	2,203,408	15.0	6	115
Mountain	761,494	91,956	669,538	11.1	2	47
Pacific	1,202,889	639,605	563,284	5.7	8	45

SOURCE: Computed from special Bureau of the Census tabulations.

Table 3–3: Selected Characteristics of Thirty 5(a) Depressed Areas

Area	1	2	3	4
U.S.	18.5	2.0	28.7	32.8
30 Labor Markets	−3.4	−15.3	29.8	31.1
Ala., Gadsden	3.3	−13.2	26.9	28.8
Ill., Herrin-Murphysboro-West Frankfort	−8.1	−13.2	34.1	31.3
Ill., Mount Vernon	−11.2	−19.0	34.2	28.5
Ind., New Castle	7.5	−5.9	29.4	30.6
Kan., Pittsburg	−9.3	−13.9	35.3	29.9
Ky., Richmond	−5.4	−19.8	24.7	29.1
Me., Biddeford-Sanford	6.3	−4.3	29.7	35.0
Md., Cumberland	−4.8	−13.4	31.1	27.1
Mass., New Bedford	0.8	N.A.ª	34.1	39.1
Mich., Port Huron	17.0	0.4	27.9	29.4
Minn., Brainerd-Grand Rapids	1.1	−13.3	30.7	26.8
Mo., Flat River	−0.8	−13.8	30.6	28.4
Mont., Butte	−4.1	−16.1	32.2	30.4
N.J., Passaic	−6.5	N.A.ª	35.9	37.8
N.Y., Amsterdam	−4.0	−10.1	35.7	37.2
N.Y., Jamestown-Dunkirk	7.5	−2.6	31.9	31.8
N.C., Lumberton	1.5	−23.2	18.6	34.7
Ohio, Ashtabula-Conneaut	18.3	3.2	29.7	29.0
Okla., Muskogee	−5.7	−15.2	31.2	34.1
Pa., Altoona	−1.6	−11.0	32.2	31.3
Pa., Scranton	−8.9	−14.8	34.6	35.9
Pa., St. Marys	8.2	−8.6	29.2	31.4
Pa., Uniontown-Connellsville	−10.8	−20.8	31.5	26.6
Tenn., Greeneville	2.7	−8.8	27.4	28.9
Wash., Aberdeen	1.5	−8.5	32.8	28.4
W.Va., Beckley	−19.2	−34.6	26.2	28.6
W.Va., Welch	−27.8	−46.5	20.7	21.3
W.Va., Wheeling	−3.0	−11.9	32.6	30.2
W.Va.-Ky., Pikeville-Williamson	−16.0	−37.9	20.3	20.5
Wis., LaCrosse	7.2	−7.5	28.5	33.8

ªNot available.

Col. 1. Per Cent Change in Population, 1950–60.
   2. Per Cent Net Civilian Migration, 1950–60.
   3. Median Age, Males, 1960.
   4. Per Cent Females in Civilian Labor Force, 1960.

SOURCE: Data for this and all following tables are computed from Bureau of the Census, *Statistical Profiles, Redevelopment Areas*. (SP Series.)

5	6	7	8	9	10	11
15.8	10.3	100.0	$1,850	$142	$219	$ 9,175
−6.4	9.1	81.7	1,466	113	116	7,843
−3.1	9.1	77.5	1,330	95	259	11,499
−3.4	8.7	76.1	1,477	118	132	5,288
−12.3	8.7	73.0	1,451	126	220	3,784
11.6	9.4	95.2	1,677	139	82	7,667
−7.7	8.9	72.9	1,450	155	79	10,442
−6.4	7.0	46.0	957	61	56	7,651
1.5	9.6	89.9	1,609	85	76	4,445
−6.5	8.9	88.2	1,549	131	212	10,000
−1.9	8.6	92.2	1,711	N.A.	N.A.	5,545
11.7	9.6	98.0	1,651	157	136	8,754
−5.3	8.8	73.8	1,283	203	128	7,572
−3.8	8.4	72.7	1,207	73	66	5,149
−14.1	10.4	93.3	1,615	131	133	9,691
−14.4	8.8	104.0	2,094	148	150	8,157
−11.9	9.4	95.6	1,730	182	108	7,515
0.7	10.0	99.4	1,782	189	176	8,126
−8.7	7.4	39.7	696	44	70	5,205
11.1	10.6	99.8	1,708	124	137	10,414
−6.9	9.1	69.5	1,374	100	188	8,834
−2.0	9.7	90.8	1,574	106	124	8,062
−7.9	9.6	86.5	1,569	95	81	5,851
0.7	10.0	101.7	1,781	84	56	6,530
−14.3	8.7	75.8	1,299	93	109	7,531
4.3	8.3	55.3	1,020	60	135	12,442
−5.4	10.3	102.0	1,928	147	163	8,627
−23.8	8.5	67.9	1,131	77	34	6,007
−41.5	7.7	69.5	1,051	84	37	6,037
−6.6	9.2	91.2	1,671	93	103	9,204
−26.7	8.0	52.6	861	63	13	5,427
−0.5	10.7	100.2	1,753	168	105	8,771

Col. 5. Labor Force, Per Cent Change, 1950-60.
    6. Median School Years Completed, Males 25 Years and Over.
    7. Median Family Income, Per Cent of U.S. Median, 1959.
    8. Per Capita Income, 1959.
    9. Local Government Per Capita General Revenue, 1957.
    10. Local Government Per Capita Debt, 1957.
    11. Manufacturing Value Added per Full-Time Employee, 1958.

Table 3-4. Selected Characteristics of Thirty-four 5(b) Depressed Areas

Area	1	2	3	4	5
34 Counties	−5.5	−23.6	23.5	29.0	−8.9
Ala., Cullman	−7.1	−20.8	26.2	26.1	−5.4
Ark., Lee	−13.7	−37.5	19.9	25.2	−26.3
Ga., Burke	−12.2	−31.9	18.8	35.6	−22.8
Ill., Richland	−3.5	−14.2	31.1	32.6	−4.8
Ind., Greene	5.6	−12.0	35.1	28.3	−2.4
Ky., Nelson	13.6	−8.7	22.4	24.3	2.7
Ky., Pulaski	−10.5	−24.2	27.1	24.4	−11.2
La., Vernon	−3.5	−33.7	27.7	25.6	−7.5
Me., Washington	−6.5	−13.1	32.5	27.3	−8.2
Md., Garrett	−3.9	−17.0	26.9	22.6	2.1
Md., Somerset	−5.4	−12.5	30.6	35.8	−14.0
Mich., Huron	2.6	−14.8	27.4	24.0	−3.0
Mich., Tuscola	13.2	−1.8	26.9	27.7	14.6
Miss., Bolivar	−13.6	−36.5	18.3	33.1	−19.5
Miss., Holmes	−18.6	−36.9	19.4	35.3	−27.4
Miss., Madison	−2.8	−26.0	18.8	34.2	−8.7
Miss., Marshall	−2.4	−26.7	18.7	27.6	−10.3
Miss., Panola	−7.9	−28.4	21.1	29.3	−8.9
Miss., Sunflower	−18.3	−46.5	20.0	32.3	−22.6
Miss., Tallahatchie	−21.0	−44.3	18.8	34.7	−16.6
N.Y., Schoharie	−0.4	−7.9	31.6	28.6	−7.2
N.C., Lincoln	4.9	−11.6	25.7	33.3	9.9
Okla., Le Flore	−17.5	−26.9	32.3	28.1	−14.6
Okla., Mayes	1.7	−9.1	31.3	26.7	−0.1
Pa., Bedford	4.1	−9.8	28.8	27.2	6.2
S.C., Lee	−5.8	−30.6	17.3	30.2	−13.7
S.C., Williamsburg	−6.6	−33.4	16.9	32.8	−18.5
Tenn., Dickson	0.2	−11.4	29.4	31.6	4.8
Tenn., Fayette	−10.7	−33.1	18.6	23.7	−20.7
Tenn., Sevier	3.7	−10.3	26.5	27.8	9.4
Wash., Stevens	−3.7	−15.6	29.7	24.7	−2.1
W.Va., Lewis	−6.5	−12.8	36.9	31.8	−6.8
W.Va., Nicholas	−8.2	−26.0	24.1	20.4	−16.2
W.Va., Randolph	−13.8	−25.8	27.3	27.9	−12.5

ᵃ Not available.

Col. 1. Per Cent Change in Population, 1950–60.
2. Per Cent Net Civilian Migration, 1950–60.
3. Median Age, Males, 1960.
4. Per Cent Females in Civilian Labor Force, 1960.
5. Labor Force, Per Cent Change, 1950–60.

6	7	8	9	10	11	12
7.8	52.0	$ 948	$ 94	$ 86	$ 5,748	—
8.3	49.9	922	71	124	3,741	70
6.2	30.8	667	57	73	3,000	58
5.4	33.4	631	86	95	1,946	69
8.9	78.3	1,534	174	163	3,682	109
8.9	72.9	1,443	130	96	9,321	98
8.3	72.5	1,063	72	56	10,882	91
8.1	42.7	872	75	90	5,358	47
7.9	50.1	929	147	156	3,143	85
9.7	63.0	1,216	82	33	7,373	82
7.9	60.9	1,077	170	114	3,547	83
7.8	60.8	1,172	105	95	3,281	106
8.6	75.5	1,235	153	97	9,593	110
8.9	89.8	1,409	130	109	5,508	109
6.0	31.8	661	74	72	8,964	75
6.9	26.1	590	74	33	3,782	45
6.9	33.5	669	58	82	5,381	49
7.2	32.1	571	66	126	5,218	27
7.5	32.4	660	60	56	4,172	46
6.1	32.2	634	85	59	5,007	69
6.1	28.6	581	89	57	1,329	59
9.1	82.6	1,459	218	162	9,634	116
8.0	69.2	1,145	44	28	3,308	84
8.1	47.6	996	112	53	3,720	59
8.7	62.4	1,196	99	82	20,617	86
8.8	76.7	1,343	127	224	N.A. *	106
6.6	30.2	504	79	16	4,072	79
6.6	29.3	537	72	19	4,541	55
8.1	59.1	1,157	70	169	3,667	72
6.4	25.5	488	64	67	3,739	51
8.1	52.0	948	80	164	5,616	63
9.4	80.3	1,398	149	53	9,536	92
8.5	63.8	1,065	54	0	4,140	71
8.3	63.1	984	72	6	3,454	64
8.6	63.8	1,063	73	29	3,424	65

Col. 6. Median School Years Completed, Males 25 Years and Over.
7. Median Family Income, Per Cent of U.S. Median, 1959.
8. Per Capita Income, 1959.
9. Local Government Per Capita General Revenue, 1957.
10. Local Government Per Capita Debt, 1957.
11. Manufacturing Value Added per Full-time Employee, 1958.
12. Farm Operator Level-of-Living Indexes, 1959.

Table 3–5: Population and Net Civilian Migration in ARA-Designated Areas

Area	Population 1960	Per Cent Change in Population 1950–60	Per Cent Net Civilian Migration 1950–60
United States	179,323,175	18.5	2.0
Non-designated Areas	146,502,215	22.1	5.3
Total ARA areas	32,820,960	4.1	−10.9
Total 5(a) areas	21,073,650	8.4	−6.3
New England	2,455,175	10.5	−1.7
Detroit, Flint, Pittsburgh	6,542,108	18.9	0.9
120 5(a) areas [a]	12,076,367	3.1	−9.7
30 5(a) areas	2,892,247	−3.4	−15.3
5 5(a) areas	487,864	−16.3	−30.0
Total 5(b) areas	11,747,310	−3.0	−18.5
34 5(b) areas	955,303	−5.5	−23.6

[a] All 5(a) areas excluding six New England areas, Detroit, Flint and Pittsburgh.

Table 3–6: Distribution of Population by Sex and Age Groups, 1960

(Percentages)

Area	Males—Age					Females—Age				
	Less than 18	18–24	25–44	45–64	65 and over	Less than 18	18–24	25–44	45–64	65 and over
United States	36.9	8.6	26.0	20.0	8.5	34.7	8.7	26.3	20.3	10.0
Non-designated areas	36.6	8.8	26.4	19.9	8.3	34.5	8.8	26.6	20.2	9.9
Total ARA areas	38.2	8.2	24.1	20.1	9.3	36.0	8.3	25.1	25.1	10.2
Total 5(a) areas	37.1	7.9	25.5	20.5	9.0	34.8	8.2	26.3	26.3	10.1
120 5(a) areas	37.4	8.4	24.2	20.3	9.7	35.1	8.3	25.2	20.6	10.7
30 5(a) areas	36.9	7.5	23.6	21.4	10.6	34.1	8.0	24.7	21.6	11.6
5 5(a) areas	41.3	6.9	22.3	20.0	9.5	38.7	7.8	25.0	19.7	8.8
Total 5 (b) areas	40.1	8.8	21.6	19.5	10.0	38.5	8.4	23.0	19.7	10.4
34 5(b) areas	42.4	8.2	20.6	18.8	9.9	40.1	8.2	22.2	19.1	10.5

Table 3-7: Labor-Force Participation Rate by Sex and Age Group, 1960 [a]

(Percentages)

Area	Total	Males—Age						Females—Age					
		Total	14–17	18–24	25–44	45–64	65 and over	Total	14–17	18–24	25–44	45–64	65 and over
United States	55.3	77.4	27.0	80.0	95.2	89.4	29.7	34.5	14.0	45.2	39.2	42.0	10.1
Non-designated areas	56.2	78.2	27.8	80.7	95.3	89.9	30.7	35.4	14.6	46.1	39.9	43.2	10.6
Total ARA areas	51.5	73.7	23.9	76.8	94.4	87.4	25.8	30.3	11.9	40.8	35.6	36.6	8.3
Total 5(a) areas	52.7	75.6	23.2	78.5	95.4	88.8	25.2	31.3	12.7	44.3	35.2	37.8	8.6
120 5(a) areas	50.0	73.2	21.5	77.8	94.5	86.9	24.5	29.8	10.8	40.3	34.8	36.5	8.4
30 5(a) areas	50.0	71.7	20.9	74.5	94.1	86.8	23.1	29.9	11.5	42.6	35.3	36.3	8.3
5 5(a) areas	39.4	57.4	11.1	64.2	90.9	78.2	16.1	20.6	6.8	30.9	24.3	23.9	5.7
Total 5(b) areas	49.1	70.3	24.8	74.1	92.2	84.9	26.9	28.5	10.6	34.5	36.4	34.4	7.6
34 5(b) areas	47.8	69.5	25.5	72.7	91.6	85.0	28.8	27.1	9.9	32.4	35.0	33.3	7.7

[a] Normally, only non-institutional population is included in calculating the labor-force participation rate, but data on institutional population were not available for designated areas; hence, total population in the respective age group was used to calculate labor-force participation rates.

Table 3–8: Distribution of Labor Force by Sex and Age Group, 1960

(Percentages)

Area	Males—Age					Females—Age				
	14–17	18–24	25–44	45–64	65 and over	14–17	18–24	25–44	45–64	65 and over
United States	3.2	12.9	46.0	33.2	4.7	3.4	16.0	41.9	34.5	4.1
Non-designated areas	3.2	13.0	46.2	32.9	4.7	3.4	16.1	41.9	34.5	4.1
Total ARA areas	3.3	12.5	44.8	34.7	4.8	3.7	15.8	41.8	34.8	3.9
Total 5(a) areas	2.9	11.8	46.2	34.7	4.3	3.5	16.3	41.4	34.8	3.9
120 5(a) areas	3.0	12.9	44.9	34.6	4.7	3.3	15.8	41.3	35.3	4.2
30 5(a) areas	2.9	11.0	44.2	36.9	4.9	3.5	15.6	40.2	36.2	4.4
5 5(a) areas	2.2	10.4	47.4	36.5	3.6	3.7	16.9	42.7	33.1	3.6
Total 5(b) areas	4.1	13.7	41.9	34.7	5.6	4.0	14.8	42.5	34.6	4.0
34 5(b) areas	4.7	13.1	41.2	34.9	6.2	4.2	14.5	42.3	34.7	4.4

Table 3–9: Labor-Force Participation and Unemployment Rates

(Percentages)

Area	Per Cent Change in Labor Force 1950–60	Per Cent Unemployment April, 1960	Females as Per Cent of	
			Civilian Labor Force	Unemployment
United States	15.8	5.1	32.8	34.5
Non-designated areas	18.9	4.8	33.3	36.0
Total ARA areas	1.8	7.0	30.8	29.6
Total 5(a) areas	4.9	7.4	31.3	29.2
120 5(a) areas	1.1	8.0	31.1	27.9
30 5(a) areas	−6.4	8.2	31.1	27.2
5 5(a) areas	−22.3	14.2	25.5	14.8
Total 5(b) areas	−3.9	6.2	29.9	30.6
34 5(b) areas	−8.9	6.6	29.0	29.6

Table 3–10: Distribution of Employment by Major Industry Groups, 1960

(Percentages)

Area	1	2	3	4	5	6	7	8	9
United States	7.0	1.1	6.2	28.2	7.2	19.0	4.3	21.8	5.2
Non-designated areas	6.5	0.7	6.2	27.9	7.3	19.3	4.6	22.2	5.4
Total ARA areas	9.8	2.7	5.9	30.1	6.6	17.8	2.9	20.1	4.0
Total 5(a) areas	4.6	2.7	5.4	34.2	7.1	18.5	3.4	20.0	4.1
120 5(a) areas	7.8	4.6	5.9	28.4	7.7	18.6	2.8	20.0	4.1
30 5 (a) areas	7.0	5.4	5.1	30.4	8.3	18.4	2.5	19.3	3.5
5 5(a) areas	4.4	22.8	4.3	15.9	8.0	19.2	2.2	20.1	3.1
Total 5(b) areas	19.8	2.7	6.9	22.1	5.7	16.5	2.0	20.4	3.9
34 5(b) areas	28.8	2.0	6.7	18.4	5.3	15.8	1.5	18.3	3.2

Col. 1. Agriculture, Forestry, and Fisheries.
    2. Mining.
    3. Construction.
    4. Manufacturing.
    5. Transportation, Communications, and Public Utilities.
    6. Wholesale and Retail Trade.
    7. Finance, Insurance, and Real Estate.
    8. Service.
    9. Public Administration.

Table 3–11: Change in Employment by Major Industry Group, 1950 and 1960

(Percentages)

Industry	U.S.	30 5(a) Areas
Total	11.8	−10.4
Agriculture, forestry, and fisheries	−38.2	−43.7
Mining	−29.8	−57.8
Construction	10.4	−3.5
Manufacturing	19.3	−.1
Transportation, communication, and public utilities	2.1	−20.0
Wholesale and retail trade	12.2	−0.4
Finance	40.4	20.7
Services	34.3	16.0
Public administration	27.4	13.4

Table 3–12: Distribution of Employment by Major Occupational Groups, 1950 and 1960

(Percentages)

Occupation	1960			1950			% Change 1950–60		
	U.S.	30 5(a) Areas	34 5(b) Areas	U.S.	30 5(a) Areas	34 5(b) Areas	U.S.	30 5(a) Areas	34 5(b) Areas
Total	100.0	100.0	100.0	100.0	100.0	100.0	15.6	−14.3	−11.1
Professional and managerial	21.1	17.2	13.9	18.9	14.2	11.0	29.0	3.8	12.4
Farmers and farm managers	4.2	4.3	14.6	8.3	6.8	30.3	−41.9	−45.7	−57.5
Clerical and sales	23.2	18.8	12.3	20.9	13.8	8.6	28.4	17.0	27.7
Service	11.9	10.7	10.6	10.4	7.9	6.9	32.8	16.3	36.8
Craftsmen and kindred	14.6	14.7	11.3	15.0	12.5	7.9	12.0	0.7	27.6
Semiskilled	19.8	26.5	18.8	19.8	35.3	14.4	15.6	−37.5	15.7
Laborers, except farm and mine	5.2	7.9	18.5	6.6	9.6	21.2	−9.6	−29.5	−22.5

Table 3–13: Unemployment Rates by Major Occupational Groups, 1960

(Percentages)

Occupation	U.S.	30 5(a) Areas	34 5(b) Areas	5 5(a) Areas	Per Cent above National		
					30 5(a)	34 5(b)	5 5(a)
Total	4.7	7.1	6.3	13.1	51	34	179
Professional and managerial	1.4	1.8	1.4	2.1	29	0	50
Farmers and farm managers	.8	.9	1.1	—	12	14	—
Clerical and sales	3.3	4.8	3.7	6.1	45	12	85
Service	5.5	6.6	5.8	8.7	20	5	58
Craftsmen	5.4	8.9	8.2	15.0	65	52	178
Semiskilled	7.3	12.7	11.7	20.0	74	60	174
Laborers, except farm and mine	12.0	16.6	10.1	35.3	38	−16	194

Table 3–14: Education

Area	Per Cent Enrolled in School		Population 25 Years and over Per Cent Completed High School	
	16–17 Years Old	18–19 Years Old	Male	Female
United States	80.9	42.1	39.5	42.5
Non-designated areas	81.2	42.0	40.8	43.7
Total ARA areas	79.6	41.5	32.4	36.3
Total 5(a) areas	80.4	40.1	35.4	38.9
120 5(a) areas	79.1	39.9	32.1	35.9
30 5 (a) areas	80.2	41.6	29.8	34.6
5 5(a) areas	74.7	32.9	22.0	25.7
Total 5(b) areas	78.3	43.6	26.5	31.1
34 5(b) areas	76.3	40.9	21.9	26.9

Table 3–15: Income

Area	Per Capita Income 1959 [a]		Per Cent Families with 1959 Income		Per Cent of Population Receiving Public Assistance, 1961
	Amount	Per Cent of U.S.	$3,000 or less	$2,000 or less	
United States	$1,850	100.0	21.4	13.0	3.3
Non-designated areas	1,925	104.0	19.6	11.6	3.0
Total ARA areas	1,512	81.7	29.6	19.5	4.6
Total 5(a) areas	1,733	93.7	21.8	13.5	3.5
120 5(a) areas	1,498	81.0	27.9	17.6	4.2
30 5(a) areas	1,466	79.2	29.2	N.A. [b]	4.6
Total 5(b) areas	1,115	60.3	30.9	44.6	6.4
34 5(b) areas	948	51.2	51.6	37.5	6.7

[a] Total money income (1959) divided by population (1960).
[b] Not available.

Table 3–16: Average Annual Wages and Salaries per Employee in Manufacturing, Retail, Wholesale, and Services, 1958

	U.S.	30 5(a) Areas	34 5(b) Areas
Average Annual Wage per Full-time Employee, 1958			
Manufacturing	$4,789	$4,189	$2,981
Retail trade	2,720	2,499	2,200
Wholesale trade	4,717	4,044	3,113
Services	3,115	2,413	2,046
Increase in Average Annual Wage, 1948–58			
Manufacturing [a]	72.5	67.2	65.7
Retail trade	35.7	42.6	53.1
Wholesale trade	40.6	45.4	58.4
Services	57.0	47.4	55.8
Manufacturing payroll as per cent of value added, 1958	52.2	53.4	51.8
Value added per employee, 1958	$9,175	$7,843	$5,748

[a] 1947 to 1958.

Table 3–17: Housing, 1960

Characteristics	U.S.	30 5(a) Areas	34 5(b) Areas	5 5(a) Areas
Per Cent				
Owner occupied	61.9	66.4	62.3	64.5
Vacant units	3.4	3.1	2.7	3.7
Substandard	13.6	29.7	52.2	38.8
Structure built				
1950–60	27.5	16.1	18.7	14.3
1940–50	14.8	12.5	16.9	16.4
Median monthly gross rent	$70.0	$54.0	$43.0	$43.0
Median value of owner occupied unit	$11,900	$7,800	$6,826	$5,800

Table 3–18: Local-Government Finances, Revenue, Debt, and Expenditures, 1957

Characteristics	U.S.	30 5(a) Areas	34 5(b) Areas	5 5(a) Areas
Per Capita [a]				
General revenue	$142.0	$113.0	$94.0	$88.1
Outstanding debt	219.1	116.0	86.0	80.8
General expenditures	148.4	119.6	95.4	86.1
Education	65.1	62.0	55.0	61.1
Public welfare	7.3	7.8	2.7	1.4
Police and fire protection	7.2	7.2	3.1	3.5
Parks and recreation	3.4	2.3	0.7	0.9
Capital outlays	41.6	22.0	17.9	9.8
Per Cent of General Expenditures Spent on				
Education	43.9	51.8	58.6	70.8
Public welfare	4.9	6.5	2.9	1.7
Police and fire protection	4.8	6.1	3.2	4.1
Parks and recreation	2.3	1.3	.8	1.1
Capital outlays	28.0	18.4	18.7	11.4

[a] Since 1957 population data for individual areas were not available, per capita computations are based on the 1960 population.

Table 3–19: Agricultural Characteristics, 1959

	U.S.	34 5(b) Areas
Value of land and buildings (average)	$34,825	$15,351
Commercial Farms		
Average value	$44,439	$20,483
Per Cent Class V and VI (sales of $50–$4,999)	40.0	61.6
Per Cent Class VI (sales of $50–$2,499)	14.4	31.8
Farm Operator Level of Living		
1959	100	74
1950	59	36
Farms operated by tenants (per cent)	19.8	25.2

SEE PAGE 84 FOR CHAPTER 3 REFERENCE NOTES.

Chapter 4

++++++++++++++++++++++

Industrial and Commercial Loans

++

The establishment of special credit facilities for firms locating or expanding in depressed areas is a basic plank in the program to aid depressed areas. During the first Senate round in the prolonged debate on the measure, William L. Batt, Jr., later the administrator of the program, referred to the need for special credit facilities in depressed areas as "the root of the problem."[20] The argument for establishing such assistance to aid expanding and new firms in depressed areas was usually based on the assertion that conventional lending facilities in the affected areas were not sufficiently venturesome to sustain economic expansion. In many cases, moreover, these lending facilities had exhausted their legal capacities for making loans. "We cannot expect very much of a financial contribution to the local unemployment problem from the banks or other financial institutions," one economist asserted.[17]

Opponents argued with equal vehemence that ample capital was available for worth-while projects. A federally financed loan program would thus either compete with private lending facilities [20] or, what was worse, finance projects of doubtful value and soundness. "Uncle Sam," Senator Wallace F. Bennett argued, "may well end up owning a lot of second-hand empty buildings in so-called distressed areas."[6]

LEGISLATIVE ISSUES AND PROVISIONS

Federal credit used to achieve policy objectives has a long history. Only outright opponents of any and all federal aid to depressed areas opposed the loan features of the bills. However, even the proponents of federal credit for depressed areas disagreed on the precise conditions under which such credit should be offered. Disagreements centered about the type of credit, the total amount, the extent of federal participation, the duration of the loans, the purposes for which credit should be extended, and the method of financing.

Guarantees vs. Direct Loans

Federal credit can be extended either directly or by guarantees. The latter method avoids competition with established credit institutions since the credit is extended by conventional lending facilities with the government guaranteeing the repayment of the loan in case of default. This is the method, for example, by which federal credit policies for housing have been achieved. Advocates of this type of federal credit argued that it would stimulate private loans instead of forcing the government to compete with private credit organizations. They also suggested that with the extension of private credit the federal dollar would be stretched to support more credit, thus permitting a more effective program. Some have opposed guarantees on the basis that guaranteed loans may constitute a subsidy to lenders without necessarily stimulating credit.

Federal guarantees, unlike direct loans, may in addition have built-in expansion features during a period of recession and may therefore be especially suitable for aiding areas with chronic unemployment or underemployment. During a period of declining business, banks have excess funds which they are reluctant to lend because of the uncertainty of business conditions. Federal guarantees might mobilize those funds during a recession or depression—at a time when loans for area development would probably be in greatest need.

But the arguments for guaranteed credit did not negate the claim that there were simply not adequate credit facilities in many depressed areas. As finally approved, the 1961 Act prohibited the extension of federal credit wherever private credit was available at "reasonable rates." Of course, since federal loans were made at a considerably lower rate than the going market rate, this provision only amounted to the usual pious endorsement of free enterprise. Nonetheless, private banks usually participate in extending credit to an enterprise backed by the ARA, and repayment of the loans made by banks may take precedence over the repayment of federal loans.

Amount and Extent of Credit

A more basic controversy centered about the amount of credit which the federal government should extend for the program. As related earlier, Douglas had originally proposed the establishment of a $100 million revolving fund from which loans could be extended to new and expanding business in designated distressed areas. The Eisenhower Administration's bill called for a loan fund of half that amount. There is no evidence that either proposal was based on any evaluation of the actual needs of the depressed areas; instead, they seemed merely to represent nice round sums, which they certainly were. When he agreed to include rural areas under the program, Douglas added another $50 million for credit facilities to these areas. Senator Fulbright succeeded in achieving "parity" for rural areas by persuading the Senate that revolving funds for rural and urban areas should be equal, namely $100 million each. Despite the rising level of unemployment throughout the country, the increasing number of depressed areas, and the consequent liberalization of the criteria for eligibility, these amounts remained in the bills throughout the next five years, with one exception. In 1960, presumably as a concession by Congress to get presidential approval of the legislation, allocations for the revolving loan funds were reduced.

There was considerable doubt whether these amounts were adequate to meet the needs which the legislation proposed to correct. When the Senate first approved the legislation in 1956, it was estimated that nineteen major labor-market areas and some fifty smaller industrial areas would be eligible to receive assistance. The best estimates indicated that the total unemployment in those areas was in excess of 300,000. There were no accurate estimates of the amount of unemployment or underemployment in rural areas and in smaller urban communities, which were not included in the original areas that would be eligible to receive assistance. This meant that if unemployment in these areas was to be reduced to 6 per cent—to the level officially designated as a "substantial" level of unemployment—the urban areas eligible for assistance would require 120,000 additional jobs. We know that the creation of new jobs has a snowballing or multiplier effect which generates additional employment. Assuming a liberal multiplier —e.g., that one hundred new jobs would generate an additional seventy jobs—the 1956 job deficit in the industrial areas would still have been about 68,000. To reduce unemployment in the larger depressed areas alone to the then prevailing level of 4 per cent would have required about 100,000 additional jobs.

The National Industrial Conference Board estimated that capital invested in the United States in corporate industry per manufacturing employee in 1956 was $12,350 and that investment was somewhat higher in non-manufacturing industries.[13] Of course, these figures are on the conservative side, since they reflect the cost of average past investments and do not reflect the current average investment per job. The creation of new jobs in 1956 would have involved a much higher investment per employee. Moreover, the average represented a wide divergence among industries. In manufacturing, for example, the range of capital invested per production worker in 1956 varied from $3,564 in apparel to $80,640 in petroleum. In utilities, it was estimated that the average investment per worker was in excess of $100,000. But even assuming that federal loans would not go to high investment industries, it would be fair to conclude that the average capital investment needed for each additional job in 1956 was about $15,000—the figures used by Senator Douglas. A capital investment of about $1 billion would thus have been required to create the 68,000 jobs needed to reduce unemployment in the larger depressed areas to 6 per cent; about $1.5 billion would have been required to achieve a 4 per cent level of unemployment. By 1962 the ARA estimated, on the basis of BES data, that there were some 1,370,000 unemployed in designated depressed areas—about 10 per cent of the labor force. It would have been necessary to create more than 300,000 new jobs to reduce the rate of unemployment in these areas to the national level, which at that time hovered between 5.5 and 6 per cent. According to the same estimates, close to 200,000 additional jobs would have been required to reduce underemployment in the depressed areas to the prevailing national level. In 1962 there existed a job deficit of at least 300,000 in designated areas, assuming again a liberal multiplier of 1.7. These additional jobs would have reduced unemployment in these areas to barely below the 6 per cent level.

None of the proponents of the legislation proposed that federal loans be used to cover the total cost of new jobs. Douglas limited federal loans to the purchase of land, buildings, equipment, and machinery; the Eisenhower Administration would have restricted it to the first two categories. In addition, the Administration proposed that the federal loans cover only 25 per cent of the cost of land and buildings, while Douglas wanted to offer loans sufficient to cover 75 per cent of the cost of land, buildings, machinery, and equipment.

Later the Administration raised the ante to 35 per cent, and Douglas reduced his proposal to 65 per cent for the respective items of coverage.

The cost of land, buildings, equipment, machinery, and other expenses varies widely from industry to industry. But broadly it has been estimated that the average investment per job in manufacturing may be distributed as follows:[4]

Land and buildings	25%
Machinery and equipment	40%
Inventory	22%
Working capital, financing, and miscellaneous	13%

Based on these very broad estimates, the reduction of unemployment to 6 per cent in the industrial areas eligible for assistance under the Douglas bill would have required a total investment of about $650 million for land, buildings, machinery, and equipment. Similarly, under the more limited assistance offered by the Administration approach, the total cost of land and buildings would have amounted to $80 million (35 per cent of $250 million). The $50 million the Administration would have allocated therefore was short of the actual need of the depressed areas.

Under the Douglas approach, the $100 million figure fell even shorter of the mark. If loans were to cover 65 per cent of the cost of land, buildings, machinery, and equipment, more than $400 million (65 per cent of $650 million) was required to fulfill the minimum needs of the larger industrial areas eligible for assistance.

Obviously, the above calculations present only the crudest estimate of the general magnitude of the funds necessary to alleviate unemployment in industrial labor-surplus areas. But, neither Douglas nor the Administration claimed that their bills would provide even the minimum investment needs of the designated areas to reduce unemployment to a tolerable level.

Crude as these estimates are, data for rural areas are even more inadequate. Where conditions of underemployment prevail, it is much more difficult to estimate the number of job deficits in any precise way.

If an attempt were made to supply working capital for new or expanding businesses in designated areas, the assistance plans would have been even further short of the mark. The reason for eliminating provisions for working capital was never clearly explained in the prolonged hearings on the legislation or during the floor debate in the Senate or the House. Strangely enough, former Senator Homer Capehart, an opponent of the bill, criticized the elimination of provisions for working capital and suggested such provisions were needed for a successful program. To be sure, Capehart used this as an argument against the legislation and proposed that the Small Business Administration, which does provide working capital, could offer more help to depressed areas than the area redevelopment bill. Douglas did not respond to this criticism but suggested that his "Republican friends are a continuous marvel. . . . We have never claimed the bill would do everything. We merely said it would make a start. . . ."[5]

Rate of Interest and Duration

Another important area of controversy relating to loans centered about the rate of interest which the government should charge. Some who favored a federal credit program to aid depressed areas, holding that the sheer availability of credit was the primary factor in encouraging redevelopment, argued that the level of interest was relatively unimportant and should therefore be determined by the market operations. Their objection to an interest rate which was lower than the one prevailing in the free-money market was that it would discourage the use of private lending facilities and be tantamount to subsidizing depressed areas through low-interest loans. The Eisenhower Administration resolved this issue by allowing the Administrator of the program to determine the appropriate interest rate. However, Douglas favored subsidization through low interest rates by making loans available at the same rate that the Treasury borrows funds, adding only a small service fee and an insurance charge to cover possible default.

Professor Seymour Harris, of Harvard, thought that Douglas' proposed interest rate was too high. He suggested that an interest rate which was lower than the going rate paid by the Federal Treasury was justified, since loans to depressed areas would reduce unemployment, increase federal tax receipts, and thereby reduce welfare expenditures. Professor Harris proposed that the interest rate be limited to 2 per cent. He reasoned that this low rate would reduce the cost of constructing new plants and thus attract new industry to depressed areas. He estimated that the reduction of 1 percentage point in the interest rate—for example, from 3 to 2 per cent—would reduce the cost of constructing a new plant by 10 per cent.[20]

Opinions also differed on the duration of the loans. Originally, Douglas suggested that loans be extended for as long as forty years, but in later versions of his bill, he reduced the duration to a maximum of twenty-five years. The Eisenhower Administration provided for a maximum of twenty years for the amortization of loans.

Local Participation

Practically all proponents of the loan program for depressed areas insisted that local citizens be required to participate and to make their contributions to private ventures which had been financed, at least in part, by the federal government. The rationale for this provision was simple. It was felt that since the local citizenry would be the chief beneficiaries from a new economic enterprise, they should be willing to make their own contribution before any federal money was expended. Local participation would also provide a good test for the soundness of any given project, it was thought, since the local people would be best able to appraise the potential success of the project for which federal assistance was sought. Furthermore, the best test of their sincerity would be to require them to contribute a share of the total money needed for the project. Hundreds of communities had already established successful economic development groups which raised funds for economic growth. It was felt that a requirement for local contributions would not constitute too heavy a burden on these communities.

There was little controversy on this subject either in the prolonged hearings or in the debates in Congress. The Eisenhower Administration proposed that the required minimum state and/or local participation be at least 15 per cent of the total cost of that part of the project for which federal money would be used. Douglas preferred that this share be cut down to 10 per cent, and that was the stipulation in the legislation as it was finally passed.

As a further safeguard for federal investment in local enterprises, the law requires that local funds take a subsidiary or inferior position to the federal funds and that no repayments can be made on the local contribution to a project until the total federal loan has been repaid. This requirement, as will be shown later, turned out to be a serious obstacle to the effectiveness of the loan program. Since the repayment of the federal loans could be extended over a period of twenty-five years, this meant that repayment of the local contribution need not be forthcoming for at least a period of twenty-five years. In effect, the law required that the local people would make a gift to the new businesses financed by the federal government. At best, the contributors could expect to receive interest on their contributions during the period while the federal share of the loan was being repaid. Under such unfavorable conditions, many communities found it difficult to raise even a small share of the total cost of projects.

The "Runaway" Shop Argument

While there was little disagreement over local participation, the debate over federal financing of businesses which relocate from one area to another area was extensive and rather acrimonious. Proponents of area redevelopment persistently held that their program represented a truly co-operative effort between federal, state, and local governments and the people in the communities involved. Douglas and his colleagues could always point to the requirement of local participation as proof of their argument. But the issue of federal financing for relocation was deep-seated and involved regional rivalries. Opponents of the program who found it inconvenient to oppose aid to depressed areas on other grounds often found refuge in the argument that the federal funds might be used to lure industry away from their own areas. Normally, this served back home as a safe justification for failing to support the program, particularly in communities which had lost industry as a result of outmigration. In these communities, "runaway" industry is an important issue and sufficient to justify opposition to the bill. On the other hand, representatives of some rural areas—particularly in the South—which have greatly benefited in recent years from the migration of industry opposed any binding prohibition against financing the relocation of industry.

Though Senator Douglas sympathized strongly with those who opposed the use of federal financing to help the relocation of industry, he candidly admitted that political considerations militated against inserting a strong "antipirating" provision in the bill. He knew that such a provision would alienate any southern support his program might attract, and as a measure of expediency, he therefore favored a mild prohibition against relocation of industry in order to break the coalition of southern Democrats and Republicans. As proposed by Douglas, S. 1 provided that ". . . financial assistance shall not be extended for working capital or to assist establishments relocating from one area to another when such assistance will result in *substantial detriment* to the area of original location by increasing unemployment" (Section 6, emphasis supplied).

This language certainly would have permitted the financing of a branch plant even if part of the original operations were transferred to the new facility. Senator Bush, of Connecticut, consistently opposed the bill on the grounds that it would permit the use of federal funds for the relocation of industry. Senator Douglas made repeated public offers to strengthen the antipirating provisions of the bill in exchange for Senator Bush's support for the revised bill. Nevertheless, Douglas suspected that a stronger provision would not buy Republican votes and at the same time would alienate whatever southern support he might have for his bill. When Senator Bush offered in 1959 to tighten the relocation provisions, the following colloquy took place:

SENATOR DOUGLAS: I wonder whether this apparently innocent proposal is meant to divide the forces which might otherwise support the bill, if you will forgive me for asking this question.

SENATOR BUSH: I am seeking to make what we call a perfecting amendment.

SENATOR DOUGLAS: A dividing amendment. A divisive amendment.[17]

And again in 1961:

SENATOR BUSH: I offered an amendment previously which would forbid financial assistance by the Federal Government . . . to assist establishments relocating from one area to another. . . .

SENATOR DOUGLAS: May I ask my good friend from Connecticut, who opposed this measure very vigorously before, if he would not support it if we were to include such an amendment as his? . . .

  As an honest broker striving to get the greatest good for the greatest number, I would like to see on which side the greater balance of political forces lay. I must say that my efforts to protect the South fell on barren ground. . . .

SENATOR BENNETT: I can now say . . . that this bill is not offered as an economic solution to our problem but it is being considered from the point of view of its political value.

SENATOR DOUGLAS: The Senator from Illinois is a realist. He believes that this bill will be of great benefit to the Nation as a whole. . . . We faced the same bipartisan coalition which has operated in both Houses for a considerable period of time. . . .

SENATOR RANDOLPH: [Since we are] talking of the North and the South and the jockeying for position, there is a rather homely story told in West Virginia which is sometimes classified as a "border State." During the War Between the States there was one man who was unable to really make up his mind as to which side he should fight with. and so he purchased or acquired for himself a blue coat. Then he also purchased or acquired a gray pair of trousers.

The result, it is said, was not good. The soldiers of the South shot him through the coat, and the soldiers of the North shot him through the pants.

So I believe we cannot jockey too much here in one position or another.[18]

These exchanges offer an excellent illustration of the sectional differences that strongly influenced debate over the depressed-area program. In 1961 a bipartisan coalition of northern supporters of the bill whose districts were victims of "runaway" industry insisted upon a stringent prohibition against assistance to relocating industries. Douglas finally yielded to proponents of a more stringent "antipirating" provision, and Senator Bush, together with fourteen other Republicans, voted in favor of the 1961 bill. The bill as finally approved prohibited financial assistance to "establishments relocating from one area to another." The Act made it clear that this would not apply to firms opening new branch plants in depressed areas, but it stipulated that the Administrator should determine that the branch plant was not intended to replace the established plant in another area.

But the prohibition against assisting relocation still left unanswered the larger question of whether the federal government was justified in financing industry in selected areas. Opponents of the program suggested that, at best, the federal program would help some areas at the expense of others; in effect, it would be a process of robbing Peter to pay Paul. Apparently this hypothesis was based on the assumption that there is a given amount of economic growth and that any federal assistance to new investment in a depressed area would reduce growth in other areas. In effect, this was a new twist on the old wage-fund theory which held that wages at any given time are predetermined by inexorable economic laws—any wage gains secured by one group of workers must be taken out from the earnings of other workers. Douglas questioned the implications of this hypothesis and repeatedly suggested that the assistance offered under his program would contribute to total economic growth, since many of the projects which the proposed agency would assist would never get under way without federal funds as "seed capital."

LOAN CHARACTERISTICS

Geographic Distribution

The ARA loan program is national in scope. By May 1, 1963, the ARA had approved loans for industrial or commercial ventures (Section 6 loans) in every region of the nation, including thirty-seven states and Puerto Rico. However, the loans tended to concentrate in the northeast and south, reflecting the unequal distribution of ARA-designated areas. Half the total ARA loans went to seven states—Michigan, Oklahoma, Pennsylvania, Florida, New York, New Jersey, and Kentucky. The ARA approved a minimum of $2 million in loans in each of these states, and the first three listed states accounted for more than a third of the total ARA commercial and industrial loans (Table 4–1).

Table 4–1: ARA-Approved Industrial and Commercial Loans by Region, Cumulative through April 30, 1963

	Investment ($'s in thousands)			Per Cent	Per Cent Distribution by Region		
	Total	5(a) Areas	5(b) Areas	5(a) Areas	Total	5(a)	5(b)
United States	$56,584	$25,398	$31,186	44.9	100.0	100.0	100.0
Northeast	13,895	12,140	1,755	87.4	24.5	47.8	5.6
New England	3,631	2,162	1,469	59.5	6.4	8.5	4.7
Middle Atlantic	10,264	9,978	286	97.2	18.1	39.3	0.9
North Central	10,792	6,877	3,915	63.7	19.1	27.1	12.6
East North Central	10,230	6,569	3,661	64.2	18.1	25.9	11.7
West North Central	562	308	254	54.8	1.0	1.2	0.8
South	22,952	4,286	18,666	18.7	40.6	16.9	59.8
South Atlantic	10,740	2,987	7,753	27.8	19.0	11.8	24.9
East South Central	4,510	1,244	3,266	27.6	8.0	4.9	10.5
West South Central	7,702	55	7,647	0.7	13.6	0.2	24.5
West	7,345	495	6,850	6.7	13.0	1.9	22.0
Mountain	3,092	0	3,092	0.0	5.5	0.0	9.9
Pacific	4,253	495	3,758	11.6	7.5	1.9	12.1
Puerto Rico	1,600	1,600	—	100.0	2.8	6.3	—

SOURCE: Computed from ARA statistical reports.

Altogether, about one of every eight designated areas was the beneficiary of an ARA-approved loan—forty-nine areas had a labor force of about 15,000 or more (5[a] areas) and seventy-nine were smaller areas (5[b]). The ARA statistics indicate that the agency had maintained the "parity" intended by Congress between 5(a) and 5(b) areas. Just over half of the loans and about the same ratio of ARA investment in these loans were made in 5(b) areas. Normally, the population of such areas is below 40,000, but in some rural areas where the work force is predominantly agricultural, the population may exceed that number. In Table 4–2, therefore, areas with a population of less than 50,000 roughly coincide with 5(b) areas.

Table 4–2: ARA-Approved Industrial and Commercial Loans by Population Size of Area, Cumulative through April 30, 1963

Population	Number of Projects	Investment (Thousands)
Total	168	$56,584
Under 10,000	17	12,102
10,000 and under 50,000	75	17,439
50,000 and under 100,000	31	9,664
100,000 and under 500,000	37	13,005
500,000 and under 1 million	1	426
1 million and under 3 million	1	271
Over 3 million	6	3,677

SOURCE: Area Redevelopment Administration.

Tables 4–3 and 4–4 attempt to examine whether the ARA has favored the relatively neediest areas in making loans. Regrettably, the agency itself has not kept such statistics. An independent check shows that almost two of every five loan dollars were invested in areas with unemployment double or more the national average in 1961. At the other extreme, more than a fourth of the value of ARA loans went to areas where the unemployment rate was less than 1.5 times the national average.

Similarly, more than a fourth of the ARA investments in 5(b) areas went to areas where the median family income was at least 80 per cent of the national average, and almost the same proportion of the loans went to areas designated because they were rural redevelopment areas. As stated earlier, many of these were relatively high-income rural areas. On the other hand, only a third of the ARA venture loans was invested in counties where the median family income was less than half of the national median. Areas which were designated on the basis of low income or low level of farm production were the beneficiaries of only one-ninth of the total ARA loans in 5(b) areas (Table 4–4).

Skimpy as these data are, they suggest that the ARA had no control over applications for loans and that it did not need to set up priorities for loans on the basis of high unemployment or low income in an

Table 4–3: Distribution of Approved Industrial and Commercial Loans by 1961 Level of Unemployment in 5(a) Areas, Cumulative through April 30, 1963

Per Cent of Unemployment in Areas Where Loans Were Approved	Number of Loans	Investment (Thousands)	Per Cent of Loans	Per Cent of Investment
Total	73	$25,398	100.0	100.0
Less than 8.0	2	2,033	2.7	8.0
8.0–9.9	12	4,872	16.4	19.2
10.0–11.9	29	8,621	39.7	33.9
12.0–15.9	12	4,744	16.4	18.7
16.0 and over	18	5,128	24.7	20.2

Source: Computed from ARA statistical reports.

Table 4–4: Distribution of ARA-Approved Industrial and Commercial Loans by County Median Family Income—5(b) Areas, Cumulative through April 30, 1963

Median Family Income Amount	Per Cent of National	Number	Investment (Thousands)	Per Cent of Loans	Per Cent of Investment
Total		95	$31,186	100.0	100.0
Less than $1,886	33.3 and less	6	2,400	6.3	7.7
1,886–2,263	33.4–39.9	10	1,612	10.5	5.2
2,264–2,829	40.0–49.9	19	7,421	20.0	23.8
2,830–3,772	50.0–66.6	16	2,693	16.8	8.6
3,773–4,528	66.7–79.9	21	8,485	22.1	27.2
4,529–5,660	80.0–100.0	18	6,151	18.9	19.7
Over 5,660	Over 100.0	5	2,424	5.3	7.8

Source: Computed from ARA statistical reports.

area. During the period under review, the ARA had more funds than eligible "clients," and therefore no need existed to set up priorities for eligibility to receive ARA help. Under the circumstances, the ARA could afford to aid applicants from all areas on an equal basis, and it is only natural that it received and approved applications from relatively more prosperous areas. Moreover, the ARA took the position that the provisions of the Act require that all designated areas be equally eligible to benefit from the program.

Size of Loans

The average size of ARA industrial and commercial loans was close to a third of a million dollars, and six of every ten loans were below $350,000 (the upper limit set on Small Business Administration loans). It would be wrong to assume, however, that the majority of ARA clients would have qualified for SBA loans. The requirements for SBA loans are much more stringent and are limited to ten years: for example, many—though not all—ARA applicants do not possess the required security to receive SBA loans, and the latter rarely extends credit to new businesses. In the event he qualifies for both, an applicant who asks initially for an ARA loan can receive the credit only from the SBA. Under the law, ARA credit is extended only as a last resort, when other sources for loans are not available.

While loans in excess of $250,000 have accounted for only 40 per cent of the total loans, they represent more than four-fifths of total ARA investments in industrial and commercial ventures. The size of the loan apparently has little relation to the ARA share of investment per job—except for loans exceeding $1 million, where the ARA investment per job exceeded $6,300, or more than double the ARA's average investment per job. The higher ARA investment per job in the larger loans primarily reflected the five motels and hotels included in this category. Hotels and motels are capital intensive and have raised the ARA's investment per job. The size of the community where the loans were made had little impact on the ARA investment per job: the average investment per job in 5(b) areas was, in fact, somewhat higher than in 5(a) areas.

Two of every three ARA-financed projects were new ventures or new branch plants of established companies, and the balance of loans were for expansion of existing businesses or reopening of businesses which had closed operations. The ARA offered to help save jobs in depressed communities as well as to start new businesses. In three cases, for example, the ARA helped businesses which were burned down and might have otherwise been lost to the communities.

Though the ARA has not published any information on the total

Table 4–5: Distribution of ARA Industrial and Commercial Loans by Size of Loan, Cumulative through April 30, 1963

($'s in thousands)

Size of Loan	Number of Loans				ARA Investment	Number of Jobs [a]	ARA Investment per Job
	Total	New	Expansion	Reopening			
Total	168	108	49	11	$56,584	18,842	$3.0
Less than $50,000	30	17	11	2	899	1,083	0.8
50,000–149,999	47	28	17	2	4,353	2,922	1.5
150,000–249,999	24	15	8	1	4,673	2,096	2.2
250,000–349,999	15	9	4	2	4,540	1,839	2.5
350,000–549,999	21	17	3	1	8,940	2,603	3.4
550,000–749,999	11	7	2	2	6,962	2,744	2.5
750,000–999,999	6	5	0	1	5,318	2,255	2.4
1 million and over	14	10	4	0	20,899	3,300	6.3
5(a) Areas							
Total	73	47	22	4	$25,398	9,288	$2.7
Less than $50,000	11	5	5	1	329	545	.6
50,000–149,999	22	15	7	0	1,988	1,551	1.3
150,000–249,999	10	6	4	0	1,936	864	2.2
250,000–349,999	5	4	1	0	1,507	832	1.8
350,000–549,999	8	5	2	1	3,419	765	4.5
550,000–749,999	7	4	2	1	4,443	1,862	2.4
750,000–999,999	3	2	0	1	2,787	1,539	1.8
1 million and over	7	6	1	0	8,989	1,330	6.8
5(b) Areas							
Total	95	61	27	7	$31,186	9,554	$3.3
Less than $50,000	19	12	6	1	570	538	1.0
50,000–149,999	25	13	10	2	2,365	1,371	1.7
150,000–249,999	14	9	4	1	2,737	1,232	2.2
250,000–349,999	10	5	3	2	3,033	1,007	3.0
350,000–549,999	13	12	1	0	5,521	1,838	3.0
550,000–749,999	4	3	0	1	2,519	882	2.9
750,000–999,999	3	3	0	0	2,531	716	3.5
1 million and over	7	4	3	0	11,910	1,970	6.0

[a] Based on number of anticipated jobs one year after completion of project.

SOURCE: Computed from ARA statistical reports.

investment which resulted from ARA-backed projects, data on the extent of ARA participation in industrial and commercial loans are available. The maximum participation of the ARA is limited to 65 per cent of the cost of land, buildings, equipment, and machinery, and the ARA extended this maximum allowable credit to 96 of its first 168 "customers." Only five successful applicants received less than two-thirds of the maximum permissible under the law, and the balance (68) borrowed between 40 and 65 per cent of the total cost of that part of the project which the ARA is permitted to finance. It was estimated earlier that, on the average, the maximum share that the ARA may contribute to a project amounts to about 40 per cent of the total cost. In actual practice, the ARA share was somewhat less than the maximum permitted by law. Assuming, therefore, that ARA loans amounted to one-third of the total cost of the projects it helped finance, it can be estimated that the $57 million which the ARA loaned to the 168 successful applicants was accompanied by an investment from other sources which amounted to double the ARA loans. On this basis, it is estimated that the $57 million ARA investment resulted in about $170 million total investment in the 128 communities which benefited from ARA loans.

Distribution of Loans by Major Industry Groups

Manufacturing industries accounted for 70 per cent of ARA's loans. Food processing, lumber, and wood products led all other manufacturing categories both in number and value of loans. These industries had a special appeal to ARA since they tended to exploit natural resources in rural areas while adding manufacturing jobs. For example, one of the first loans made by the ARA was to finance a wood-products plant in Mingo County, West Virginia. The ARA anticipated that the new factory would use the lumber products in the area and thus provide additional sawmilling jobs. The single largest ARA loan in the wood-products industry—$1.3 million—was to help finance the building of a particle-board plant in Sutton, West Virginia. The intense competition that prevails in the industry and the existing overcapacity in related products, such as plywood, subjected the ARA to considerable criticism from established producers. But industry projections indicated an increased demand for particle-wood products, and the ARA was willing to chance the financing of a new industry in an area of high unemployment which lacked other potential for the generation of jobs.

While manufacturing accounted for about three times the value of loans that were aimed at expanding recreation and tourism facilities (Table 4–6), loans in the latter industry attracted wider public atten-

Table 4–6: ARA-Approved Industrial and Commercial Loans by Major Industry Groups, Cumulative through April 30, 1963

($'s in thousands)

Industry	Number of Projects	Invest-ment	Jobs	Investment Per Project	Per Job	Per Cent of Total Investment
Total	168	$56,584	18,842	$337	$3.0	100.0
Manufacturing	133	39,737	14,351	299	2.7	70.2
Apparel	14	2,050	1,520	146	1.3	3.6
Chemicals and minerals	6	3,293	583	549	5.6	5.8
Electrical and electronic	10	3,041	1,647	276	1.8	5.4
Fabricated metal products	13	1,770	1,103	136	1.6	3.1
Food	24	5,751	1,635	240	3.5	10.2
Furniture and fixtures	6	1,663	790	277	2.1	2.9
Leather and leather products	1	474	600	474	0.8	0.8
Lumber and wood products	26	11,408	2,770	439	4.1	20.2
Paper and allied products	5	3,047	777	609	3.9	5.4
Primary metals	3	2,063	460	688	4.5	3.6
Printing and publications	2	771	350	385	2.2	1.4
Rubber and plastics	8	1,985	1,017	248	2.0	3.5
Stone, clay, glass	8	1,824	450	228	4.1	3.2
Transportation equipment	4	442	320	110	1.4	0.8
Other manufacturing	3	155	329	91	1.5	0.3
Recreation and tourism	25	14,180	2,662	567	5.3	25.1
Research and scientific	4	1,328	1,349	564	6.0	2.3
Services	4	933	408	590	8.7	1.6
Mining	2	406	72	203	5.6*	0.7

SOURCE: Area Redevelopment Administration.

tion. This was due to the fact that tourism is a capital intensive industry and that it provides relatively low paying jobs, frequently on only a seasonal basis. Some questioned the wisdom of investing ARA's meager resources in an industry which would provide only a questionable base for sound economic development. For example, the ARA approved a $1.2 million loan to help develop a $2 million ski resort in Summit County, Utah. The two major employment sources in the area—agriculture and nonferrous mining—had declined sharply since 1950. The new ski facility was to employ over one hundred people, or most of those unemployed in the sparsely settled area. However, the anticipated jobs will be largely seasonal, and it is doubtful whether it will prove feasible to train ex-metal miners for the skills required by the ARA-financed project—ski instructors, mechanics, cooks, and waiters.[11]

ADMINISTRATION OF THE LOAN PROGRAM

The details of processing loan applications were delegated to the Small Business Administration, an agency created in 1953. Under the enabling law, SBA loans must "be of such sound value or so secured that repayment will reasonably be assured." The agency interpreted this to mean that the liquidating value of the collateral required for an SBA loan be adequate to cover the portion of the SBA loan. Congress imposed less stringent requirements for ARA loans: the agency was to determine only "that there is a reasonable assurance of repayment" (Section 6[b][6]).

In this area, as in most other operations, the ARA did not attempt to establish any ironclad criteria as to what "reasonable assurance of repayment" would mean. The ARA decided to handle loan applications on a case-by-case basis. In general, the agency's policy was that an applicant would be eligible for a loan if the proposed enterprise had a reasonable assurance of success and if the loan did not involve relocation.

The SBA did not make the final determination on ARA applications, which is the responsibility of the ARA Administrator. Each processed application is returned by the SBA to the ARA accompanied by different and sometimes conflicting recommendations. These recommendations are prepared by the loan processor in the regional office, the national loan expert, and, finally, in case of larger loans, by the SBA official in charge of the ARA loan program. The final approval of an application for a loan is made by the ARA Administrator and his staff based upon these recommendations. It takes the SBA about three to four months to process an application. Frequently the delays are due to the applicant's failure to submit the proper information that is needed to evaluate the requested loan. The applicant must show that conventional lending facilities have refused to supply the needed capital and that community participation—the 10 per cent requirement—is assured; he must describe precisely the collateral offered and demonstrate that the project has a reasonable chance of success. At best, preparation of this package of information and guarantees is time-consuming; but after all the information is gathered and collected, there still remains the determination as to whether a given project has a reasonable assurance of success.

Availability of Private Capital

Congress has given the ARA Administrator broad powers in administering the loan policy. *Any* industrial or commercial project which would create jobs in a designated area is eligible to receive an ARA loan, as long as private capital is not available to finance the undertaking. The ARA Administrator is therefore required in each case to determine whether private capital is available. A number of applicants, particularly in smaller rural or urban areas, at first assumed that sufficient proof of the unavailability of private capital could be demonstrated by presenting letters from two local bankers certifying that they could not supply the applicant the desired credit. The ARA realized that small local banking facilities may not be in the practice of extending long-term loans for new businesses and, therefore, has required applicants to seek credit from at least two banks, or other commercial lenders, having a lending capacity large enough to finance the loans. The ARA has also insisted that applicants attempt, if necessary, to obtain their credit from lending institutions outside their immediate community. In case these private lending institutions do not desire or are unable to supply the total needed capital, the ARA has encouraged applicants to secure at least part of the capital from conventional lending institutions.

SBA Participation in ARA Loans

In addition to acting as ARA agent in the processing of commercial and industrial loans, the SBA has also contributed funds to ARA projects. While the ARA has not lacked funds during its first two years of operations, SBA participation offered a distinct advantage to the applicants. ARA loans are limited to 65 per cent of the cost of land, buildings, equipment, and machinery and cannot contribute to the working capital. However, there are no such limitations on SBA loans.

In addition to making loans to individuals, the Small Business Investment Act of 1958 authorized the SBA to make loans to state and local development companies to assist small businesses (Section 502).

There is no limit to the number and total amount of loans which the Small Business Administration can make to local development organizations as long as the amount of assistance going to any individual firm does not exceed $250,000. The SBA also makes loans to local development companies for the construction and development of property. The duration of such loans may be for as long as twenty-five years—the same as ARA loans—but the SBA share of the loan does not normally exceed 80 per cent, and the local development corporation has to provide 20 per cent of the total cost of the project.

The SBA shared in the first ARA loan made to West Virginia. The applicant was to produce furniture in Mingo County. The total capital needed by the company was in excess of $1 million, but the total equity that the owners could invest was limited to $200,000, which was insufficient to provide the needed working capital. The ARA contributed the maximum under its enabling law, and the SBA, together with three local bankers, contributed $288,000 to be used primarily for working capital. The State of West Virginia contributed the 10 per cent local funds. The SBA participated similarly in other ARA-supported projects where lack of working capital was a stumbling block to the successful initiation of the enterprise.

The ARA and the SBA also combined forces on a project in Berwick, Pennsylvania. Early in 1962 the community of Berwick, population about 13,000, faced economic disaster when the American Car and Foundry Company (ACF), the major employer in the community with 1,900 workers, announced that by October 1, 1962, it would close its plant. Several of the executives of the corporation, working with community leaders, formed a new corporation to continue a portion of the ACF production under a defense contract. The ARA loaned $504,000 to the Berwick Industrial Development Association, which, together with an ACF loan and local funds, made it possible for the new corporation to continue with some of the ACF defense work and thus save an immediate three hundred jobs for the community. To provide working capital for the newly formed corporation, the SBA then made a loan of $350,000. Altogether, the SBA participated with the ARA in almost one of every five loans.

Community Participation in ARA Loans

The Act requires, as previously stated, that either the state or the local citizenry must supply 10 per cent of the aggregate cost of commercial and industrial projects financed by the ARA. In many areas, raising "the ARA 10 per cent funds" became a major local activity that was headlined by the local newspapers and participated in by local chambers of commerce, Kiwanis Clubs, and other organizations. The campaigns were played up as major news stories by the local papers. For example, when Mitchell County, North Carolina, applied for an ARA loan early in 1963, the local weekly headlined stories about the campaign during six consecutive weeks.[15] The headlines, all in one-inch block print, were as follows: "ARA Leaders to Sell Stocks as Required by Government in ARA Plant" (February 14, 1963); "Mitchell County Making Progress in Sale of Stocks Required ARA Plant" (February 21, 1963); "Deadline Extended to March 18 for Raising ARA Funds in Mitchell" (March 7, 1963); and "Eleven Days Left to Sell Stock for ARA" (March 14, 1963).

The ARA was sympathetic with the difficulties experienced by communities in raising funds and permitted them, in lieu of the 10 per cent funds, to use prior investments for the development of industrial sites or shell buildings. This policy was established in connection with one of the ARA's first loans, which was made to the Technical Tape Corporation in Carbondale, Illinois. In this case, the city asked that its investment to expand and to rehabilitate a vacant city-owned building for the prospective customer be applied to the 10 per cent contribution required by the law. The ARA approved this application.[1]

The states were slow in mobilizing resources to help their depressed communities raise the 10 per cent share. By the end of 1962, only seven states—Kentucky, Maryland, Minnesota, New Jersey, Oklahoma, Pennsylvania, and West Virginia—had taken steps toward contributing state funds to help finance the local share of ARA loans. West Virginia passed the broadest law, allowing the use of state funds where federal contributions are contingent upon state or local participation. Minnesota and Pennsylvania made provisions for state contributions to cover the total 10 per cent required by ARA legislation. Maryland and New Jersey limited state participation to 50 per cent of the total local share; the communities were supposed to contribute the other 50 per cent.

Secretary Hodges appealed to the governors of all the states to sponsor enabling legislation that would make state funds available to meet some part of the 10 per cent which the states or localities have to contribute to ARA loans.[9] Two governors followed the Secretary's suggestion by proposing appropriate bills to their legislatures, but in both states their recommendations were rejected.

The ARA authorities looked upon the requirement that 10 per cent contributions take a subordinate position in repayment to ARA loans as a major impediment to the agency's activities. This is evidenced by the fact that in the spring of 1963, when the ARA requested Congress to authorize additional funds for the operation of the agency, it asked Congress for only one substantive change in the law which dealt with the 10 per cent requirement. The bill proposed that local and state contributions for industrial or commercial projects could be repaid concurrently with the ARA loan. The ARA hoped that the enactment of this provision would help communities in raising their share. This proposal was still pending before Congress when this study was completed.

Relocation

The prohibition against offering assistance to firms relocating from another area also offered administrative problems. It is frequently difficult to determine in advance what constitutes relocation, as compared with expansion of a new business. However, the ARA established careful controls to ferret out applications which might involve relocation, and it is to the credit of the agency that not a single loan involved a relocation.

The apparel industry, which accounted for more than one of every ten loan applications, posed especially knotty problems. Entry into this industry requires very little capital. It has been estimated that the initial investment required to start manufacturing women's blouses may be as little as $15,000. Many small manufacturers in this industry operate more than one producing unit, frequently transferring work from one unit to another.

The structure of the apparel industry also makes it particularly difficult to determine the distinction between a relocation and an expansion of a production unit. Most of the production in this industry is done by contractors that work for a large manufacturer who markets the goods. The contractor normally does not sell in the open market. Many contractors work for only one manufacturer, while others work for several. Thus, a manufacturer who decides to expand his own productive capacity may reduce the work of the contractors who supplied him with his stock. In such a case, ARA assistance to the expanding capacity of a given apparel manufacturer might result directly in contraction or even bankruptcy for the contractors who supplied him with the same stock in the past. On the other hand, expansion assistance to the contractor could be risky because the market of a contractor is extremely limited and is subject to wide fluctuations. Employees hired in the expansion may become unemployed as the fortunes of the contractor fluctuate.

The unions in the apparel industry have exercised a policing role aimed at minimizing employment fluctuations due to these changing relations between manufacturers and contractors. Congress has recognized the salutary impact of the union policing functions by exempting these unions from certain proscriptions of what would be considered secondary boycotts in other industries.[10] The unions have succeeded in persuading members of the employers' association not to expand their activities unless the parent plant and the contractor or contractors supplying the parent plant with products are fully supplied with work. Under the terms of this agreement expanded facilities can be utilized only when the regular labor force existing prior to the expansion is fully employed. Should work be reduced for any reason, employees in the parent plant must be given work first.

In an effort to break away from contractual relationships with unions, some apparel employers have tried to establish new plants in non-union areas. Frequently these moves have been halted by unions through the use of arbitration awards which have been upheld by the courts. Despite union policing activities, the trend during the past few decades has been for the apparel industry to move to rural communities, notably in the South. This has been particularly true in the sectors of the industry which produce work clothes, shirts, and lower-priced dresses. Most of the requests for ARA credit have come from employers who desired to expand their productive capacities in the South. In most cases, it was quite apparent that the success of a new operation would reduce employment in other areas. Usually, the reduced employment would not affect employees working directly for the loan applicant but would cause unemployment among the contractors who relied upon the manufacturer for their work.

The ARA did not succeed in devising specific criteria for making loans in the apparel industry. It examined applications on a case-by-case basis and was normally caught between the desires of the employer to get credit and the union interests which normally opposed the spread of the industry into areas where the union was weak. Altogether, during the first two years, the ARA approved fourteen loans in the apparel and finished-goods industry out of a total of thirty-one applications. In addition, many more potential applicants were discouraged in the field from filing formal applications.

LOAN CRITERIA

From the beginning it was quite apparent that the processing of loans was going to present a very serious problem to the ARA. Few successful corporations applied for ARA assistance, and the high mortality rate of small business compounded the arduous task of determining whether federal funds should be loaned for any given project. The ARA official must therefore live dangerously. A tight or "sound" lending policy would prevent the ARA from carrying out its mission of providing venture capital to help expand economic activity in chronic labor-surplus areas. However, too loose a policy might involve the loss of public funds and fail to bring any lasting improvements to the depressed areas. The bankruptcy of an ARA-backed project, accompanied by a loss of jobs, would not only subject the ARA to congressional and public criticism, but it would also have an adverse impact on the communities which the ARA is trying to help.

Investment per Job

A thorny problem facing ARA policy-makers was the maximum amount of funds per job the ARA should invest to create new employment. Of course, average investment per job varies widely from industry to industry, ranging, in manufacturing industry, from about $4,200 in apparel to $100,000 in the production of petroleum. Assuming an average investment of $15,000 per job, the maximum ARA contribution for the "average" job might be expected to be about $6,000.[1]

ARA statistics indicate that the agency's actual share of the investment per job during its first two years of operation amounted to $3,000, or only 50 per cent of the theoretical $6,000. This was partially due to the fact that a significant proportion of ARA-approved industrial loans were concentrated in low-capital investment industries, such as wood products and apparel, and that in many cases ARA-financed enterprises utilized vacant buildings which were frequently available in depressed areas (Table 4–6). In addition, the ARA's customers have themselves contributed appreciably to reducing the

[1]ARA loans are limited to covering 65 per cent of the cost of land, buildings, equipment, and machinery, which constitute about 60 per cent of the total cost of generating a new job. The rounded $6,000 average is therefore based upon the assumption that the maximum ARA investment per average job is roughly 39 per cent of the total.

average investment per job. Many applicants apparently believed that their chances of getting ARA approval for a loan would be enhanced if they claimed particularly optimistic employment potential for their planned ventures. In many cases it is difficult to disprove the claims of the applicants, but there is little evidence that the ARA tried to secure realistic estimates of the future employment to be derived from the applicants' projects. The ARA claimed that it helped to provide two hundred permanent new jobs in Butler, Pennsylvania, by extending a $16,088 industrial loan to the Butler County Community Development Corporation in order to acquire a tract of land in an industrial park for a new packaging plant. The ARA cost per job, according to this claim, was exactly $80.44.[3] Such claims cast doubt on the credibility of ARA statistics relating to average investment per job.

But since one of the ARA's major sales points to Congress and the public at large is the number of direct jobs that are "created" by ARA help, it would be beyond the call of duty to expect ARA officials to reduce the estimate of the number of jobs attributable to ARA assistance. Since the ARA measures the investment per job on the basis of anticipated employment one year after a project has been in full operation, it has thus far been impossible in most cases to compare the anticipated number of jobs with the actual number created. Nor has the ARA attempted to make any such comparisons.[16] Spokesmen for the agency have denied that ARA statistics overestimate the potential direct employment which will result from ARA-backed projects. They have asserted that since the employment estimates are part of a loan application, penalties for submitting false information deter businessmen from filing overoptimistic claims.

The ARA had to confront the problem of whether it would establish any formal limits on investment per job where capital intensive industry was involved. The ARA decided not to establish arbitrary limits and not to apply stringent criteria regarding the maximum investment per job when estimating the economic effect of a proposed project. A test case soon arose in the form of an application for a $6 million loan for an aluminum-producing facility in eastern Kentucky, one of the most depressed economic areas in the United States. The total number of jobs that would have been directly generated by the project would have been relatively small compared with the total investment requested. In this case, the ARA decided that the investment factor should be balanced against other aspects of the proposed project, as follows:

1. the anticipated use of basic indigenous natural resources not fully exploited previously;

2. indirect employment resulting from the supplying of raw materials, power, and transportation to the new facility;

3. additional industries that might be attracted to the area to supply the ARA-financed project or to use its end product;

4. the wages paid by the industry; and

5. alternative opportunities for the development of the area.

On the basis of these criteria, the ARA would probably have approved the loan. The economy of the area had been based upon the bituminous coal industry, in which employment had declined precipitously since the end of World War II; and there were no other immediate development opportunities for the area. In this particular case, however, the loan was not made because the prospective investors could not raise their share of the capital needed to finance the venture.

Even though the aluminum undertaking did not work out, it illustrates the difficult (indeed, dangerous) policy decision which resulted in an ARA investment of over $10 million to help build a recreation center in Oklahoma. The theory behind this loan was that the development of the recreation center would generate secondary jobs in the area. It was estimated that the number of direct jobs resulting from the recreation center would be only five hundred, at an average investment of more than $20,000 per job. The approval of this loan left the ARA open to considerable criticism in Congress as well as in the press.[2] In a dramatic fashion it raised the issue of whether the ARA should limit its assistance to labor intensive industries to the exclusion of capital intensive investments.

It also left open to question the "seed" theory approach, whereby the initial ARA investment would supposedly generate additional private investments in an area. Even though the "seed" approach may be sound, its fruits may come too slowly to enable the ARA to withstand both legislative and public criticism of the high investment per job necessitated by its application. Thus it would appear that the "seed" theory, which to Senator Douglas was a basic justification of the program, may be discarded if the ARA is compelled to justify each loan on the basis of immediate results. Such a conclusion may be premature. The ARA could establish some arbitrary limit on its in-

[2]Technically, this project involved a public facility and will be discussed in the next chapter.

vestment per job, and still succeed in "seeding" successful ventures which would bear fruit. The ARA adopted such a policy in connection with tourism projects.

Possibly the greatest amount of controversy was evoked by two ARA loans to finance the construction of a hotel and a motel in Detroit. The ARA contributed $3 million to construct these luxury facilities—despite the fact that a market survey showed that the rate of occupancy in Detroit hotels was only 54 per cent. The ARA justified the loan on the basis that a new luxury hotel—the first to be built in Detroit since 1928—would attract conventions to the city. Rather than competing with the older hotels, the new facility would attract an excess of visitors which would spill over into the older hotels. Moreover, the same group of investors had been unsuccessful for five years in obtaining the necessary credit. The ARA investment per job created by the new luxury hotel amounted to $4,200, and its share of the total cost of the venture was only 18 per cent—almost a fourth of the maximum that the agency could have contributed under the law. Wise as the investment might prove to be in the future, the ARA could not withstand the congressional attacks and public criticism that followed the financing of luxury hotels and recreational facilities.

As a result of these experiences, the ARA decided to establish criteria regulating the financing of tourism projects, as follows:

1. To determine the direct full-time jobs created by the tourism facility, the total annual anticipated payroll and gratuities were to be divided by $3,700.

2. The estimate of the indirect jobs created by the facility was to be based on the anticipated tourist expenditures in the area divided by $10,000. These estimates were to be based on appropriate feasibility studies regarding total additional funds that added tourists would bring to the area.

The ARA was then to limit its share of financing to between 50 and 65 per cent of the cost of the project, or $6,000–$7,500 per job, whichever is lower, depending upon the extent of unemployment or the level of income in the area.[2]

Competition and Excess Capacity

A difficult, double-edged problem which the ARA faced was the extent to which it should infringe upon competition among rivals and the extent to which it should let the existing and potential capacity of an industry be a guiding factor in the consideration of a loan application. The law specifically prohibits the ARA from extending assistance to establishments relocating from one area to another or to firms desiring to expand their productive facilities if the expansion of production in new areas "will result in an increase in unemployment in the area of original location or in any other area where such entity conducts business operations. . . ." (Section 6[a]).

But the ARA could cause decline in business and reduction in employment among established firms by financing new competitors. Though the business community officially views competition as the "life blood" of the American economy, potential or imagined victims of ARA loans have complained about the competition generated by the government. And there has been ample sympathy in Congress for businessmen who complained about ARA loans to potential competitors. The ARA had to face the fact that the usual attitudes concerning the desirability of competition do not extend to a toleration of governmental assistance to one's competitors.

The ARA considered the extension of a loan for the establishment of a new soybean processing plant, whose product would be used for poultry feed, in the Delmarva Peninsula on the eastern shore of Maryland. The region was a major producer of poultry and accounted for about 30 per cent of the total poultry production after World War II. But since then Delmarva's share of poultry sales has slipped to only 10 per cent of the total as a result of competition from other regions with access to cheaper poultry feed. The ARA reasoned that the intensified competition and increased production of soybeans would reduce the cost of production in the area and result in cheaper feed grain. The whole area would thus benefit, even if a few established producers suffered. Harold W. Williams, deputy ARA administrator, commented: "We don't necessarily consider competition or price declines bad things."[12] The ARA justified the consideration of the loan on the basis that it would be helpful to the area in which the plant would locate.

An established soybean producer in the area did not see the situation in the same way. Three years prior to the establishment of the ARA, this particular businessman had borrowed funds from conventional lenders at 6 per cent interest to be repaid over a five-year period to establish his business. When the ARA considered extending a loan to a potential competitor, the businessman charged: "I don't suppose there is much point in taking a risk like that when somebody else comes along and gets money on a 20-year, 4% loan; why they could drive me right out of business while I am pinching pennies to pay off my mortgage in five years." But the clinching argument of the businessman was: "We could hardly complain if this were a privately-financed operation, but it just isn't fair to use our tax money to build the plant to drive us out of business."[12]

The ARA consequently announced that it was denying the loan for the soybean plant. The official reason for the denial was that it involved too high an ARA investment per job—$38,000. Public criticism, however, was probably crucial in discouraging the ARA from making the loan. It became quite apparent to the ARA policy-makers that they would have to be most careful in financing the expansion of capacity if the newer facilities made possible by ARA loans would offer stiff competition to existing businesses.

The Senate Committee on Banking and Currency also struggled with the problem of competition and excessive capacity that might be generated by ARA loans. In reviewing the first two years of ARA activity, it cautioned that the ARA had not exercised sufficient caution in extending loans in industries where overcapacity already existed. The committee admonished the ARA to "take great care to insure that any new production capacity created [by ARA loans] will not be *obviously excessive* to drive other efficient producers in the industry out of business."[19, emphasis supplied]

This admonition was a general warning rather than a specific guideline. It left the ARA with the task of developing appropriate criteria for the extension of commercial and industrial loans. Ideally, if the ARA were to follow the committee's admonition and were to minimize the impact of its approved projects upon existing establishments, it would limit loans to industries which operate at full capacity and where projections indicate future growth and expansion of demand for the product of the industry. This would be a tall order indeed, given the generally slack economy in which the ARA has operated.

But even if the ARA had tried to limit loans to industries operating at full capacity, it is doubtful that, in most cases, it could have obtained the data required for sound estimates of current capacity and for projections of demand for a given product. Such data are most elusive, and the determination of appropriate rules is necessarily subject to arbitrary criteria.[3] In every industry, part of the total pro-

³As a matter of public policy, we try to encourage technological innovation and change, and the 1962 tax laws encouraged business to modernize plant and equipment through the use of tax credit for such investments.

ductive capacity is technologically outmoded and inefficient. The question was, therefore, whether the ARA should consider *all* the available facilities for the production of a given product, or just the capacity of efficient producers, as the Senate Committee suggested. But if the ARA were to follow the committee's suggestion and consider the productive capacity of efficient producers only, it would not have resolved the basic problem of complaints, since it can be anticipated that the most likely complainants against new competition would be the least efficient producers.

The ARA normally relies upon the Small Business Administration, the agency which processes ARA industrial and commercial loans, to determine whether a loan is approvable by the ARA. But when larger loans are involved, the ARA also seeks expert advice, either from other government agencies or from private consultants. This advice serves a double function: it seeks to establish the venture's chances for success and to determine the impact upon established producers. For example, in considering the application for a gypsum-producing plant in Duke, Oklahoma, the ARA sought expert opinion about the capacity of the industry, the return of investment enjoyed by established firms, the cost of transportation, the potential demand for the product, the capacity of the firms who would be competing with the applicant, and the raw material resources available to this company. The loan was approved only after the ARA was satisfied that the company could operate successfully and that there was an adequate market for the applicant's products.

The return on investments and other financial data as well as projections of future demand for gypsum were relatively easy to find, since the industry is highly oligopolistic and is dominated by U.S. Gypsum, which produces 50 per cent of the total national demand. In other industries, such data are difficult to obtain because the line of demarcation between the relevant national, regional, and local considerations becomes blurred, and extraneous influences sometimes intrude.

The difficulty of establishing pertinent capacity critera is illustrated by an application from a poultry producer for a relatively small loan. Poultry capacity in the nation had expanded widely during the decade prior to the establishment of the ARA, and as a result, the price of poultry had declined precipitously. At the same time, advancing technology had made small units of poultry production uneconomical, and for that reason many poultry producers turned to the ARA for credit in order to expand their productive capacity. There was no question, however, about the over-all national glut of poultry supply, though the excess varied among different regions.

A producer of poultry from Ohio applied for a loan to expand his facilities. In support of his application he presented data showing that the extra supply could be sold within his immediate market, where cost of poultry was higher than in other areas. The expansion of his capacity would have supplied additional jobs to the depressed area in which his business was located. It appeared that this application had sound economic justification because, even though the potential market of other suppliers would have been reduced, the applicant could have sold his product at a lower cost in his immediate area. Moreover, conflicting federal programs complicated the decision-making process. The government financing of a multimillion chick-producing unit was contrary to the policies of the U.S. Department of Agriculture, which places a higher priority on the perpetuation of small family producers than on efficiency of production or reduced consumer costs. The ARA could approve the loan only over the objections of the Department of Agriculture, and declined to do so, although it never officially stated the reasons for its rejection of the application.

Controversy over capacity data has not been limited to products sold in wide regional markets. Appropriate criteria for products whose market is essentially local also generated disagreement. The ARA did approve some loans to coal producers in spite of the well-known over-capacity and unemployment in the industry. In March, 1963, the ARA announced a loan for $325,000 to the Columbine Coal Company in Carbon County, Utah. The mine was idle when the ARA announced the loan because of financial difficulty resulting from undercapitalization and from a fire which had destroyed its tipple. The ARA was subjected to considerable criticism for extending this loan. On the face of it, the criticism appeared rather sound. Competing coal mines in the area had laid off employees just prior to the time when the ARA made the loan. But a closer examination revealed that the Columbine mine had special locational advantages. Whereas most of the other mines shipped their coal by railway, the Columbine mine was attractive to truckers because it was 20 miles closer to the market areas of central Utah, which saved a 15-mile pull up a rugged mountain canyon. The mine will have an even greater advantage in the future since a new interstate highway will close the existing canyon road and require an additional 12-mile detour to competing mines. In its request the Columbine mine was able to present letters from various truckers expressing their willingness to purchase its coal. However, an independent observer expressed doubt about the wisdom of this ARA loan and concluded that "the expansion of employment and production at the Columbine mine would doubtless be offset by declining sales in other mines now serving the truckers."[11]

Another loan which aroused considerable criticism against the ARA involved assistance, to the tune of $418,000, to construct a paper-tissue mill in Tomahawk, Wisconsin. When the loan was announced, the local newspaper came out with a banner headline, "Extra—ARA Approves Loan. Extra—Tomahawk to Get New Paper Industry."[14] But the rejoicing in Tomahawk was not shared by other paper-tissue producers. The association complained that the industry was operating at only 85 per cent of capacity and that the establishment of the Tomahawk plant would reduce employment elsewhere. Congressman John W. Byrnes, of Wisconsin, tried to resolve this perplexing ARA problem by proposing an amendment which would prohibit ARA help "in an industry operating below normal capacity while meeting existing demand."[7] Congressman Byrnes explained that his amendment would prevent the ARA from using "taxpayers' money to shift unemployment from one part of the country to another. This is what happens when a loan is granted to build a plant in a depressed area which will make products that can be sold only by preempting the markets of an industry operating below the normal capacity."[7]

The opponents to the Byrnes amendment retorted that such an amendment would be impossible to administer. "What is normal capacity and how would it be determined? . . . How in the world can you determine [industrial capacity] with the long lead necessary to establish an industry, based on an ever-changing market?"[7] The amendment would have virtually prevented the ARA from making loans. For example, the total potential capacity of the ARA-financed Tomahawk plant equaled only 0.2 per cent of the industry's capacity, which had grown about 5 per cent annually during recent years. The Byrnes amendment was rejected by a teller vote of 195–95.

But not all the cases presented such ponderous dilemmas. The ARA had its lighter moments. A producer of butter applied for an ARA loan, noting in support of his application that there would always be a market for his product since the U.S. government guarantees that it will buy any surplus he might produce. The applicant did not show that additional butter capacity was needed nationally or even in his own area. The ARA concluded that it would not be proper to finance additional butter production which would merely be turned over to government warehouses, even though the facility might supply additional jobs to a depressed area.

APPRAISAL OF LOAN POLICY

It is evident but not crucial that during its first two years of operation the ARA failed to develop definite criteria on which to base loans. Members of Congress and the academic community have been especially critical of the ARA for this failure. A closer analysis of ARA policies would indicate that such criticism has largely been unjustified. Economic development is complex and varied, and the ARA needed flexibility and empirical experience in order to execute its program. Under the circumstances, it would appear that the reluctance of the ARA to develop binding criteria and formulas which would control the issuance of loans was justifiable.

It is indeed very doubtful whether economists or financial analysts could supply sound criteria to the ARA for the approval of loans; the tools of economic analysis are inadequate for such determination. Professor Fred Cottrell's thoughtful comments on the subject are worth reflection:

> The ARA was created to correct some conditions that arose as a result of the operations of the market. A considerable part of the flow of goods and services results from decisions made by men who are ultimately responsible not to the consumer in the market place but to the voter in the polling place. It is *his* hierarchy of values that must be discovered and catered to for the generation of the system, not those of the economic man.[8]

But the difficulties of spelling out precise criteria should not have prevented ARA policy-makers from announcing general guidelines which would control the agency's loan policies. Such guidelines were necessary to help prospective applicants to understand the types of loans which the ARA would approve and were also essential for effective and efficient operations. The absence of general guidelines left ARA field representatives and, particularly, SBA staff men who processed ARA loans in confusion as to ARA policies and marred the image of the agency. The failure to develop general guidelines caused the approval of some questionable applications which subjected the ARA to wide criticism and forced it to adopt rigid criteria with regard to loans for tourist facilities.

At best, therefore, it will take years of experience and the application of interdisciplinary techniques before adequate criteria may be developed to govern the ARA's loan and other policies. And given political realities, it is rather doubtful whether it would be feasible for the ARA to develop such criteria rapidly. Congress has not spoken with one voice on this matter; and the sponsors of the ARA have shown an inclination to eat their cake and have it too. Having tried to escape the vicissitudes of a free-market economy by establishing the ARA, the advocates of the program have since insisted that the ARA should live by the rules which Congress apparently considered ineffective in economically depressed areas.

REFERENCES

1. U.S. Department of Commerce, Area Redevelopment Administration. "Previously Acquired Land and Buildings," ARA Policy Guideline No. 3. January 15, 1962. (Mimeographed.)
2. ———. "Limitations of ARA Section 6 Financial Assistance for Tourism Projects." ARA Policy Guideline No. 23. June 24, 1963. (Mimeographed.)
3. ARA Press Release. April 4, 1962 (ARA 62–61).
4. U.S. Chamber of Commerce. *Investment for Jobs.* Washington: The Chamber, 1959, p. 10.
5. *Congressional Record.* March 14, 1961, p. 3651.
6. *Congressional Record.* March 15, 1961, p. 3783.
7. *Congressional Record.* June 12, 1963, p. 10118 (Congressman John W. Byrnes); p. 10119 (Congressman Albert Rains).
8. Cottrell, Fred. Letter to Victor Roterus, ARA assistant administrator for planning and research. December 14, 1962.
9. Hodges, Luther. Letter to Governors dated January 10, 1963.
10. Labor-Management Disclosure and Reporting Act, 1959, Title 7.
11. Mangum, Garth L. Brigham Young University. Memorandum to the author on the impact of the ARA in Utah.
12. Moffitt, Donald A. "Redevelopment Woe," *The Wall Street Journal,* April 11, 1963, p. 1.
13. National Industrial Conference Board. *Business Record,* May 1960, p. 6; and *The Economic Almanac.* New York: Conference Board, 1962, p. 244.
14. *The Tomahawk Leader* (Wisconsin). February 14, 1963.
15. *The Tri-County News* (Mitchell County, N.C.). February 14, 1963, through March 14, 1963.
16. U.S. House of Representatives, Committee on Appropriations. *Hearings on the Department of Commerce Appropriations for 1964.* 88th Cong., 1st Sess., Washington: U.S. Government Printing Office, 1963, p. 180.

17. U.S. Senate, Committee on Banking and Currency. *Hearings on Area Redevelopment.* 86th Cong., 1st Sess., 1959, pp. 1255 (Leo Fishman), 105.
18. ———. *Hearings on Area Redevelopment.* 87th Cong., 1st Sess., 1961, pp. 93–95.
19. ———. *Area Redevelopment Act Amendments of 1963.* Report 250, 88th Cong., 1st Sess., 1963, p. 14.
20. ———. Committee on Labor and Public Welfare. *Hearings on Area Redevelopment.* 84th Cong., 2d Sess., 1956, pp. 1074, 112, 875, 329.

++++++++++++++++++++++

Chapter 5

Loans and Grants
for Public Facilities

+++

In addition to supplying venture capital for new and expanding businesses in depressed areas, the area redevelopment program also called for federal assistance to improve the infrastructure of these communities. As originally conceived by Senator Douglas, a total of $100 million was to be allocated to grants or loans for public facilities. The bill originally contained no provision for dividing the $100 million between the two types of assistance. But as the scope of the program was expanded and rural communities became eligible to receive benefits under the legislation, two separate funds were established for the improvement of public facilities: a $100 million revolving loan fund and an additional $75 million for grants.

LEGISLATIVE ISSUES AND PROVISIONS

As with most of the provisions of the legislation to aid depressed areas, basic differences over the need for financing public facilities developed during the early stages of the debate. Proponents of the legislation were convinced that depressed communities could not afford to carry out a program of economic reconstruction with their own resources and that federal assistance was needed if such communities were to develop a comprehensive economic development program. It was assumed that depressed communities would have to be attractive to industry in terms of labor supply, public services, and other needs of new or expanding business. However, the absence of public facilities might serve to discourage prospective industries. Because of its deteriorated tax structure and inability to remedy the situation, the depressed community might lose out to more prosperous communities which could meet the specific needs of a given industry or business. Douglas and his colleagues therefore wanted to make federal money available to aid the depressed communities in such cases.

On the other hand, opponents argued that adequate federal aid was already available through the Housing and Home Finance Agency and, more particularly, through the Community Facilities Administration—the latter provides capital to improve the public facilities of depressed communities and other areas. They suggested that even in the absence of such legislation, most communities could raise the needed funds. Pointing to the tax-exempt status of communities, they maintained that community-facility bonds were most attractive to investors in the higher-income brackets and cited cases of depressed communities which had succeeded in raising funds at interest rates comparable to those paid by the federal government. In 1961, for example, the Republican minority in the House Committee on Banking and Currency noted that some of the most severely depressed communities had succeeded the previous year in borrowing funds at rates of interest ranging from 2.5 to 4 per cent. The Republicans therefore concluded that there was no economic need for federal assistance to finance community facilities, declaring that such a policy would be a "step in the direction of federalizing municipal finance."[13]

For his part, Douglas viewed federal financing of the infrastructure of depressed communities as a sound investment which might never be undertaken in the absence of federal aid. He pointed to southern Illinois, where the shortage of industrial water had been a major obstacle to economic development. This shortage was overcome in one section of this region during the nineteen-thirties when the region's Congressman (Kent E. Keller, 1931–41) secured funds from the WPA, the PWA, and the CCC to dam a creek which then provided a lake and a permanent water supply in Crab Orchard. According to Senator Douglas, opponents deprecated the Congressman's efforts at the time, referring to the lake as "Keller's frog pond" or "Keller's folly." However, the lake not only provided drinking water for three communities in the immediate area but also encouraged several industries to locate there. And during World War II the lake made it possible for the War Department to establish an ordnance plant in the area. After the war the ordnance facilities were taken over by a new industry which moved into the community and provided 3,000 jobs in an area of chronic unemployment.[1, 15]

Based on his own observations of southern Illinois, Douglas continued to stress the importance of the development of industrial water as a first step in the industrial regeneration of depressed communities. Fully cognizant of the diverse needs of the many depressed communities, however, he refused to limit federal assistance for public facilities to any specific program. He therefore insisted that such federal assistance be linked with the establishment of new jobs in these areas and that the facilities not be used to provide "make-work" for temporary alleviation of unemployment or underemployment.

During the first round of hearings on the proposed legislation, Douglas sought the advice of experts concerning the advisability of limiting public-facilities assistance to specified types of projects. The following exchange was typical:

> SENATOR DOUGLAS: Would you feel that this section [public facilities] should be restricted to purposes which would make it more possible to get new industry; or whether it should be in its present form so that . . . it should include schools and such things?
>
> MR. [WILLIAM L.] BATT: I think it should include everything. I have seen companies go into the areas because of the good schools. And I have seen companies stay out because of rotten schools.
>
> Industrial development strikes at the very heart of the community's whole. . . . There is very little that doesn't relate to industrial development.[15]

The lack of specific limitations on the type of public facilities to be assisted opened this part of the program to broadside attacks by its opponents. The Republican minority on the House Committee on Banking and Currency found "this provision of the bill . . . fantastic"[13] because it would dissipate federal funds for useless projects which would not help the economic development of the communities that the program was designed to assist. They feared the worst as a result of the bill: "They [the bill's administrators] could even go so far with this bill as to construct public schools. . . ."[3] The attack on the public-facilities program on the basis that it might "even" assist in the building of schools was understandable. This section of the Act had considerable appeal to southern congressmen whose districts were in particular need of improving the economic infrastructure of their communities, and it was apparently hoped that raising the issue of federal assistance for the construction of schools might alienate some of these southern supporters. But Congressman Albert Rains, of Alabama, who favored the bill, assured his colleagues that "schoolhouses are left out."[4] However, neither the legislation itself nor any criteria presented in the House and Senate committee reports justified Congressman Rains' assertion. The eligibility criteria for public facilities are as follows:

1. The project must tend to improve the opportunities for the successful establishment or expansion of industrial or commercial plants or facilities.
2. The funds sought must not otherwise be available at reasonable terms.
3. The project must conform with the economic development program of the depressed community.

From these criteria, it would appear that if the Administrator determined that improved school facilities were needed in order to attract new jobs to a depressed area and that the success of the program was dependent upon the availability of improved school facilities, he would be within his power in approving the financing of school construction under the public-facilities program of the Act.

Interest Rate

The interest rate to be charged on public-facility loans raised little controversy. According to the Douglas bill, the effective interest rate would have amounted to 4.125 per cent and was based on the then current average yields of outstanding long-term marketable obligations of the United States plus one-quarter of 1 per cent for servicing the loan. The House bill provided for a lower interest-rate charge by limiting the interest rate to the average annual interest rate on *all* interest-bearing obligations of the United States. The House bill also provided for an effective interest rate of 3.25 per cent, plus the same one-quarter of 1 per cent service charge. Senator Sparkman, of Alabama, favored the lower interest rate and introduced an amendment to that effect during the Senate debate on the bill. This amendment was acceptable to Senator Douglas and was adopted without any debate or roll call.[2]

Grants

The provision for making grants aroused the greatest amount of controversy surrounding the public-facility provisions. Direct subsidies were justified by the argument that the tax base in some communities had deteriorated to the point where additional funds could not be raised to provide needed public facilities. In addition, many witnesses testified that because their communities had reached the limit of their power to borrow under existing state law, they had been unable for many years to improve or to build new public facilities. Representative Carl D. Perkins, of eastern Kentucky, claimed that many mining communities in his district lacked adequate funds to maintain their city governments, let alone build new public facilities. He suggested that similar conditions existed in other areas. According to Congressman Perkins and others, these localities had no way of borrowing funds in the open market and thus depended on federal grants.[4]

In short, proponents of the grants provision argued that grants for the development of public facilities for severely depressed areas would be in line with the established historical practice of using federal grants for clearly specified and important national objectives. Indeed, they argued, it would be ironic to establish a federal program to aid depressed areas while denying them the very assistance which would make it possible for the most needy communities to rehabilitate themselves. They proposed that grants be limited to localities that could not raise money from private sources and which were not in a position to repay the principal and interest on a federal loan. It would be unrealistic, according to this argument, to ask a depressed community to burden itself with additional debts and interest payments. By requiring the community to export sorely needed capital, such burdens would only retard community rehabilitation and negate the very purpose of the area redevelopment program. Opponents saw a real danger in this type of program. The grants would constitute a subsidy, not only to new or expanding firms in depressed areas, but to all private industry in these areas, since industries in other communities would have to pay taxes in order to support the grants. Federal funds would thus be used to build up industry in the affected area, giving it a competitive advantage over industries in other areas. This argument seemed so persuasive that opposition to the grants provision was voiced by several legislators who supported the over-all legislation: In 1961, for example, Senator Frank J. Lausche, of Ohio, announced that he would be ready to vote for the bill, but only if the grants provision were eliminated.[2]

Critics also argued that public-facilities grants would in fact stifle the efforts of communities attempting to rehabilitate their economies.

They claim that grants, even more than loans, would rob communities of their initiative by making them more dependent upon federal aid.[2] And, of course, there was always the "foot-in-the-door" argument which foresaw dire consequences of a grant program. Senator John L. McClellan argued: ". . . if we ever begin permitting the government to enter one area, one community, and foot the entire cost of a project, then we shall have every community in the country appealing to the federal government for the same treatment."[2]

Neither House nor Senate majorities were persuaded by these arguments to delete the grants provision. But in 1961 the House voted to limit grants to 65 per cent of the total cost of the project, while according to the Senate version, 100 per cent grants were allowed for projects unable to attract other funds. It was no secret that the House proponents of the depressed-area legislation, though favoring 100 per cent grants, reduced the maximum to 65 per cent as a tactical measure to blunt the attacks of opponents. The program was sold as an attempt by the federal government "to help the people in depressed areas to help themselves," with the understanding that it would be a cooperative effort between private enterprise and local, state, and federal authorities. The 100 per cent federal grants provision hardly fit this pitch. The conferees charged with ironing out the differences between the House and Senate versions of the bill readily adopted the 100 per cent grants provision for projects which "fulfill a pressing need" in the depressed area.

CONDITIONS FOR MAKING GRANTS

As in the case of public-facility loans, approval of grants was contingent upon the likelihood that new industrial or commercial jobs would be generated within the community. Beyond this, Congress did not spell out the specific circumstances under which a grant or a loan would be given. The law provides the following three general qualifications for receipt of a grant:

1. that the community requesting the grant must contribute to the cost of the project in proportion to its ability to contribute to its completion;

2. that there must be a finding that there is ". . . little probability that such project can be undertaken without the assistance of a grant . . ."; and

3. that the grant shall be limited to the difference between funds which can be "practicably obtained" from other sources (including loans from the ARA) and the amount necessary to complete the project.

The ARA had to deal with the keen competition that exists among communities in attracting new industry. Communities frequently offer a variety of concessions to lure new businesses. The most common of these concessions are free or subsidized plant sites, buildings and public utilities, and exemption from local taxes for a period of years.

Community Resort to Subsidizing Industry

The ARA questioned the wisdom of those communities which offered tax exemptions in order to lure new industry. Such tax exemptions and similar concessions are fraught with danger to the economic development of the community. They deplete its tax base and hamper its future development at a time when the needs for conventional public facilities and schools may be increasing as a result of additional industry. Nor was the ARA alone in questioning the wisdom of such policies. An executive of a major American manufacturing corporation observed that "a town that offers tax concessions or giveaways is merely robbing Peter to pay Paul and we know that sooner or later we will have to pay Peter."[10]

By 1962, ten states permitted communities to offer tax exemptions to new industry. Twenty-one states had enacted laws authorizing political subdivisions to finance the location of business through various tax concessions, including the sale of tax-exempt general obligations and revenue bonds.[8]

Mississippi was the first state (1936) to adopt a state law permitting municipalities to build plants through the sale of tax-exempt bonds. The majority of the states authorizing municipalities or counties to finance plant location through the sale of bonds are located in the southeast and border states. But the New Mexico law has the broadest application. It permits municipalities to acquire "industrial property," which may include the company's entire assets. All other states limit the use of bonds to the purchase of lands or real estate.

Financing new industrial growth through municipal bonding has some obvious advantages. Since municipal bonds are exempt from federal taxes, municipalities can market their bonds at a lesser rate of interest than private industry, thus reducing the cost of developing and building the new industrial site. Frequently the bonds are purchased by the industry for which the building is being constructed, giving the industry a double tax advantage. The building is sold to industry on a lease-purchase basis, thus freeing corporate funds for operating capital that would otherwise be tied up in capital investment. At the same time, the municipality usually retains the title to the new building until the bonds are retired, which exempts the property from local property taxes.

Some have defended the practice of using municipal tax-exempt bonds to finance new industry on economic grounds. Tax concessions are often justified as a community investment in jobs and payrolls; such concessions can thus be used as a countervailing force to wage rigidities created either by government fiat or unions.[9] In a free market, according to this theory, high levels of unemployment in a community would tend to drive wages down and would offer such communities a competitive advantage in attracting new industry. But wage rigidities, according to this argument, tend to eliminate such advantages. To compensate for the "extra" cost of wages, it was suggested that subsidies should make up the difference between the "natural" level of wages and the higher level created by wage rigidities. Of course, this assumes that there is a "natural" level of wages.

The practical application of such schemes has also been questioned. The theory fails to suggest yardsticks by which a community could measure the marginal cost of wages due to wage rigidities and the extent to which new industry is to be subsidized. Moreover, if subsidies to industry are justified because of wage rigidities, it would indeed be difficult, on the basis of equity, to limit such subsidies to new industry, since that would discriminate against established employers.

But whatever the merits of the above arguments, the· ARA questioned whether it should use federal funds to assist communities which already offer tax concessions to new business. A community which offers tax concessions and then requests a federal grant, on the ground that it cannot afford further expenditures for economic development, would receive a double advantage if the grant were made. The ARA could not, formally, question the soundness of the federal tax policy that permitted tax exemption of municipal bonds and the attendant "windfall" to private companies at the expense of the federal treasury; but it could—and did—warn communities that it would review carefully any applications for grants where tax concessions were involved.

Grants vs. Loans

Other problems centered on the conditions under which grants should be made as well as the proportion of the total cost of the project that would be subsidized by the grant. During the legislative debate, defenders of grants justified the provision on the basis that it would be used: "In extreme cases of need . . . the extent to which the Federal Government would provide such grants would depend upon the ability of the community and the State to contribute."[16] The Community Facilities Administration, the agency which was delegated the chore of processing applications, therefore felt compelled to search for a formula to determine the eligibility of a community to receive grants.

In the absence of any congressional criteria for limiting the extent of grants, the CFA technicians set out to establish administrative guidelines for determining the extent of a community's "ability to pay" (i.e., contribute to the cost of a project). The CFA found the following four criteria suitable for determining the extent of ARA grants: (1) the net total per capita debt of the community; [1] (2) the ratio of net total debt to full property evaluation; [2] (3) the tax rate per thousand full property evaluation; [3] and (4) the ratio of per capita net total debt to per capita income.[4]

The CFA then proceeded to determine the median and the lower quartile for each of the above criteria based on the financial reports of Moody's and of Standard and Poor's. It proposed that a community be entitled to receive a grant if its tax rates and per capita debt burdens

[1] The term "net debt" relates to the net tax-supported debt secured by the full-faith credit and taxing power of the local government unit plus the gross overlapping debt of the other taxing authorities whose geographical boundaries overlap those of the local government.

[2] "Full evaluation" is to be contrasted with "actual evaluation" or "assessed evaluation." The latter is usually appreciably below the actual value of the property. To offset this practice, most state governments have devised what is commonly referred to as an "equalization factor," which reflects what the state assessors regard as the ratio of assessed evaluation to actual evaluation in the community. Adjustment of the assessed-evaluation figures of the local government, by this equalization factor, gives the full real property evaluation of the community.

[3] This criterion represents a measure of local fiscal effort in measuring the ratio of taxes levied to real property value. While the CFA recognized that the relative importance of property taxation is declining, it still accounted in 1959 for 58 per cent of total local tax revenue.

[4] This criterion is self-explanatory and recognizes the fact that the fiscal capacity of a community is largely dependent upon the aggregate of personal income of its citizens.

were heavier than those of 50 per cent of all municipalities for three of the above-listed criteria. The extent of the grant would vary from zero to 75 per cent, depending upon the fiscal circumstances of the applicant and the cost of the project. But the authority of the ARA to limit grants to 75 per cent may be questioned in view of the legislative history of the Act. As stated earlier, the House originally limited grants to 65 per cent of the cost of any project. But the Act, as finally approved, included the Senate provision for a maximum of 100 per cent grants.

It took the ARA only a short time to realize that it could not live with these complicated though elegant formulas. At best, it would be most difficult to explain them to the people of a community. And even community leaders who would understand the basis of the formulas could not help but question their arbitrary quality. Moreover, the ARA did not want to be in the position of having to judge the eligibility of communities on the basis of their comparison with other communities in the United States. The ARA thought that communities should determine their own tax and indebtedness policies and that it should not meddle in such internal community affairs through the eligibility criteria.

A closer examination of the legislation might also have led the CFA to question whether the formulas were justified. Apparently the CFA technicians failed to distinguish between congressional rhetoric and the actual wording of the legislation. The Act provided that $100 million be expended for public-facility loans and $75 million for grants. It did not require sophisticated calculations to recognize that a four-to-three ratio hardly justified the conclusion that grants were to be made only in "extreme" cases. A proposal by Congressman James E. Van Zandt (H.R. 6975—Eighty-fifth Congress), a Republican advocate of federal aid to depressed areas, attempted to establish levels of eligibility based on the extent of unemployment in an area, but it was never seriously considered. According to this proposal, only areas with the highest and most persistent unemployment would have been eligible to receive grants.

Congress thus refused to develop criteria spelling out the circumstances under which depressed areas would qualify to receive either loans or grants for public facilities. The law provides, in the words of the House Committee on Banking and Currency, that when "a community's needs are so great or its financial resources so limited that it is not practical to improve or expand its public facilities entirely on the basis of borrowed funds,"[13] it will be eligible to receive federal grants. The Act does not state that a community must exhaust its resources before it becomes eligible for a grant. The history of the Area Redevelopment Act indicates that the framers of the legislation assumed that all depressed areas had equal claim upon the resources allocated for the program and that it was up to the administrators of the program to parcel out the limited resources to areas where federal aid would do the most good, according to criteria which they would establish.

The debate between the CFA and the ARA about the appropriate use of grants centered on exegeses of legislative intent. Economists might have questioned the germaneness of the CFA criteria, which were based on three factors: property taxes, per capita debt, and per capita income. The theories underlying the criteria were that a community should not be entitled to receive grants if its property taxes are relatively lighter than those of half of all U.S. communities and that the community applying for ARA grants must have incurred less per capita debt, in relation to income, than the median community. However, the CFA criteria included only property taxes, which account for less than a half of the total general revenue received by local governments. Under the CFA criteria, if a community decides to secure a greater proportion of its revenue from non-property taxes, it would automatically disqualify itself from receiving ARA grants.

The ratio of per capita income to local indebtedness is an even more questionable criterion. The property-tax criterion tends to encourage reliance on this source of revenue as compared with other sources, while the per capita debt criterion fails to take into consideration the financial structure of depressed areas. An examination of the financial structure of these communities would have disclosed a direct relationship between community prosperity and indebtedness. The deterioration of the economic base of depressed communities seems to preclude the ability to borrow funds. As shown earlier (Chapter 3), the ratio of per capita income to per capita debt of local communities is about six to one. In the thirty 5(a) areas and thirty-four 5(b) areas, the comparable ratio of income to debt was found to be twice as high. Thus, under the CFA proposed criterion of per capita income ratio to debt, Pikesville, Kentucky, would not have qualified for grants because its ratio of per capita income to debt is about sixty to one, ten times the national average. But unemployment in the area has averaged more than three times the national average during recent years, and its population declined by 38 per cent between 1950 and 1960.

The ARA therefore had to formulate a more workable policy for the issuance of grants than the one proposed by the CFA. It approached the problem from the point of view of its mission of reducing unemployment in depressed areas and concluded that a public-facility project which would reduce unemployment at a reasonable cost per job should be eligible for a grant if the project was not self-liquidating. On this basis, an application for public-facility aid would first be studied to see if it could fully qualify for a loan. The community would be required to charge fair user rates for the services offered by the ARA-financed public facility. If the full cost of the project could not be supported by the revenue, based on actual user charge, then a grant would cover the difference.

An example would best illustrate this ARA policy. Suppose a new plant desires to move into a community but requires a new water main to service it, which the community promises to supply. If the main can be built from the amortized revenue forthcoming from the prospective user of the new water facility, then the ARA would supply the financing on a loan basis. If the fair user charges do not cover the full cost of the project, however, the difference between the total cost and that part which can be regained from revenue would be covered by an ARA grant. Thus, if the cost of the water main is $100,000 and if the community charges the new employer fair rates for services to be provided, the project would yield revenues amounting to $60,000 over the forty-year maximum period during which the ARA loan has to be amortized. In such a case, the ARA would finance the project with a 60 per cent loan and a 40 per cent grant.

What if the community promised the new employer a concession and agreed to supply him the water facility at less than the fair rate in the community? In such cases the ARA refuses to meddle in the affairs of the community, but it holds that the concessions offered by the community should not be borne by federal funds. In the above example, if the community agreed to charge the employer a rate which would yield only $35,000 over the same period of amortization rather than the fair rate which would have yielded $60,000, under the ARA policy the ratio of the loan to grant would be the same as in the first case. It remains to the community to bear that portion of the cost of the project which it agreed to give to the employer. In this way, the community itself has to make up for the cost of the concession to the new employer, and the grant is made just as if the community had charged the employer the fair rates for the services.

The ARA took the position that, practically speaking, it would be difficult to distinguish between tax concessions and other inducements which a community might offer to lure industry—such as free or reduced rents, reduced property assessments, free or below-cost utilities, or loans with exceptionally low interest rates. Moreover, the ARA did not think that it should discourage a community from assuming additional tax burdens resulting from tax concessions or other inducements. However, it refused to subsidize concessions made by a community in order to attract new industry. The ARA reasoned that the community itself can best decide its policies for rehabilitating and expanding its economic base.

The advantages of the ARA policy are self-evident. The rules are simple and can be easily explained to the community. The ARA is not required to meddle with internal affairs, yet all communities are treated alike. Finally, the ARA avoids the pitfall of making special concessions or giving grants to communities which offer tax or other concessions. Of course, this assumes that estimates of potential future use and fair charges can be made with reasonable precision. The ARA policy also failed to satisfy the opponents of tax or other concessions which communities use as a means of attracting industry.

The "great debate" over the appropriate extent of loans and grants provides an excellent exercise in futility for the lawyers of the ARA and the HHFA. In the legislative history, which fills hundreds of pages of debate in the *Congressional Record,* thousands of pages of hearings, and eight separate reports by the congressional committees, either side could find justification for its interpretation. Regrettably for the execution of the program, both agencies wasted much time in quibbling over the meaning of congressional utterances, which were frequently made to argue a point on a specific issue. The basis of the debate is not clear, though it may have been merely an old-fashioned bureaucratic jurisdictional dispute. The ARA's proposal of making loans based on fair user charges encroaches upon CFA activity, since the financing of a new water main may also involve receipts from household consumers. But according to the law, the ARA is supposed to provide public facilities only for prospective commercial and industrial users, while the CFA retains jurisdiction over household public facilities. The CFA tried to differentiate sharply between consumer and commercial public facilities, but the ARA occasionally found the distinction impractical and artificial. By limiting grants to "extreme" cases, the area of competition between the ARA and the CFA would be reduced, along with the effectiveness of the ARA's public-facility program.

The debate between the ARA and the CFA on the proper use of grants was not resolved by the time this study was completed. A series of interagency "summit" conferences failed to produce a solution of the differences. It is difficult to estimate the extent to which this squabble between the ARA and the CFA affected the ARA's public-facility program. But it does illustrate the impracticability and the difficulties involved in delegating ARA activities to other agencies. It was clearly a case of too many cooks.

THE USE OF PUBLIC-FACILITY FUNDS

Since the Area Redevelopment Act fails to define or restrict the meaning of public facility, the policy-shapers of the agency determined to apply the term broadly. By May 1, 1963, the ARA had approved a total of ninety-two applications that had been filed by private non-profit and public organizations under the public-facility program. Seventy-nine of these applications were for the development of indus-trial parks and the construction of utilities, including sewerage systems, water mains, and port facilities. But these projects accounted for barely half of the value of loans and grants made under the program. The balance of the successful applications were for the development of recreational facilities and for research projects. The former category of projects proved to be the most controversial and costly. The seven recreation and tourism projects required an ARA investment of $18 million, at an average estimated cost of $13,400 per job, which was ten times the ARA investment per job in other public facilities.

The most prominent tourism project was the development of a recreational center in Oklahoma. It involved a $9 million public-facility loan and a $1.3 million grant to the Oklahoma Lake Rede-velopment Authority to build two luxury resort hotels on Lake Eufala, a 143,000 acre man-made lake. The hotels were to provide five hundred jobs, which meant a direct cost of over $20,000 per job. The ARA justified its action on the basis that its initial investment, though high, would stimulate private investment in the area.

To the charge that the project should have been financed from industrial loan funds, the ARA replied that public-facility loans and grants are usually given to facilitate the entrance of new business into a redevelopment area. In other words, public-facility loans and grants are used to lure private investment into depressed areas. Similarly, the Eufala Lake project was designed to entice private enterprise into building similar resorts, for without a "proof" project, private capital would not, in all likelihood, be used to bring tourists to Lake Eufala; instead, small, inconsequential enterprises would spring up around the lake: in which event, the area's potential would not be fully exploited.

The second largest, and no less controversial, public-facility project involved the construction of a convention center in Duluth, Minnesota, with a $3 million grant. Initially, the ARA approved an additional $3.1 million loan to construct the auditorium, but Duluth floated a public bond at a lower interest rate, which made the ARA loan unnecessary.

The purpose of the auditorium is to make Duluth a convention center, particularly for regional conventions. It is estimated that the auditorium will eventually bring $4 million annually to Duluth, a city which, even without adequate facilities, had a $1.6 million income from conventions in 1961. Since Duluth is the major population center in the northern regions of Minnesota, Wisconsin, and Michigan, the ARA felt that the prospects for further growth in tourism and in conventions in the city were especially good. By helping provide a meeting place, the ARA hoped to stimulate secondary investment in facilities for the accommodation of visitors.

Based on the conviction that its public-facilities program should include more than sewer lines, water mains, and access roads, the ARA has utilized public-facility funds imaginatively for aiding the development of infrastructure in designated areas. It made a $400,000 grant to assist in the construction of a private university graduate training laboratory in Wilkes Barre, Pennsylvania. ARA investigators found that the expansion of existing electronics and associated new-growth industries has been hindered largely because of the reluctance of technicians and scientists to accept positions in a community where opportunities for continuing advanced education and research were not available at any nearby center.

Another project of the same type was a grant of $960,000 to build a marine research center at Yaquina Bay, Oregon. This center hopefully will have multiple roles in the economic rehabilitation of that area. In addition to generating several hundred jobs, the center will provide information to fishermen about ocean currents and the location and species of fish in the area; it will investigate undersea geological structures for oil and minerals; and it will try to solve the waste-disposal problems of the local timber industry, which has been polluting local waters with its refuse. Finally, the ARA expects an oceanographic research complex to spring up around the research center, as has happened in other communities which already had such facilities. The Public Health Service and Oregon state wildlife agencies plan to establish branches connected with the center, and the whole complex is expected to attract tourists to the area.

The ARA also made a grant of $642,000 to the University of Kentucky to establish a wood-use demonstration center as part of a state-wide program for the conservation and development of timber resources. Studies of the Kentucky timber industry showed that the wood resources of the state were not being used to best advantage. The forest service estimated that with better forest management more than twice as much wood could be cut and sawed annually, thus increasing the resources available to existing firms and providing room for new ones. Further, the demonstration center will also upgrade the skills of the workers engaged in the industry and help management improve production techniques.

An inventive application of the public-facility concept was devised by the ARA to aid Berwick, Pennsylvania. It combined the use of private and public loan funds. When the American Car and Foundry Company (ACF) announced in 1962 that it would close its operations in Berwick (Chapter 4, p. 117), the company offered to sell its facilities to the community at a price appreciably below cost, which would leave the ACF facilities for new industry that might move into the town. The alternative was to dismantle the facilities for scrap. But Berwick did not have the $2.4 million necessary to buy the ACF facilities. To prevent the dismemberment of the facilities, the ARA extended a loan of $951,000 from its public-facility funds to the Berwick Industrial Development Association, and the ACF took a second mortgage on the property for $619,000. The ARA determined that keeping the ACF complex intact was an essential public facility for Berwick. The $400,000 local contribution to the purchase was evidence of local support for the ARA's position.

Of course, the closing of the ACF operation in Berwick constituted a serious setback to the local economy. But with the existing first-rate industrial facilities, the Berwick Industrial Development Association expects to be in a position to attract a new industry which will diversify the local economy and replace the jobs that were lost. According to the latest available information, several prospective employers have indicated an interest in utilizing the Berwick facilities.

The above projects illustrate the broad application ARA policymakers gave to the public-facility program. Some involved significant allocation of federal resources and attracted considerable attention and criticism. The ARA response was that it could not limit its assistance to building sewers and water mains; and in some cases, more imaginative and costlier projects were necessary to rehabilitate depressed areas.

STATISTICAL SUMMARY

During the congressional debate over the area redevelopment legislation, congressional members from southern and border states expressed the greatest interest in the public-facilities part of the program. They anticipated that a federal program aimed at assisting the

Table 5–1: Distribution of ARA-Approved Public-Facility Loans and Grants by Region, Cumulative through April 30, 1963

($'s in thousands)

		Loans		Grants	
	Total	Investment	Per Cent 5(a) Areas	Investment	Per Cent 5(a) Areas
United States	$46,322	$26,207	70.5	$20,115	61.4
Northeast	5,517	2,395	97.7	3,122	91.3
New England	1,844	746	100.0	1,098	100.0
Middle Atlantic	3,673	1,649	96.7	2,024	86.5
North Central	10,610	5,725	73.4	4,885	73.4
East North Central	2,965	1,663	66.1	1,302	42.2
West North Central	7,645	4,062	76.3	3,583	84.7
South	25,772	15,382	76.8	10,390	54.8
South Atlantic	5,659	2,026	19.0	3,633	50.8
East South Central	6,590	3,279	71.1	3,311	73.2
West South Central	13,523	10,077	90.3	3,446	41.4
West	4,423	2,705	4.6	1,718	12.3
Mountain	412	125	100.0	287	73.9
Pacific	4,011	2,580	0.0	1,431	0.0

SOURCE: Computed from ARA statistical reports.

development of the infrastructure in depressed areas would be most beneficial to the lesser-developed areas in the country. During the first two years the ARA fulfilled the anticipations of the representatives from the southern region. The total ARA investment in public-facility projects through April 30, 1963, was $46.3 million, and 57 per cent of these funds was allocated to the South, though only a third of the population in designated areas lived in that region.

Seventy-three areas were the beneficiaries of the ninety-two public-facility projects—twenty-nine were 5(a) areas and fifty-four were 5(b) areas. Two-thirds of the projects and an equal share of the total investment were allocated to smaller urban areas and rural counties with a population of less than 50,000.

The ARA invested an average of close to $500,000 per public-facility project. Grants accounted for two of every five dollars of the total funds expended for public facilities. The average ARA investment per job, according to the agency's claims, amounted to $1,800. There appeared to be a close relation between size of project and ARA investment per job. On projects of less than a quarter-million dollars,

Table 5–2: Distribution of ARA-Approved Public-Facility Loans and Grants by Size of Loan, Cumulative through April 30, 1963

($'s in thousands)

Size of Loan	Number of Loans and Grants	Total	Per Cent Grants	Number of Jobs [a]	ARA Investment per Job
Total	92	$46,322	41.0	25,121	$ 1.8
Less than $50,000	14	421	71.0	1,078	0.4
50,000–149,999	21	1,853	66.0	3,208	0.6
150,000–249,999	15	3,131	62.0	4,305	0.7
250,000–349,999	11	3,285	29.0	7,860	0.4
350,000–549,999	13	5,524	50.0	2,587	2.1
550,000–749,999	7	4,630	77.0	2,450	1.9
750,000–999,999	3	2,718	65.0	132	20.6
1 million–2,999,999	6	8,329	23.0	2,975	2.8
3 million and over	2	16,431	27.0	526	21.2

[a] Anticipated number of jobs one year after completion of project.

Source: Computed from ARA statistical reports.

the average ARA investment per job amounted to $600, compared with $7,000 on projects of a million dollars and higher. The high investment per job on the high-cost projects was largely due to the Eufala Lake and Duluth projects.

Areas with relatively high unemployment were favored with a higher proportion of grants than areas with lower unemployment. In areas where unemployment exceeded 12 per cent of the work force, grants accounted for five-sixths of ARA contributions to public facilities. These areas received a third of the total funds allocated in grants for 5(a) areas, but only 4 per cent of the total loans (Table 5–3). For 5(b) areas, the inverse relation between the low level of income and the extent of grants was not as pronounced. Designated areas with a family income of less than half of the national median received a fourth of the total public-facility loans made in 5(b) areas and a third of the grants (Table 5–4).

Table 5–3: Distribution of Approved Public-Facility Loans and Grants by Level of Unemployment in 5(a) Areas, Cumulative through April 30, 1963

($'s in thousands)

Per Cent Unemployment	Loans		Grants		Per Cent Grants	Per Cent of Total	
	Number	Amount	Number	Amount		Loans	Grants
Total	21	$18,478	32	$12,342	40.0	100.0	100.0
Less than 8.0	3	1,846	2	511	21.7	10.0	4.1
8.0–9.9	2	3,450	5	3,647	51.4	18.7	29.5
10.0–11.9	11	12,449	12	3,914	23.9	67.4	31.7
12.0–15.9	3	393	9	2,848	87.9	2.1	23.1
16.0 and over	2	340	4	1,422	80.7	1.8	11.5

SOURCE: Computed from ARA statistical reports.

The law does not limit the share that the ARA may contribute to the cost of a public-facility project, and the agency has covered 86 per cent of the total cost of the projects approved through March 31, 1963. Other federal agencies and private capital have each contributed another 3 per cent of the cost, and the balance was covered by state and local governments and non-profit organizations. It may therefore be estimated that the $46 million the ARA has obligated for public facilities by May 1, 1963, will add another $8 million in direct investment. However, ARA-financed public facilities are related to new economic activity in a community, and the benefits to the community are supposed to result from the added commercial and industrial ventures. But by May 1, 1963, barely a tenth of the total approved funds for public projects was actually disbursed. The benefits that will come to the communities from these projects will therefore be delayed for some time.

Table 5–4: Distribution of Approved Public-Facility Loans and Grants by County Median Family Income—5(b) Areas, Cumulative through April 30, 1963

($'s in thousands)

Median Family Income		Loans		Grants		Per Cent	Per Cent of Total	
Amount	Per Cent of National	Num-ber	Amount	Num-ber	Amount	Grants	Loans	Grant
Total		40	$7,729	47	$7,773	50.1	100.0	100.0
Less than $1,886	33.3 and less	2	70	3	128	64.6	0.9	1.6
1,886–2,263	33.4–39.9	2	416	1	889	68.1	5.4	11.4
2,264–2,829	40.0–49.9	15	1,563	17	1,712	52.3	20.2	22.0
2,830–3,772	50.0–66.6	10	2,452	12	2,164	46.9	31.7	27.8
3,773–4,528	66.7–79.9	3	468	5	901	65.8	6.1	11.6
4,529–5,660	80.0–100.0	6	930	3	250	21.2	12.0	3.2
Over 5,660	Over 100.0	2	1,800	6	1,729	49.0	23.3	22.2

SOURCE: Computed from ARA statistical reports.

ACCELERATED PUBLIC-WORKS PROGRAM

The ARA is involved in another public-works program, under the Public Works Acceleration Act (P.L. 87–658, September 14, 1962). The expenditures authorized under this program dwarf the ARA's own public-facilities program. The purpose of P.L. 87–658 is to speed up and expand public works in communities with substantial unemployment, primarily to provide "immediate useful" employment, but also to aid industrial development and make them "better places in which to live and work" (Declaration of Purpose).

P.L. 87–658 originated as an antirecession measure and was part of a program proposed by the Administration to grant the President stand-by authority for tax reduction and for the inauguration of public-works programs in order to prevent imminent recessions.[6] But, despite the over-all economic recovery, the disturbingly high level of unemployment that persisted in early 1962 (more than 4.5 million persons remained unemployed) persuaded the President to propose that an accelerated public-works program should not be delayed and that such a program should be combined with the stand-by authority to combat future recessions. The accelerated public-works program was to be geared to aid areas designated by the ARA as well as communities with "substantial" unemployment ("federalese" for 6 per cent unemployment or higher) for a year or longer.

The President distinguished between the established ARA and the newly proposed accelerated public-works program:

The area redevelopment program . . . is a continuing effort to help communities to attract new and permanent jobs to solve their long-range economic problem; it is not primarily designed to provide immediate relief of distress caused by unemployment, or to assist in the general rehabilitation and improvement of public facilities. I believe that a further Federal effort is necessary, both to provide immediate useful work for the unemployed and the underemployed, and to help these and other hard-pressed communities, through improvement of their public facilities, to become better places to live and work.[20]

Congress had little enthusiasm for relinquishing control over pork barrel legislation, as implied by the proposed presidential stand-by authority. Though the Senate did adopt a watered-down version on May 28, 1962, the House Committee on Public Works did not report it out, stating that ". . . while sympathetic to the purposes of the legislation, the method of financing deserves more extensive study than could be given to it. . . ."[14] The bill, as approved by Congress, omitted any provisions for stand-by authority.

The accelerated public-works program was enacted broadly along the lines requested by the President. The principal modifications of the President's proposal included:

1. The funds authorized were increased from $600 million to $900 million, with the terminal date left open.

2. A requirement was added that at least a third of the funds, $300 million, had to be allocated to rural and small urban areas designated under Section 5(b) of the Area Redevelopment Act. On the other hand, eligibility of larger cities was relaxed by qualifying such communities to receive assistance if their unemployment rate exceeded 6 per cent in nine of the twelve preceding months (instead of the proposed twelve or more months). The funds that could be allocated to any one state were limited to 10 per cent of the total appropriations.

3. Grants to localities were limited to 75 per cent of project costs; the Administration proposal made no such restriction.

Congress appropriated a total of $850 million in two steps for the accelerated public works. An initial $400 million was appropriated shortly after the passage of the enabling legislation, an additional $450 million on May 17, 1963. The second appropriation was passed by the House over the objections of its Appropriations Committee by a 228–184 vote (208 Democrats and 20 Republicans voted for the $450 million supplemental appropriation, while 151 Republicans and 33 Democrats opposed it). [5]

Funds under the Accelerated Public Works Act are due to expire by June 30, 1964, and no funds can be obligated after that date. Assistance is largely limited to projects which require state and local matching. To retain congressional control over projects that are traditionally financed by the federal government, the initial appropriation set a limit of $400,000 on projects financed entirely by the federal funds.[11] Supplementary appropriations placed further emphasis on local projects, in effect limiting federal projects to conservation (basically forestry work) administered by the Agriculture and Interior Departments.[12]

Role of the ARA

The accelerated public-works program represents an extension of the philosophy underlying the ARA. In both pieces of legislation, Congress recognized that the concentration of high levels of unemployment in local communities is a national problem. The areas eligible for assistance are virtually the same under both acts, though the public-works program adds about 150 communities, with a population of 22 million, which are not eligible for assistance under the Area Redevelopment Act.

The two programs differ, however, with respect to goals. The ARA is a long-term program aimed at expanding economic growth in depressed areas, while the central objective of the public-works program is to provide "immediate useful work" for the unemployed and underemployed; and projects financed under the latter program must be initiated or accelerated within a reasonably short time and be 50 per cent completed in twelve months. The Act establishes other eligibility criteria: the project has to meet "an essential public need," contribute significantly to reduction of local unemployment, and not conflict with any locally approved comprehensive development plans. Also, the federal funds are available only where the local share of funds for the project represents a net increase in the locally-planned public-works programs that year.

The enabling legislation made no provision for the administration of the accelerated public-works program. The appropriations were made to the President, who in turn was expected to allocate funds to agencies which normally handle public-works programs. The President assigned the co-ordination of the program and the establishment of regulations to the Secretary of Commerce,[7] who in turn assigned the administrative responsibilities to the ARA.

Theoretically, it would appear that the ARA was the logical choice to co-ordinate the program. It was already concerned with the economic development of most of the areas eligible for assistance, and it was already working with some of the agencies responsible for public-works programs. But alternative administrative arrangements were available. Possibly the most logical candidate for the administration of the APW program was the CFA, which in the end handled half of the appropriated funds. But William Batt, ARA Administrator, expressed a keen desire to co-ordinate the accelerated public-works and area redevelopment programs and received permission to do so. Since the ARA was already familiar with the problems of the areas, it was expected that the agency would be in a favorable position to expedite the program.

Whatever the logic of the choice of the ARA, it became apparent that the agency had taken on a very sizable new responsibility at a time when it was heavily burdened in getting its own redevelopment program moving. A large portion of the time of the ARA's top staff was drawn into development of the regulations, procedures, and interagency consultations required by this multiagency program, and those tasks had to be carried out without additional staff during most of 1962. This necessarily drained the resources which would have been invested in its regular program at a time when it may have been ready to move ahead more quickly. What remains to be seen is if this loss will be more than repaid in the longer run by the advantages of having the ARA participate actively in this additional program.

The ARA exercised only a minor role in the selection of projects which would tie in with its over-all mission. The function of the agency was largely limited to the mechanical chores of assuring compliance with the statutory provisions which require allocation of one-third of the funds to 5(b) areas and which limit the total funds allocated to any state to 10 per cent. The ARA was also responsible for publishing progress reports on APW operations.

Program Operations

The judgments on distribution of funds at the start of the program were influenced primarily by what projects were ready to get under way. But as the flow of applications increased, priority questions

became increasingly significant. What should be the order of preference among different types of projects: water systems vs. hospitals vs.
community swimming pools? What if a needy area seeks funds for a
swimming pool, while one with less unemployment seeks funds for a
project of greater economic utility?

No fixed formulas were developed. The judgment was made that
wide geographic distribution—a "fair share" for all—was to be the
principal guide. Funds were tentatively earmarked so that areas with
the greatest unemployment and the lowest income would be eligible
for the most assistance. The specific amounts are not made public, to
avoid any impression that a definite amount is "coming to" particular
areas and to permit flexibility in the distribution of funds. The relative
merits of projects submitted by communities are not decisive; if a
project is approvable, and funds earmarked for the area have not been
used up, it is approved without comparing its economic merits to
projects in other areas.

As between projects within a single area, the ARA understandably
favors those which contribute most to long-run economic development; but this preference has to be tempered frequently in light of
the community's own preferences, the speed and amount of immediate
employment involved in alternative projects, and the size of the
tentative projects (a small one may fit within a fund's ceiling, where
a larger one may not).

Speed and timeliness are often influential elements in the APW
program. A community may want to expand its public-works program
with, say, a water system and a courthouse. But if the water project
must be delayed because it has to be approved in a referendum or
await authorization of a bond issue, preference might be given to the
courthouse, even if its potential impact on the economic development
of the community may not be discernible. The amount of on-site
employment is another important factor in choosing among projects.
Wherever possible, the preference is for projects which will create
the most number of immediate jobs, i.e., those with the highest ratio
of on-site employment costs to total costs. Added consideration may
be given to the jobs which may be generated as a result of the completion of the project.

The ARA was particularly concerned that communities might switch
from the ARA public-facility program to the more liberal financial
aid possible under the APW program. The ARA discourages communities from withdrawing ARA applications for resubmittal to the
APW, except where it has found that the application could not qualify

for ARA assistance. The ARA emphasizes that the APW program was intended to increase public works and not to replace other aid programs. The agency has stressed the tighter APW criteria—particularly the aspects of speed in initiation, early completion, and the requirement that the project represent a net increase in the community's planned public works.[19]

The federal share of project cost varies from 50 to 75 per cent of the total, depending upon the level of unemployment in the area and the per capita income; one of every four communities, predominantly 5(b) areas, are eligible to receive a grant of more than 50 per cent. The limitation on the extent of grants does not apply to projects which have been traditionally in the federal domain, such as the construction of post offices and conservation work. The cost of these projects is covered fully by federal funds and has accounted for about a fourth of total APW fund commitments. In addition, some federal projects were financed by a combination of APW and regular agency appropriations.

A total of 3,661 projects was approved by May 1, 1963, at an estimated cost—exact figures are not available—of close to $680 million, including $383 million in APW funds and the balance in state and local matching funds and allocations from federal agencies. The estimated average cost per project was almost $200,000. But the cost of individual projects varied widely, from $1,000 for a repair job to $4.6 million for the construction of a hospital in Lafayette, Louisiana.[18]

Funds handled by the CFA (49 per cent of the APW total) are allocated for public facilities. Such projects are particularly suitable for an accelerated program. They can be started and finished quickly, can employ more workers, and represent needed public projects. HEW handled 23 per cent of the funds; these grants were divided equally between hospital and other health-facility construction under the Hill-Burton Act, and sewage treatment works under the Water Pollution Control Act.

The funds allocated to the Agriculture and Interior programs (18 per cent) were utilized primarily for conservation measures. These projects permit flexibility in rounding out APW allocations because they provide work for relatively large numbers of workers, can be undertaken quickly, and can be allocated to areas which have not come up with sufficient proposals of their own—a significant consideration in meeting the Act's requirement that at least one-third of total funds be allocated to 5(b) areas. The remaining 10 per cent of APW funds was divided among the Commerce Department, the Army Corps of Engineers, the General Services Administration, the Post Office, TVA, the Coast Guard, and the Veterans Administration.

The approved projects were distributed over some nine hundred areas. Three-quarters of the project funds were allocated to ARA areas, with the other quarter going to areas of substantial unemployment which were not eligible for ARA assistance (Table 5–5).

Table 5–5: APW-Approved Projects by Type of Area as of May 1, 1963

($'s in thousands)

Area	Number of Projects	Estimated APW Cost		Estimated Man-Months On-Site Employment
		Amount	Per Cent	
Total	3,661	$382,515	100.0	548,178
5(a)	980	136,750	35.8	180,058
5(b)	2,060	135,522	35.4	207,512
Indian reservations	80	11,629	3.0	17,622
Labor surplus	541	98,614	25.8	142,986

SOURCE: Area Redevelopment Administration.

The total of $284 million allocated to ARA areas under the APW program in seven months of operation was three times as large as the total funds the ARA committed to these areas in loans and grants under its original program during the first two years.

Although the APW eligibility criteria put primary emphasis on immediate contribution to employment, a major part of the APW projects do serve basic economic development needs. The bulk of APW approvals have been for the types of projects—notably water, waste-treatment, and sewerage systems, etc.—which serve the same development purposes as contemplated by the ARA public-facility program (Table 5–6).

The wisdom of the administrative structure is difficult to assess. There are patent disadvantages, but there are also some values. From the ARA's standpoint, the task of co-ordinating programs involving relationships with many agencies, while using criteria different from its original program, was complex and time-consuming, and detracted from staff resources which might otherwise be available for the ARA program. At the same time, however, this role enabled the ARA to give the APW projects more of a long-term development flavor as well as greater compatibility with other ARA programs than would otherwise have been the case.

The involvement of several agencies in the program precluded the development of uniform criteria in processing projects. But the use of established agencies involved a minimum loss of money and time in inaugurating the program.

It is impossible from this vantage point to evaluate the impact of the accelerated public-works program. The $850 million of federal outlays appropriated by Congress will almost be matched by state and local expenditures, reflecting both the stipulation that most communities are eligible to receive maximum grants of 50 per cent of

Table 5–6: Distribution of Approved APW Projects by Function as of May 1, 1963

Type	Projects	APW Funds
Total number	3,661	$382,515,000
Total per cent	100	100
Construction		
Utilities (water, sewage and other)	20	30
Roads and streets	14	13
Waste treatment works	9	12
Hospital and health facilities	4	11
Courthouses, post offices, and other buildings	7	11
Recreational facilities	3	5
Fish and wildlife facilities	10	2
Water resources projects	1	2
All other construction	11	5
Repairs	11	6
Conservation	10	4

SOURCE: Area Redevelopment Administration.

project cost and the stringent limitations on financing federal projects. Total outlays generated by the program will therefore amount to about $1.5 billion. ARA officials in charge of the program have estimated that these outlays will directly generate 250,000 man years of employment. While this expectation might prove somewhat overoptimistic, it can hardly be questioned that the program will increase the demand of unutilized capacity and stimulate employment in areas where forced idleness is a major problem. Because the benefits of the program are spread thinly over some nine hundred areas, its contribution to the immediate expansion of employment in individual communities is necessarily limited.

Crucial to the over-all evaluation of the program is the extent to which new programs have been undertaken that would not have materialized had the accelerated public-works program not been in effect. On this point it is possible only to speculate. The evidence seems to indicate that the APW program led many communities to step up their public-works programs to take advantage of the offered financial aid, with the result that the demand exceeded the appropriations. The extent to which success of the accelerated public-works program will reduce future demand cannot be determined. But meanwhile, many depressed communities will enjoy public facilities which they certainly could not have afforded without outside help.

REFERENCES

1. *Congressional Record.* March 9, 1961, p. 3378.
2. *Congressional Record.* March 15, 1961, p. 3789 (Senator Sparkman); p. 3769 (Senator Lausche); p. 3758 (Senator Saltonstall); p. 3743 (Senator McClellan).
3. *Congressional Record.* March 28, 1961, p. 4740 (Congressman Brown).
4. *Congressional Record.* March 29, 1961, p. 4935 (Congressman Rains); p. 4936 (Congressman Perkins).
5. *Congressional Record.* April 10, 1963, p. 5806.
6. *Economic Report of the President.* Washington: Government Printing Office, 1962, pp. 17–20.
7. Executive Order 11049. September 14, 1962.
8. McAuliff, Joseph L. "States Assisting Local Areas in Financing Area Redevelopment." Unpublished study. The Area Redevelopment Administration, August, 1962.
9. Moes, John E. *Local Subsidies for Industry.* Chapel Hill, N.C.: University of North Carolina Press, 1962.
10. Sullivan, Joseph D. "Plant Woers Woe," *The Wall Street Journal,* March 2, 1962.
11. U.S. House of Representatives, Appropriations Committee. *Conference Report on H. R. 12900.* Report 2531, 87th Cong., 2d Sess., October 4, 1962, p. 22.
12. ———. *Conference Report on H. R. 5517.* Report 290, 88th Cong., 1st Sess., May 3, 1963.
13. U.S. House of Representatives, Committee on Banking and Currency. *Area Redevelopment Act.* Report 186, 87th Cong., 1st Sess., 1961, p. 23.
14. U.S. House of Representatives, Committee on Public Works. *Accelerated Public Works.* Report 1756, 87th Cong., 2d Sess., June 2, 1962, p. 4.
15. U.S. Senate, Committee on Labor and Public Welfare. *Hearings on Area Redevelopment.* 84th Cong., 2d Sess., 1956, pp. 1076–77.
16. U.S. Senate, Committee on Banking and Currency. *Area Redevelopment Act.* Report 61, 87th Cong., 1st Sess., 1961, p. 6.

17. U.S. Senate. *Hearings on Area Redevelopment Act.* 87th Cong., 1st Sess., 1961, p. 365.
18. U.S. Department of Commerce, Area Redevelopment Administration. *Accelerated Public Works Program, Directory of Approved Projects.* May 1, 1963. Washington: The Department, 1963.
19. ———. "Relationship between ARA Public Facility Projects and APW Program." Policy Guideline No. 16. November 26, 1962. (Mimeographed.)
20. White House Press Release. March 26, 1962.

Chapter 6

++++++++++++++++++++++

Training the Unemployed for Jobs

++

During the past few years there has taken place a radical transforma-
tion of attitude toward adult vocational training and the role that
such training must play in a dynamic labor-market policy.

Today, the need for providing adult vocational training and retraining facilities to help workers adjust to technological changes and
to upgrade their skills is commonly accepted. It is no longer a subject
of partisan controversy. However, this was not true in 1955, when
Senator Paul H. Douglas introduced his first bill to aid depressed
areas. Senator Douglas considered the training of unemployed persons in depressed areas an integral part of the program to aid chronic
labor-surplus areas. He repeatedly asserted, during the six-year legislative debate over the bill, that financial subsidies to attract new or
expanding firms to the depressed areas would not be effective unless
provision were also made to train or retrain the unemployed in these
areas in order to provide them with the skills needed by the new
industry.

Federal support for vocational training is not a new concept: it dates
from the Smith-Hughes Act of 1917.[1] By the time the ARA was
established in 1961, the federal government was contributing close
to $50 million a year for vocational education. About a fourth of
the federally supported vocational education was devoted to out-of-
school youths and adults. But some of these funds were expended for
training unemployed workers to help acquire new skills.

---

[1]The Smith-Hughes Act has been amended and expanded, notably by the
George-Deen Act, 1936, the George-Barden Act, 1946, and the National Defense
Education Act, 1958.

LEGISLATIVE ISSUES AND PROVISIONS

Training Provisions (Section 16)

At first, Senator Douglas wished to limit vocational training to unemployed persons in depressed areas who were preparing to fill local job vacancies. A number of witnesses suggested that this limitation would restrict the value of the training program and would deprive unemployed persons in depressed areas of the opportunity to fill job vacancies in more prosperous and growing communities.

Secretary of Agriculture Orville Freeman suggested that the training provisions be further expanded to include the underemployed, an idea which Senator Douglas readily adopted. As a result, the Act requires (Section 16) that the training and retraining needs of depressed areas shall be determined by the needs of the unemployed and underemployed in the area and shall not be limited to the job skills needed in the depressed areas alone.

Congressman Joseph M. Montoya, of New Mexico, emphasized the training needs of the underemployed in rural areas by pointing to the continuing decline of work opportunities in agriculture. He proposed that the training and retraining program "shall give consideration to the special needs of individuals who are agricultural workers or are engaged in other seasonal occupations. . . ." Congressman Montoya's amendment was also incorporated into the Act (Section 16[f]).

While many witnesses representing different interests testified in favor of the training provisions,[9, 12, 13] Mayor David L. Francis, of Huntington, West Virginia, presented possibly the most persuasive arguments in favor of vocational training.[1] Francis favored the depressed-area bill but insisted that federal subsidies to attract new industry to the depressed areas in West Virginia and eastern Kentucky would at best be a slow process and would do little to alleviate the economic distress of the 100,000 unemployed who constituted about a sixth of the labor force in these areas. He therefore proposed a crash program to train annually some 10,000–15,000 unemployed in West Virginia and eastern Kentucky. He declared that such training would enable these unemployed workers to accept jobs either within the local community or in other parts of the country. "These unemployed must be made vocationally mobile so that they can properly seek employment in areas where job opportunities are available."[1]

Little opposition was voiced in principle to the training and retraining program, though some expressed skepticism concerning the
potential of the program. Senator Wallace F. Bennett, of Utah,
pointed out that prospective employers would be particularly concerned with the attitude of an employee to be hired. According to
Senator Bennett, when an employer hires a new employee, he is
looking for "a man who is willing to do a day's work for his pay, who
is reasonably happy in his home surroundings, and all these things."
[12] He maintained that retraining would not change employee attitudes. On the floor of the Senate, however, Senator Bennett stated
that retraining provisions of the depressed-area bill contained "the
only really worthwhile idea in the bill."[1] Nevertheless, he did not
seem to think the problems of the unemployed sufficiently pressing to
rush into any legislation, because he proposed only further study.
Moreover, he averred that he opposed immediate action on procedural
grounds: since matters pertaining to training are within the jurisdiction of the Senate Committee on Labor and Public Welfare, the
Senate Committee on Banking and Currency, which was handling the
bill, had no business recommending legislation pertaining to training.[2]

The House Republicans also supported the principle behind the
vocational training program, but they would have liked to have
accomplished it without any further federal expenditures. The minority pointed out that the federal government was already appropriating
$30 million (actually the amount was closer to $50 million) annually
for this purpose. Therefore, they saw no reason for authorizing additional expenditures.[8] Even the witness for the U.S. Chamber of
Commerce did not oppose the expenditure of federal funds for
vocational training "if state funds are inadequate to accomplish the
need." But he stressed that this represented his personal opinion and
not that of the Chamber of Commerce.[12]

Congress also had to resolve jurisdictional problems in designing a
vocational training program for depressed areas. Involved were the
jurisdictions of several established federal and state agencies, each of
which wanted to obtain the maximum authority under the Act. The
vocational educators argued that the administration of the training
provisions should be delegated to the state vocational education authorities. The Department of Agriculture insisted that it should be
consulted on any program which involved rural areas, and the Depart-

²Five months later, when the Senate Committee on Labor and Public Welfare
reported out the Manpower Development and Training Act, Senator Bennett still
voted against the bill.[3]

ment of the Interior wanted to supervise training activities on Indian reservations.

The Act parcels out responsibilities in the following manner: The Secretary of Labor is delegated the authority to determine training needs and potential job vacancies. The need for a given training program having been established, the Secretary of Health, Education and Welfare then determines the course content of the training program and contracts with the appropriate state authorities for its administration. Because the agricultural lobby was on the job, the Secretary of Labor is required to consult with the Secretary of Agriculture regarding the determination of training needs in rural areas. The Secretary of Interior's spokesmen were apparently not as effective, since he is not mentioned in the training provision. In practice, however, the Bureau of Indian Affairs has been consulted on all training projects involving Indian reservations. In establishing apprenticeship and journeymen on-the-job programs, the Secretary of Labor retains full jurisdiction. Since, as will be shown later, the effective training period under the provisions of the Act is limited to sixteen weeks, the provision (16[d]) for the establishment of apprenticeship programs is not clear. Apparently, this provision was included to utilize the expertise of the Bureau of Apprenticeship in practical training matters. Similarly, the Agriculture Department was asked to participate in the training programs because of its involvement in rural training through its extensive extension programs.

The amount of money to be authorized for the training provisions was another subject of some controversy. Douglas proposed an annual authorization of $4.5 million and held to this figure throughout the six years the bill was pending in Congress. Experts on vocational education believed that an effective program could be developed slowly but that a $10 million annual authorization would be a more appropriate figure (with $5 million as a minimum).[11] Congressman William B. Widnall, of New Jersey, in the final discussion of the bill in 1961, proposed a $10 million annual authorization.[2]

Strangely enough, criticism of the inadequacy of the $4.5 million annual authorization for the training program came also from Senator A. Willis Robertson, of Virginia, a consistent opponent of the bill. The gist of Senator Robertson's argument was that the training provisions would necessarily be ineffective, since the program could at best take care of only a small proportion of all unemployed who need retraining; the $4.5 million to be appropriated annually would thus be spread too thinly. His solution was to do nothing, rather than to pour $4.5 million a year down the drain. Senator Douglas' reply to this argument was his favorite quotation from the Chinese philosopher Mencius: "a journey of a thousand miles begins with one step."[12]

Subsistence Payments (Section 17)

The greatest controversy in connection with the depressed-area training program related to the provision of paying subsistence benefits to unemployed workers undergoing training or retraining. Douglas took a page from the G.I. Bill of Rights which similarly provided for the payment of training benefits to veterans. He reasoned that it would be unrealistic to expect an unemployed worker to undergo an effective training program without providing him with any means of subsistence. If the federal government were to undertake responsibility for the retraining of unemployed workers in depressed areas, then it could not deny them the means of subsistence.

When Douglas first introduced his depressed-area bill, every state except Michigan and the District of Columbia denied unemployment benefits to otherwise eligible workers if they were undergoing training.[3] The law in all these states provided that an unemployed worker must be available for work if he were to receive unemployment compensation. The fact that he was undergoing training would mean that he was not available for work. Under the circumstances, a federal training program alone would have been self-defeating, since a worker would be forced to wait until he exhausted his unemployment insurance before undertaking a training course. Douglas therefore provided that unemployed workers who undertook a vocational training course would be eligible to receive federal subsistence payments equal to the average unemployment benefits in his state. The average rate was specified for purposes of administrative simplicity and also to assure that workers who had not previously received unemployment insurance would be eligible for training as well as subsistence payments. Originally, Douglas limited the subsistence payment to thirteen weeks. Though seemingly arbitrary, this duration was 50 per cent of the prevailing period of unemployment insurance benefits, which in most states was limited to twenty-six weeks. In 1959, after the federal government added temporary unemployment compensation benefits of up to thirteen weeks, Douglas increased the duration of benefits under the training program to sixteen weeks. The subsistence payments were to be paid from federal funds. Within a year after the Area Redevelop-

[3]By 1962, eighteen additional states passed such laws.

ment Act became law, Congress approved a much more ambitious program that provided for up to a year's training and which was not limited to depressed areas—the Manpower Development and Training Act of 1962.

The 1956 and 1958 bills contained no limit upon the total amounts to be expended for subsistence benefits. The reason for this was very simple. In the absence of any experience, there was no sound way to estimate the proper relation between the cost of training and the cost of subsistence benefits. This opened the bill to the charge that "unlimited amounts" would be expended for the payment of subsistence; and in 1958, therefore, as part of the deal to get the House bill free of the Rules Committee, the proponents of the legislation promised to eliminate the provision for subsistence payments. Howard Smith, chairman of the House Rules Committee, felt that one extension of unemployment insurance (the Temporary Unemployment Compensation Act of 1958) in one year was more than enough.

To prevent further attacks on the subsistence provision, members of Douglas' staff consulted with experts who advised that an appropriate ratio would be $4.5 million for administrative and instructional expenses and $10 million for subsistence. As will be shown later, experience has shown that the advice of the experts was not correct.

As finally enacted, the legislation provided that workers undergoing training under the ARA program would be eligible to receive subsistence benefits equal to the average unemployment insurance rate in their respective states for a maximum period of sixteen weeks, even though the actual period of training may last for a longer period of time. But for most practical purposes this limited ARA vocational training courses to sixteen weeks duration, although about one of every eight projects approved during the first year of operations provided for training in excess of sixteen weeks.

THE ADMINISTRATION OF TRAINING

The Area Redevelopment Act charges the Secretary of Labor with the responsibility of determining the training needs of unemployed persons in depressed areas. The initiative for providing training to local unemployed workers under the ARA program, however, is normally assumed by the local employment service office, which determines skill shortages in occupations suitable for ARA training courses with a maximum of sixteen weeks duration. Local advisory committees drawn from management, labor, employment service, and vocational education frequently play an active role in selecting courses and determining content. Theoretically, once the local employment office determines the presence of labor shortages in a given occupation where training is suitable, it notifies the state employment service of the need for a course. The state employment service then asks the state vocational authorities to prepare a course curriculum and to handle the details of the course, including procurement of facilities and instructors. In practice, the local employment office and the vocational education authorities usually work out these details and then present their respective state offices with the detailed information about the prospective course.

Once the respective state agencies approve the course, they forward the proposed training project to Washington for final approval and allocation of funds. In Washington, several agencies get involved in the act of reviewing the course proposal before final and formal authority is granted by the Office of Manpower, Automation and Training, the agency designated by the Secretary of Labor to administer ARA training. The technical aspects of training are reviewed by the Vocational Education Division in HEW's Office of Education. However, if the proposed training course is offered in a small urban or rural area (5[b] area), the Agriculture Department insists on reviewing the proposed course; the Bureau of Indian Affairs in the Department of the Interior similarly reviews training courses for unemployed or underemployed Indians residing on a reservation. The Bureau of Apprenticeship Training may also offer technical advice; and the Area Redevelopment Division in the Bureau of Employment Security co-ordinates the processing of the training proposal.

While this review process seems cumbersome, it involves decision-making by a committee representing several agencies rather than by a single administrator. Spokesmen for this procedure claim that it makes possible the utilization of diverse types of expertise which have been developed by the several agencies. Critics assert that it is a product of an attempt to protect the jurisdictional claims of the agencies and that it results in an unnecessary diffusion of responsibility.

The ARA itself took only a minor role in the administration of the training program, since the Act specifically allocates this responsibility to the Secretary of Labor. During the first year of its operation, the ARA assigned only one part-time person, a special assistant to the Administrator, to maintain liaison with the Departments of Labor and HEW in connection with the development of training programs. When this official left the ARA, one full-time professional member of the staff was assigned to ARA training activity. However, ARA field staff viewed the training program as an integral part of their responsibilities.

Federal-State-Local Relations

The diffusion of responsibility at the federal level for approval of training courses, with the frequent accompanying delay in processing course proposals and the federal "meddling" in vocational training, has been a source of irritation to some local vocational education authorities.[4] No doubt some of these complaints represent narrow institutional views of the vocational educators who oppose the intrusion of employment services in matters pertaining to training.

The burden of the complaints from local and state vocational education authorities centers around the delay in processing training proposals and the excessive paper work required for the filing of applications. Local vocational authorities have to prepare from fifteen to twenty-seven copies of training proposals—ten copies go to Washington and the rest to state employment services and vocational education offices. Local vocational education directors have complained that their applications must go to six different offices before final approval of a course proposal is given.

Another complaint of the local vocational authorities is that the advance costs of preparing a course outline have to be defrayed from the funds of the local vocational education office. And when the course is not approved, the local office receives no reimbursement for the outlay. Some local authorities have therefore maintained that the federal government should supply their offices with "get ready money" for the planning and preparation of ARA training courses. Local vocational educators also complain that they are required to include, in the cost proposal, exact prices of the minor equipment to be purchased. In the interests of efficiency and flexibility, they think it would be desirable to have these requirements relaxed, so that a general estimate of these costs would be allowed. Department of Labor

---

[4]The following discussion is based on some forty letters that were written by state and local vocational educators and which were supplied to the author on a confidential basis.

spokesmen have asserted that they do not require detailed cost estimates of minor equipment, and that the complaint is not based on facts. The Labor Department rebuttal has been substantiated by checking a random sample of applications.

Delay in the approval of proposed courses has also been a source of common complaint. After processing at the state level, an average of three to four weeks is required to secure course approval from Washington, exclusive of mailing time. No data were available concerning the time of processing a proposed course at the state level; but a number of local vocational education directors have stated that it takes about two months for the approval of a program after it is originally submitted. The delay, according to the Labor Department, has frequently been due to the fact that many proposals were sketchy and lacked necessary information as to the availability of jobs in occupations for which training was proposed, course content, and such essential information as to whether the training was intended to aid an establishment which has recently relocated from another area. The Department of Labor has asserted that after the organizational channels were set up, "clean" projects cleared Washington within two weeks. But even after the Labor Department approves a training proposal, the local vocational authorities have to wait another month—frequently longer—before they receive HEW's check for the cost of instruction.

Possibly the most important source of irritation on the part of local vocational education authorities is their resentment of meddling by the "feds" in matters which are presumably local in nature and which the local authorities consider their exclusive jurisdiction. The theme that there is "no reason for the Labor Department to receive copies of course outline and course content" is repeated frequently by local directors in commenting upon the ARA training program. One local director states that "I resent deeply sending down people from Washington to help us plan a vocational education course. . . . It appears to be a design to make us look as though we don't know all the answers. . . ." The Bureau of Employment Security claims that it became involved in planning the contents of a few courses at the request of the local and state vocational educators who applied for assistance in cases where they had no previous experience.

A vocational education superintendent of a large state testifies that the new training programs—ARA and MDTA—impose new burdens upon the meager resources of local authorities and force them to "spread themselves out even thinner." And a colleague from another state suggests that in many cases trainees could be absorbed by existing vocational training facilities. "There are many classes where we could add two or three, maybe more, individuals and give them opportunity to develop suitable skills in ongoing programs. It seems unwise to establish competing programs. . . ." The basis for this complaint is not clear, since there is nothing in ARA legislation that would have prevented the local educational director from doing exactly what he proposed. Nevertheless, some vocational education directors have organized separate courses for ARA trainees, even in cases where it would appear feasible to enroll them in courses offered under established programs. The reason for this is not clear: possibly vocational authorities are opposed to mixing students under their traditional programs with ARA trainees, who receive subsistence payments while undergoing a retraining course.

The complaint, no doubt, alluded to the vocational training program that operates under the George-Barden Act of 1946. According to the Vocational Education Division in the U.S. Office of Education, some 57,000 unemployed and underemployed men and women, including out-of-school youths, have been trained under this program during 1962 alone. Regrettably, there is little information available on the quality of the training and the characteristics of the trainees. In his sample studies of ARA trainees, Professor Gerald Somers found very few persons who have had any previous useful vocational training.[5]

The 1946 legislation, which expanded the Smith-Hughes Act (1917) and the George-Deen Act (1936), provides annually for $8 million in federal funds, to be matched by the states, for training out-of-school youth and adults in trade and industry, agriculture, home economics, and distributive occupations. In 1962 thirty-two states and Puerto Rico offered vocational training courses to the unemployed in areas where there was a reasonable expectation of employment upon completion of training. Twenty states now make provision in their laws allowing trainees to receive unemployment benefits while they are undergoing occupational training.

The Department of Labor spokesmen and other "feds" gladly concede the contributions to vocational education made under the George-Barden Act, though in some cases they question the effectiveness of

---

[5]Professor Gerald Somers, of Wisconsin University, is now conducting a thorough study of ARA training under a Ford Foundation grant. This study will, no doubt, present more thorough data on the program than are available in 1963 as well as an evaluation of the whole ARA training program.

many of the courses developed under this legislation and the extent to which local vocational educators are job-oriented in planning training courses. Moreover, they insist that many of the depressed areas do not have effective vocational training programs, that in the majority of the states the trainees lose unemployment benefits if they enroll for training courses, and, of course, that many of the unemployed, particularly in depressed areas, have long exhausted their unemployment benefits before they apply for a vocational training course. The proponents of the ARA training program—the same applies to the MDTA—insist that it is unrealistic to expect that an unemployed person could undergo an effective training program without any means of subsistence. Generally, advocates of the new federally sponsored training programs acknowledge the contributions made under the George-Barden Act, but they suggest that present-day needs require additional and more ambitious programs to retrain the unemployed and underemployed.

Federal authorities have insisted that the ARA program is necessarily a co-operative program. Upon the inauguration of the program, Dr. Louis Levine, the director of the U.S. Employment Service, stated: "[T]his is above all a cooperative program. It is cooperative in every sense of the word. It includes state and federal officials. It involves inter-agency relationships at each level of administration and within various departments of government. Indeed, the real test of effectiveness of this program is going to be—the extent to which we have good cooperation."[6]

This was no mere exhortation. Federal authorities have insisted that the spirit of co-operation be adhered to at all levels of government and that no training program be "forced down the throats" of local people, no matter how strong the provocation. In late 1961, early in the ARA training program, the Labor Department approved a program to train some 1,200 farm workers who had been displaced by agricultural mechanization to operate farm machinery. The training program would have equipped displaced agricultural workers and underemployed farm laborers with the skills needed on mechanized farms. The training program was planned for the Mississippi-Yazoo Delta. But since a majority of the potential trainees were Negroes, the training program was to be racially integrated. This was enough to raise a political controversy, with objections coming from many of the planters as well as from the State Farm Bureau Federation. The training program was killed, despite the urgent need for workers who could operate tractors and other mechanized farm equipment. It was reported that half of the male population in the Yazoo Delta was either jobless or underemployed.

This was possibly the most ambitious single program planned under the ARA training provisions during its first two years of operations. There is no need to comment upon the position of the Labor Department authorities in this controversy; though one might sympathize with the righteous indignation of a newspaper commentator who suggested, before the program was killed, that the deep-seated local controversy could be easily resolved "in a one minute conversation between JFK and Abe Ribicoff, assuming their willingness to tell off the Farm Bureau Federation's Mississippi branch and its local fellow travelers. . . ."[16]

But the federal authorities refused to "tell off" the local authorities; and if they had tried, there was little chance of success, since the state returned the federal funds and refused to offer the training program. Apparently, federal officials felt that a co-operative program could not be carried out effectively if they enforced their will whenever the local authorities disagreed with them. The Mississippi incident was only the first major one in the ARA training program. The ARA training program encountered other obstacles, some of a philosophical or political nature. Massachusetts and New York had long-established and effective vocational training programs, and the administrations in both states were unsympathetic to the acceptance of federal assistance. But four training courses did materialize in Massachusetts under local initiative. For example, a training committee that was set up in New Bedford to prepare the local Overall Economic Development Program (which every depressed community must complete before it is eligible to receive ARA assistance) discovered a shortage of metal machine operators in the labor market, despite the high level of unemployment that prevailed in the area. A hundred unemployed workers were initially selected for the training course. Seventeen dropped out before completion, but fifty obtained jobs immediately upon the completion of the training course as machine-tool operators or in related jobs. In New York, which had eleven designated depressed areas, more than a year elapsed before state authorities agreed to start the first ARA retraining course. Louisiana refused to co-operate with the program. At first the ARA also encountered difficulties in New Mexico, where the state authorities refused to co-operate in the federally sponsored program. But the state administration finally agreed to approve proposals for retraining which were worked out at the local level under the state employment service guidance.

In the final analysis, the initiative to develop training courses rests with local and state authorities. This was clearly brought out in the following colloquy during the course of the Senate Manpower subcommittee hearings:

SENATOR CLARK: If you have a State administration which is not sympathetic to a retraining program, you are defeated, are you not?

MR. GOODWIN [administrator, Bureau of Employment Security]: Well, you have got two strikes against you, at least.

SENATOR CLARK: And if you have a local school board that does not want to cooperate in adult retraining because of financial implications, you are also defeated, are you not?

MR. GOODWIN: Yes, I think that this is particularly true in the ARA program where the initiative is in the local community.[14]

Need for a National Program

Labor Department officials in charge of training refused to abrogate their responsibilities under the legislation. They considered it only proper that the training proposals include a complete estimate of costs relating to facilities, equipment, and instruction. They held that under the Area Redevelopment Act, the Secretaries of Labor and HEW are responsible for expenditures of federal funds, thus requiring their authorized representatives to exercise control over training expenditures.

In fact, federal officials are in a poor position to review knowledgeable cost estimates that are provided by local vocational education authorities and which are approved at the state level. Nevertheless, modifications of local cost estimates occurred frequently because local vocational educators, who often have to work with obsolete equipment, understandably tried to take advantage of federal funds by equipping their shops with materials that were not essential for the ARA course or by padding overhead costs. One community proposed a course to prepare some two hundred unemployed workers to gain employment in a new factory in the town. The application was approved at the state level without modification, but when it reached Washington, Labor Department officials thought that the training costs were too high and that the duration of training was too long. It took several conferences to cut down the initially proposed cost by as much as 50 per cent. Needless to say, the local training officials were miffed at the federal cut. Added to this was the fact that the state employment service would select pupils to attend "their" schools and would then take credit for finding employment for "graduates," who are frequently placed by the vocational educators. (Traditionally, one of the functions of a local vocational education director is to place those who have successfully completed training courses.)

But the impediments to ARA training caused by frictions can be overemphasized. While these differences have certainly been an important obstacle to effective development of ARA training courses in some areas, in most cases the hope of the federal officials that the ARA program would be a truly co-operative program, at all levels of government, has been realized.

It would certainly be a mistake to leave ARA training completely to the local and state vocational education systems. Our labor market is becoming increasingly more national in scope; in some occupations it is already national. As for depressed areas, the only real hope for some of the unemployed and underemployed in these regions is to secure jobs outside of their areas. Retraining these people may equip them to find jobs in other areas, but this would require the co-operation of state employment services and a more effective national employment service. Even for those who will remain in their local areas, more effective co-operation between training and placement authorities than has existed in the past will be necessary.

During its first two years the ARA operated in a generally loose labor market. With only limited shortages in occupations for which the unemployed and underemployed persons in the depressed areas could be trained, there had been little training for relocation by 1964. Nevertheless, a number of training courses were approved under the ARA program with a view to relocating the trainees in other areas. Nearly a hundred trainees in metal-working occupations, machine-tool operators, and welders were trained in northeastern Minnesota to satisfy needs in the Minneapolis-St. Paul area. Clerk-stenographers were trained in eastern Kentucky and West Virginia for jobs in Washington, D.C.; some were trained in southern Indiana to be employed in Indianapolis. Farm-machine operators were trained in Laredo, Texas, to be employed in other parts of the state. Machine-tool operators were trained in Bluefield, West Virginia, with the expectation that most of the trainees would take jobs in the Norfolk, Virginia, shipyards. Indians from New Mexico and Arizona reservations were trained in Los Angeles for employment as electronic wirers and solderers in various parts of California.

All these programs for migration involved only a few hundred persons, but they indicate a potential that may exist when the high level of unemployment which has prevailed throughout the United States drops perceptibly. While Congress has not approved any funds for relocation of unemployed workers from depressed areas, it has provided that the training program be geared to the needs of the national labor market rather than exclusively to the needs of the area. Area labor surpluses will remain even after a nationally tolerable level of unemployment has been achieved, and the only realistic hope for many of the unemployed in the depressed areas is to secure gainful employment through relocation. The acquisition of useful skills through retraining will make such relocation possible when general economic conditions improve. This will require close co-operation between vocational training and placement authorities. It will also require knowledge of existing job vacancies outside of the depressed areas. Local and state vocational authorities cannot expect to develop expertise in these matters. The very modest ARA training programs for relocation indicate the possibilities of finding work for the unemployed workers by acquiring a useful skill, even in the loose labor market that has prevailed during the period they were being trained.

STATISTICAL SUMMARY

Altogether a total of 387 separate projects were approved to train 19,329 unemployed and underemployed workers in 170 occupations; about 14,000 persons had either enrolled or completed ARA training courses during the first two years of the program, while the other 5,000 selectees were awaiting the opening of programs. West Virginia, Pennsylvania, and Michigan accounted for almost a third of the total enrollment, and six other states—Arkansas, Connecticut, Kentucky, Minnesota, Oklahoma, and Rhode Island—contributed about the same proportion of trainees. The balance of the trainees was selected from thirty-three other states, Puerto Rico, and American Samoa. Training courses were offered in 169 different redevelopment areas and 7 Indian reservations. A regional distribution of ARA training is found in Table 6-1.

One out of every six selectees was to be trained as a machine-tool operator. Other occupations for which training was most often provided included typing and stenography, sewing-machine operation, welding, and nurses' aides. About two out of every three trainees was

Table 6–1: ARA Training: Amount Expended and Number of Persons Selected for Training by Region, Cumulative through April 30, 1963

| | Total | | | Areas with Work Force | | | | | |
| | | | | 15,000 and More (5[a]) | | | Less than 15,000 (5[b]) | | |
	Cost [a] (Thousands)	Number of Trainees	Cost per Trainee	Cost [a] (Thousands)	Number of Trainees	Cost per Trainee	Cost [a] (Thousands)	Number of Trainees	Cost per Trainee
United States	$10,960	19,329	$567	$7,514	12,937	$581	$3,029	5,794	$523
Northeast	2,901	4,719	615	2,700	4,263	633	201	456	441
New England	1,509	2,293	658	1,488	2,223	669	21	70	300
Middle Atlantic	1,392	2,426	574	1,212	2,040	594	180	386	466
North Central	3,108	5,330	583	2,001	3,612	554	918	1,442	637
East North Central	2,482 [b]	3,844 [b]	646	1,783	2,674	667	687	1,086	633
West North Central	626 [b]	1,486 [b]	421	218	938	232	231	356	649
South	3,874	7,545	513	2,276	4,238	537	1,370	2,985	459
South Atlantic	1,769	3,630	487	1,466	2,743	534	303	887	342
East South Central	902 [b]	1,760 [a]	512	466	934	478	329	683	482
West South Central	1,203 [b]	2,155 [b]	558	344	561	613	738	1,415	522
West	926	1,416	653	421	525	802	505	891	567
Mountain	719	1,067	674	271	316	858	448	751	597
Pacific	207	349	593	150	209	718	57	140	407
Puerto Rico and American Samoa	151	319	473	116	299	388	35	20	1,750

[a] Exclusive of administrative outlays.
[b] Total includes training courses that were allocated on a state-wide basis and which are not included in either 5(a) or 5(b) areas.

SOURCE: Computed from ARA statistical reports.

male, a ratio similar to the sex distribution in the labor force as a whole.

Although about one of every six selectees who entered training dropped out before completing the course, 6,747 of the 9,747 "graduates" (69 per cent) obtained jobs shortly after they completed the course, usually in the occupations for which they had been trained. Of course, many of those who remained unemployed completed training just before the accounting period was closed and may have found jobs later. By the same token, some of the trainees who have found jobs may have lost their jobs shortly after they secured them.

The average instructional cost per trainee, exclusive of federal administration, amounted to about $250. Subsistence payments made to trainees averaged $317, or close to $30 per week, since the average duration of training was 10.5 weeks. A distribution of the approved courses by hours of training was:

Hours of Training	Per cent Distribution
40–90	3.1
100–180	22.9
200–280	14.3
300–390	21.0
400–480	21.3
500–560	14.9
Over 660	2.5

Most training projects provided for thirty to forty training hours a week, but in some cases training was limited to twenty hours a week. The controlling factor was the availability of training facilities. In some cases ARA training had to be provided at night because facilities were already fully utilized. "We have been asked to run a machine shop class from 10 p.m. to 4 a.m., five nights a week, because the shop is already in use from 9 a.m. to 10 p.m. every day and all day Saturday," one educational director testified.[10]

Three out of every four trainees were nineteen to forty-four years old. Eight per cent were eighteen years or younger, and the balance (10.2 per cent) was forty-five years or older. More than a third of the trainees had completed a high school education; 15 per cent had less than nine years of formal education, and half that number had over twelve years of education. About half of the trainees may be considered hard-core unemployed or underemployed; 38 per cent had been unemployed for half a year or longer—one out of every four had been unemployed for more than a year—prior to enrollment for retraining; another tenth of the trainees were underemployed farm workers. A statistical summary of the characteristics of the trainees is presented in Table 6–2.

Table 6–2: Characteristics of Trainees Enrolled in or Completing ARA Courses, Cumulative through April 30, 1963 [a]

Characteristics	Per Cent of Trainees
Age (in years)	
Under 19	7.6
20–34	59.0
35–44	18.6
45 and over	10.2
Not reported	4.6
Education (in years)	
Under 9	15.4
9–12	34.8
12	38.8
Over 12	6.8
Not reported	4.2
Unemployment (in weeks)	
Less than 5	15.5
5–14	19.2
15–26	12.6
27–52	12.5
Over 52	25.7
Underemployed and family farm workers	9.7
Not reported	4.8

[a] The first ARA training course was offered in November, 1961. The Area Redevelopment Act was signed into law on May 1, 1961. However, Congress delayed the appropriation of funds for the program until September 30, 1961.

SOURCE: U.S. Department of Labor, Bureau of Employment Security, May, 1963.

EVALUATION

The above data concerning the characteristics of ARA trainees have led some to question the effectiveness of the program. Advocates of the program have been disturbed by the fact that only a tenth of the ARA trainees were forty-five years or older and that only 15 per cent had less than nine years of formal education. It has been suggested that the employment services have failed to select hard-core unemployed for training because of their desire to show a good re-employment record for the program. It has also been noted that many of the hard-core unemployed have not been responsive to the training program. In Huntington, West Virginia, the first area to receive an ARA-approved training program, more than a thousand long-term unemployed were invited to participate in the retraining program. Only 640 appeared for the aptitude tests and of these only 240 qualified for training.

The fact that four out of ten of the long-term unemployed did not even respond to the invitation for training may indicate that many of the poorly educated and unskilled unemployed are improperly motivated and psychologically unprepared to participate in formal training. It also reflects poor communications between the employment agencies and some segments of the unemployed. The high proportion of rejections—three out of five—led some to conclude that the training program was designed for the better-motivated and better-educated unemployed and that the ARA training program was not geared to help the least educated, who might need assistance to gain re-employment the most.[15]

A more careful analysis of the early ARA training program and the climate in which it operated might lead one to question these pessimistic conclusions. The meager data available disclose that more than half of the total ARA trainees during the first two years of operation were from among the hard-core unemployed—if more than half a year unemployment preceding the training and underemployment with less than $1,200 annual income are taken as the criteria. An additional 13 per cent had been unemployed for fifteen weeks or more. This means that almost two-thirds of the total trainees were long-term unemployed or underemployed. Considering that most of the training was for job vacancies within the depressed areas, the fact that two-thirds of the trainees received jobs after the completion of the training period is not too bad a record. On the other hand, only one of every ten ARA trainees was forty-five years or older, while the ratio of long-term unemployed in this age group in 1962 was at least twice as high. This would indicate that the cream of the unemployed were selected for ARA training. Or, more specifically, that age was a very formidable barrier to participation in retraining.

The fact that most employment services and local vocational education systems had very little prior experience in this type of program was a serious obstacle to the early ARA training. At the same time, considerable friction existed—some still remained in 1964—among and within the various levels of authority involved in planning and approving ARA training courses. Despite the initial difficulties, considerable pressure was brought to bear to get the program working without delay. During the first half year of operation, Congress was considering a much more ambitious training program which was enacted as the Manpower Development and Training Act of 1962. Proponents and opponents of the new program therefore carefully scrutinized the operations of ARA training to find support for their respective positions. The early training programs were thus developed and executed in a fishbowl atmosphere which was certainly not conducive to effective planning or to ironing out the diverse administrative problems.

Most employment services were not prepared for the program. The service in Providence, Rhode Island, was one exception: it made advance preparation for the training program even before the legislation was enacted. The state department of employment security conducted studies of occupations in short supply in the area and applied for ARA grants almost immediately after the legislation was approved. As a result, 365 unemployed workers in the city were enrolled in training courses within a few months after the program started.

Imaginative Projects

Despite serious obstacles and the program's inherent limitations— the training of unemployed workers in chronic labor-surplus areas for local hire and the general high level of unemployment which prevailed throughout the country—a number of imaginative courses have been developed which indicate the potential of the program. In Hammonton, New Jersey, the state employment service organized a training course for twenty-five farm workers to operate, maintain, and repair farm equipment. The age of the trainees ranged from eighteen to forty-eight, and the average educational level attained by the trainees was the middle of the ninth grade; two had completed only two years of school. The trainees were farm laborers, some of whom were migratory laborers based in New Jersey. Twenty of the twenty-five trainees who initially enrolled completed the course successfully and secured jobs in the area. The success of the New Jersey training program led to the development of similar courses in Arkansas, Oklahoma, and Texas. The New Jersey employment service applied for a second course in another community; as planned, the new course was to include some training in literacy. The significance of this type of training is that it improves the efficiency of the labor force in basic industry and provides the base for expansion of employment in service industries.

A more ambitious course was developed for thirty-five Indians from eight reservations in New Mexico and Arizona. This involved the co-operation of California vocational education authorities, the U.S. Department of Labor, and the Bureau of Indian Affairs. The last-mentioned agency moved the trainees to Los Angeles, California, and secured housing for them in the new location. The California authorities contracted with the RCA Institute, a privately owned organization, to train the selectees to work as electronic solderers and wirers, in the hope of placing them in various California labor markets. In this case, the course was designed for twenty-four weeks: ARA training funds supplied the subsistence for the first sixteen weeks (the maximum allowed under the ARA), while the Bureau of Indian Affairs picked up the tab for the balance of the training period.

But despite the few "success" stories, it should be recognized that the ARA training program is extremely limited and that it contains some inherent problems. As contemplated by Congress, the training program was designed to be associated with the other types of assistance under the Act; training was to be provided for new or expanding plants locating in depressed areas. During the first two years of the ARA little opportunity arose to train workers for the newly expanded facilities, in part because of the limited hiring by ARA-financed enterprises in full operation—by May 1, 1963, about fifty such enterprises were in operation with about 7,000 employees. Moreover, training programs were usually found inappropriate for ARA-generated employment. The ARA automatically notifies the U.S. Bureau of Employment Security concerning every approved commercial and industrial loan. The BES, through its affiliated state employment services, then asks the loan applicant about his training needs. Almost invariably it has been found that the needed skills are available or that the employer had to do little training. In some cases the employer had brought in skilled workers from the outside. The bulk of the training has therefore been limited to providing manpower for expanding enterprises and for replacements.

On-the-Job Training

Another difficulty in integrating training with new commercial and industrial facilities financed by the ARA lies in the legislation itself.

The Act failed to include a provision which would have authorized on-the-job training in connection with the development of new job opportunities. As a result, products made under ARA training programs are prohibited from use in commerce. This is a carry-over both from earlier vocational training experience and from the George-Barden Act, which prohibits utilizing "the services of vocational trainees for private profit" (P.L. 79–586, Section 8). The Wage and Hours Division of the U.S. Department of Labor has interpreted the law as requiring that minimum wages be paid to employees being trained for work that would be used in commerce. Consequently, every approval of an ARA training course, where appropriate, contains the provision that "instructional materials must be consumed in the process of instruction, or if not consumed, donated to tax-supported institutions. Trainees may not work in commerce or in the production of goods for commerce."

In only one case where training was integrated with an ARA loan were special provisions made to overcome the prohibition against performing work in commerce. For one of the largest training projects approved under the ARA program, in Carbondale, Illinois, the difficulty was resolved by dividing the working day into work performed on the job that was paid for by the employer, and time devoted to training where subsistence was paid under the approved program.

In order to strengthen the ARA package of tools for attracting new industry to depressed areas, consideration should be given to expanding on-the-job training by combining subsistence benefits with wage supplements. These supplements would offer employers a sufficient inducement to train workers and, at the same time, would avoid the undermining of prevailing wage rates or statutory minimum wages. But adequate safeguards must be provided to assure that government outlays are used to broaden the skills of workers and that the government expenditures are not used to pay their wages when they are actually employed in productive work.

In some cases, the states have co-operated in contributing toward the cost of instructional material for the program; the products of the trainees are then used for distribution in state-supported institutions. For example, a proposal to train sewing-machine operators stipulated that the state would acquire dresses valued at approximately $63,000 for use at state institutions.

Aside from legal impediments, the ARA training experience has shown that it is difficult to synchronize training with the actual opening of new operations. A considerable amount of time may elapse between the approval of an ARA loan for a new commercial or industrial venture and the time when the new company is ready to hire new employees. In some cases, the training program was completed before the company was ready to hire employees, and the trainees had to look for jobs elsewhere.

The greatest difficulty of on-the-job training programs involved sewing-machine operations. Vestibule training is usually the most desirable and economical method of training in this occupation. This is particularly true where a single employing establishment is involved.

But the life of a company in this industry is known to be extremely short, with geographic mobility very common. The Area Redevelopment Act prohibits financial aid for the relocation of plants, and this ban has been administratively interpreted to apply to all the benefits provided under the Act. But even in cases where the new needle-trade plant did not involve relocation, the Labor Department authorities were reluctant to approve the training of sewing-machine operators lest the employment provided by the new facility prove to be only temporary. The Office of Manpower, Automation and Training therefore prepared informal guidelines which would be helpful in reviewing training projects for sewing-machine operators. The guidelines, which illustrate the type of problems the Labor Department has encountered in approving training courses, included the following:

1. Duration of course: Training courses for sewing-machine operators are normally limited to 120 hours. The course was normally devoted to the training in the basic operation of power sewing machines, with the training of specialized skills left to the prospective employers. However, exceptions were made. For example, the OMAT approved 150 hours of training that involved former coal miners in Pennsylvania. Since the potential trainees were middle-aged and older unemployed workers, it was assumed that they would need extra training in order to qualify for the new occupation.

2. Course materials: Expendable instructional materials were limited to 20 cents per trainee hour.

3. Consultation: The appropriate unions in the needle trades were to be consulted prior to the approval of a training course. In many cases it is difficult to identify a relocation or "runaway" shop in this industry because of formal changes in corporate ownership. In some cases the OMAT found conflict between the national and local union views: the national officers, aware of existing unemployment among union members in established needle-trade centers, opposed

the opening of new facilities, while the local union officers welcomed new potential membership in their own areas.

Need to Broaden Program

The ARA experience has shown that the formula under which the Congress allocated funds for training proved to be unrealistic. It will be recalled that, following the advice of experts, Congress authorized $4.50 to administer and to operate the training program for every $10.00 paid in subsistence. Experience during the first fiscal year of ARA operations proved that the actual relation of training costs to subsistence was about four to five. This was due mainly to the fact that in many instances adequate facilities and equipment were not available to the local vocational training authorities. This necessitated the expenditure of extra funds for obtaining new or used equipment as well as for renting or renovating new facilities. As a result, during fiscal 1962 the ARA expended almost all the funds appropriated for vocational training but less than half of the funds allocated for the payment of subsistence benefits. The actual cost of training, including subsistence payments, depends upon the type of course offered and the availability of facilities and equipment. It would have been more efficient if Congress had authorized a lump sum for training, thus allowing flexibility in the proportioning of funds between the subsistence and other costs connected with the training program. During fiscal 1963 Congress "resolved" the problem by appropriating only $6 million for subsistence payments, instead of the authorized $10 million, along with the $4.5 million for the administration of vocational training courses.

The passage of the Manpower Development and Training Act in the spring of 1962 (funds were not appropriated until late summer) created another problem in connection with ARA training. The MDTA allows fifty-two weeks of training, while ARA subsistence payments are limited to sixteen weeks, thereby restricting the effective training period to the same duration. One possible course would be to drop the ARA training program and to limit training under the more ambitious MDTA program. But this would be contrary to the philosophy of the ARA's authors, who attempted to assemble a package of tools to aid depressed areas. It would also subject training in depressed areas to some of the restrictions imposed under the MDTA—for example, the limitation of subsistence payments to youths between the ages of nineteen and twenty-one, and restriction of the remainder of the program to persons who have had three years of experience in the labor market and who are heads of families. The MDTA also provides that beginning in July, 1964, states and localities will have to match federal contributions. Many depressed areas will not be able to match these contributions.

Another solution would be to retain the ARA program but to extend training under it to fifty-two weeks and to provide for defraying transportation costs of trainees who attend courses outside of their communities, which is done under the MDTA. Congress will no doubt have to confront this problem when it considers the revision of ARA legislation in 1965, when the Act is due to expire.

The immediate scope of the ARA training program is obviously extremely limited. At an estimated annual cost of $567 per trainee, exclusive of federal administrative expenditures, only some 12,000–15,000 unemployed workers in depressed areas can receive direct benefits from the program each year, given current appropriation levels. Even under ideal circumstances only part of this small group of trainees would be from among the hard-core unemployed. Considering the magnitude of unemployment and underemployment in depressed areas, the ARA training program will reach annually only about one out of every sixty unemployed in these areas.

IMPLICATIONS OF ARA TRAINING

The ARA training program has, however, much broader implications than the quantitative limitations would indicate. A major contribution of the ARA training provisions lies in the fact that the program has emphasized the relationship among existing but hitherto independent programs: employment services, including counseling and guidance, vocational education and manpower projections. The Manpower Development and Training Act, which followed closely on the heels of the ARA, further stressed the interdependence of these agencies and institutions and the need for close co-operation if each is to succeed in carrying out its assigned mission.

Bringing out the obvious relationships among employment services, vocational training, and placement should also focus greater public attention on the inadequate scope and dubious quality of much of our public vocational education system. While our educational system as a whole is not exactly wallowing in luxury, vocational education is treated as a stepchild of the system, and too frequently only the shabbiest facilities are allocated to it. In many communities, equipment is of pre-World War II vintage, consisting of leftovers from the National Youth Administration.

The new ARA and MDTA training programs have stretched the meager available public vocational training facilities to the extreme. It is no doubt a tribute to our much-maligned vocational educators that they could adjust their programs on short notice to satisfy the increased burdens placed on them.

The ARA has tied training to economic growth and has emphasized the harsh fact that our educational and vocational facilities have not kept pace in developing skills for our changing technology. As a result, significant sectors of the labor force are left out of the mainstream of the changing American economic life. The increase in the number of youths entering the labor market during the immediate years ahead presents a challenge to our educational system and particularly to vocational training to devise new ways of preparing the youth for a productive life and equipping them for the needs of the labor market of the future.

The limited ARA training experience suggests the need for strengthening vocational education. It indicates that many presumably "unemployables" are salvageable, given the proper training opportunities. But it is also quite apparent that in many, possibly most, United States communities adequate training facilities are not available for those unemployed who could benefit from them. The ARA and MDTA training programs point out the weaknesses in present facilities. To be sure, only part of the currently unemployed will be reached even by an expanded and improved training program; but the dollars invested in training bear sound returns.

The ARA training experience has also indicated that some of the hard-core unemployed will not be absorbed by private enterprise in the immediate years ahead, even assuming a higher growth rate than we experienced in 1952–62. A sample study of 2,000 unemployed by the Michigan Employment Security Commission has suggested that even if the total unemployment rate is reduced to 4 per cent, there will still be 1 per cent—or more than 700,000—who are hard-core unemployables. Sixty-five per cent of the unemployed workers included in the Michigan sample study were unskilled or semiskilled, 50 per cent were Negroes, and 35 per cent lived on relief.[17]

This suggests the need for additional public programs to absorb the hard-core unemployed as a matter of sound economics, since the alternative to finding useful employment for them is to expand welfare expenditures. One step in this direction is the youth employment bill, which is currently being considered by the Congress. By providing employment opportunities to out-of-school and out-of-work youth, some of these youths will be able to acquire desirable work habits which they would not have an opportunity to develop under existing conditions.

Another desirable program would be the gradual increase of federal grants for vocational education. In the final analysis, the effectiveness of training under the ARA, the MDTA, and the Trade Expansion Act will depend upon the resources allocated to traditional vocational education programs. A reappraisal of these facilities along the lines recently proposed by a group of experts appointed by the Secretary of HEW and by several bills introduced in the Eighty-eighth Congress is long overdue.[7, 4] The tide of the new youthful entries into the labor market is already upon us. This points up the need of devising new formulas for allocating additional vocational education grants to depressed areas.

Availability of needed training facilities will help many youths as well as adults in acquiring skills which are in demand. While many economists have questioned the validity of Say's Law that supply creates its own demand, there is little doubt that our current unemployment problems would be reduced if our educational and vocational training institutions could succeed in closing the gap between the skills acquired by their products and the dynamic changes in demand for occupational skills which our economy has experienced in recent years.[6]

Nevertheless, some economists have questioned the efficacy of retraining in combatting unemployment. They argue that the creeping unemployment which the American economy has experienced during the past decade is a function of inadequate expansion in demand and that expanded growth would generate sufficient jobs and eliminate excessive unemployment. This view was possibly best expressed in a Joint Economic Committee study:

> Many of the jobs in expanding activities like trade, services, and government do not require extensive training but can be filled by individuals possessing only moderate amounts of formal education and skill. . . . If employers do prefer teenagers or women, displaced industrial workers will find themselves at the

[6]For an excellent brief statement on the need to allocate additional resources for vocational education and related federal policies to stimulate skill development and worker mobility, see U.S. Congress, Joint Economic Committee, *1963 Joint Economic Report*, 88th Cong., 1st Sess., Senate Report 78 (Minority Views), pp. 89–92.

back of the hiring queue. . . . *In an expansion period of any duration,* the unemployment rate should eventually approach the earlier full employment neighborhood of 4 percent. [11, emphasis supplied.]

No doubt the above Kalachek-Knowles analysis would be correct if, for some unforeseeable reason, "an expansion period of any duration" should materialize. In a prolonged tight labor market, employers will hire marginal workers. But even in 1953, a year of full employment, there remained a number of chronic labor-surplus areas, while serious labor shortages existed in many other areas. The transition to full employment can be achieved less painfully yet more rapidly if adequate training is offered to those who have never acquired the skills needed in expanding occupations. The Joint Economic Committee study ignores the fact that economic growth is retarded because many unemployed are ill-equipped to fill existing job vacancies and because they fail to queue up to look for jobs as they do not expect to find employment. Labor-force data for depressed areas indicate that a significant proportion of the unemployed drop out of the labor force and that others do not enter the labor force because they know that job openings are not available for the skills which they possess.

Employment service studies further suggest that the desired expansion in demand is arrested because employers do not choose to assume the costs of training potential employees and thus fail to expand their activities. ARA, MDTA, and other vocational retraining may provide unemployed workers with the skills needed in order to line up effectively in the "hiring queue."

However, it could hardly be hoped that the token ARA training program could meet the needs of the unemployed in the depressed areas. A much more ambitious and comprehensive program is needed to retrain the unemployed in these areas. Nils Kellgren, a member of the Swedish Parliament and an expert on manpower problems, who recently acted as a consultant on manpower problems to the U.S. Secretary of Labor, suggested the need of annually retraining, under public auspices, 1 per cent of the labor force. This would require retraining some 700,000 workers annually.[5] Since the depressed areas contain close to a third of the total U.S. unemployed, and presumably a larger proportion of the underemployed, the Kellgren proposal would indicate a need to retrain annually some 250,000 persons in ARA areas. Moreover, an effective training program will also require an appreciable extension of the training period, to fifty-two weeks and possibly longer. Such a program, in addition to upgrading the skills of the work force in depressed areas, will also have the effect of stimulating income maintenance and consumer demand.

REFERENCES

1. *Congressional Record.* March 15, 1961, pp. 3780, 3782.
2. *Congressional Record.* March 29, 1961, p. 4933 (Section 15, H. R. 5943).
3. *Congressional Record.* August 23, 1961, p. 15709.
4. U.S. Congress. H. R. 3000 and S. 580 (Administration bills), H. R. 4955 (Carl D. Perkins), and S. 1222 (J. Caleb Boggs). 88th Cong., 1st Sess., 1963.
5. Kellgren, Nils. "An Active Labor Market Policy." A Memorandum to the U.S. Secretary of Labor, 1963, p. 71. (Mimeographed.)
6. Levine, Louis. "Manpower Aspects of the Area Redevelopment Act." Address delivered at Providence, Rhode Island, November 20, 1961. (Mimeographed.)
7. Report of the Panel of Consultants on Vocational Education. *Education for a Changing World of Work.* Washington: Government Printing Office, 1963.
8. U.S. House of Representatives, Committee on Banking and Currency. *Area Redevelopment Act.* Report 186, 87th Cong., 1st Sess. Washington: Government Printing Office, 1961, p. 25.
9. ———. *Hearings on Area Redevelopment Act.* 87th Cong., 1st Sess., 1961, pp. 169–77.
10. U.S. House of Representatives, Committee on Education and Labor. *Hearings on H. R. 4955.* 88th Cong., 1st Sess., March 18, 1963 (Statement of Burr D. Coe). In Print.
11. U.S. Congress, Joint Economic Committee. *Higher Unemployment Rates, 1957–60.* 87th Cong., 1st Sess., 1961, p. 13 (Edward D. Kalacheck and James W. Knowles).
12. U.S. Senate, Committee on Banking and Currency. *Hearings on Area Redevelopment Act.* 87th Cong., 1st Sess., 1961, pp. 182–83 (Governor David Lawrence, of Pennsylvania); pp. 196, 310 (Robert P. Lee); pp. 399–400 (M. D. Mobley, executive director, American Vocational Association); p. 606 (Senator Paul H. Douglas).
13. U.S. Senate, Committee on Labor and Public Welfare. *Hearings on Area Redevelopment Act.* 84th Cong., 2d Sess., 1956, p. 1155 (Professor William Miernyk).
14. ———. *Hearings on Nation's Manpower Revolution.* 88th Cong., 1st Sess., 1963, Part 3, p. 865.
15. *Wall Street Journal.* February 16, 1962, p. 1.
16. Wechsler, James A. "1,200 Lives," *New York Post,* January 24, 1962.
17. "Who Are the Unemployables?," *Business Week,* February 9, 1963, pp. 68–70.

Chapter 7

++++++++++++++++++++++++

Community Planning:
The Unlocking of Resources

++

Before a designated community is eligible to receive financial assistance, it is required, under the Area Redevelopment Act, to prepare an over-all economic development program which must receive both state and ARA approval. The Act further requires that every project for which financial assistance is subsequently requested must be consistent with this over-all economic program (Section 6[b] [10]).

It might have been expected that this provision—which makes communities engaged in long-range economic planning subject to state as well as federal approval—would generate considerable debate in Congress. Yet, strangely enough, this far-reaching provision was considered only sparingly in the prolonged legislative hassle over depressed-area legislation.

LEGISLATIVE ISSUES AND PROVISIONS

While most of the substantive provisions of the Area Redevelopment Act originated in the Senate, the planning provision was a product of the House.[1] The House Committee on Banking and Currency considered the planning provision to be "one of the most constructive for

[1]Reportedly, the planning provision was "sold" by Solomon Barkin, secretary of the Area Economic Expansion Committee, which played a key role in lobbying for the area redevelopment legislation. There is no evidence that Senator Douglas was wholeheartedly sympathetic with the idea, though it was included in his 1961 bill. He never elaborated on the planning provision in his discussion or comments on the bill.

long-term recovery."[14] The committee's report spelled out the legislative intent of the provision in detail:

This requirement for careful studies and advance *planning* should assure, first, a real knowledge of the economic potentials of the area—whether they lie in the commercial or industrial field. It should point out the strong and weak points of the area, in both the skills of its manpower and its resources in materials, location, and facilities. Such *planning* should take into account the potentials of the area. . . .

It is, moreover, essential that each program be appraised realistically, and approved by the Secretary [of Commerce], in order to make the wisest use of limited public funds and to give maximum help to the area. *This is "seed money,"* to give impetus to a broad program which, if the unemployed are to be re-employed, will call for private and local public efforts many times the size of this federal program.

. . . .

While economic planning carries no guarantee of success, this provision insures that careful attention will be given to the problems of the area and to the steps that need to be taken to restore prosperity. It will be a reasonable guarantee that the development of the area is feasible and that the project for which assistance is sought will make a real contribution to the long-term expansion of industry and employment.[14, emphasis supplied.]

Presumably, the committee intended that the long-range economic program was to be prepared by the people of the community. Originally, the Douglas bill of 1955 required that the community organization in charge of local economic development be appointed by the federal administrator of the program. The state was not to be involved in the community's economic planning. The rationale for this requirement was that many economic units, such as labor markets or designated rural areas, do not coincide with political boundaries. However, the appointment of local development committees by the federal administrator and the by-passing of state channels were generally opposed by witnesses who commented on these provisions, which opened the bill to wide criticism by both its opponents and friends. Assistant Secretary of Commerce Frederick Mueller stated that "the Federal Government . . . should not interfere in local matters."[17] Governor G. Mennen Williams, of Michigan, who favored the bill, felt "strongly" that applications for financial assistance should be processed through state agencies.[17] William L. Batt, Jr., who expressed no opinion about "states rights," still preferred that the Administrator be required to approve local committees rather than to appoint them.[17]

In light of these criticisms, Senator Douglas dropped the requirement that local committees be appointed by the federal administrator. As finally enacted, the legislation provided that applications for assistance require prior approval by "an agency or instrumentality of the state or political subdivision thereof in which the project to be financed is located . . ." (Section 6[b] [2]). This provision assured that the depressed-area program would be a co-operative effort of local, state, and federal authorities.

Technical Assistance

Closely related to the requirement for economic planning is the provision of the Area Redevelopment Act which authorizes an annual expenditure of $4.5 million for technical assistance. As in the case of over-all economic planning, the provision for technical assistance evoked very little debate, and only minor opposition to the proposal was expressed throughout the voluminous and prolonged hearings on the bill. Both Douglas' bill and the one introduced by the Eisenhower Administration included the provision for technical assistance. Even the Chamber of Commerce, which found little merit in either bill, approved the principle of federal technical assistance. However, the Chamber of Commerce was not ready to endorse an annual federal expenditure of $4.5 million for such assistance.[17] Similarly, the Republican minority of the House Committee on Banking and Currency, which also opposed any new federal legislation to aid depressed areas, recognized the desirability of technical assistance to depressed areas and suggested that existing federal facilities for such assistance might be expanded.[14]

Possibly the most articulate advocate of technical assistance was Solomon Barkin. He considered effective technical assistance basic to the whole program and argued that an annual $4.5 million appropriation would be inadequate. He thought that carefully conceived planning should precede any request for direct financial assistance and that an inadequately financed technical assistance program would create bottlenecks in the development of the over-all depressed-area program. Barkin therefore proposed a $10 million annual appropriation.[15]

As conceived by Senator Douglas and the other proponents of the legislation, technical assistance would aid communities in developing their economic potential. While all the other provisions of the Act are

intended to aid designated depressed areas, in the case of technical assistance the Administrator is authorized to extend aid to all areas
"which have substantial need for such assistance" (Section 11).

Congress seemed to have only a vague idea as to the potential function of technical assistance. Only two comments were made on the
subject during the 1961 congressional debate. Congressman Wright
Patman, House floor leader for the bill, thought that technical assistance would help communities in attracting new industry.[4] And Senator Robert Byrd, of West Virginia, considered technical assistance an
important tool in aiding economic recovery by helping communities
realistically evaluate their economic potential.[3]

The eight reports prepared by the appropriate House and Senate
committees between 1956 and 1961 were largely repetitious and vague
as to the intent of the technical assistance provisions. They broadly
asserted that technical assistance should help to pinpoint the compara-
tive advantages of communities and to help local leaders develop economic growth and expansion on the basis of an intelligent appraisal of
their community's physical and human resources. It was also thought
that sound technical assistance would encourage the expansion of indigenous industry by helping firms in depressed areas increase their
efficiency and develop new products and services.[16, 14] This paucity
of comment on technical assistance reflects the relatively undeveloped
state of community economic planning in the United States.

Research

Specific provisions for long-range research dealing with the causes
and cures of depressed areas were inserted into the bill at the eleventh
hour. During the hearings on the bill a number of witnesses called attention to the need for special research to aid the Administrator in
effectuating the purposes of the legislation. For example, in 1956 Senator Everett M. Dirksen urged that modest grants be offered to universities and colleges located in depressed areas to help develop the
resources of their regions.[17] Similarly, Solomon Barkin called attention to the emerging "regional science" and suggested that insights developed by this new discipline should be helpful to the Administrator
in developing the program to aid depressed areas. He urged that a
special provision dealing with research be included in the Act.[17]

Similar suggestions were made by other witnesses during subsequent
hearings. It was generally assumed that the provision for technical assistance, along with the general powers granted the Administrator,

would be adequate to provide for any long-range research that was needed. In the 1961 House debate on the bill, however, Congressman Joseph M. Montoya, of New Mexico, proposed an amendment directing the Administrator to conduct continuing research programs "designed to assist in determining the causes of unemployment, underemployment, underdevelopment, and chronic depression in the various areas of the nation and in the nation . . . as a whole. . . ."[5] The amendment was adopted without debate. The conference accepted the Montoya research amendment but required that research be concentrated on designated areas and not "in the nation as a whole."[6]

COMMUNITY OVER-ALL ECONOMIC
DEVELOPMENT PROGRAMS

The provisions for over-all economic development programs, technical assistance, and research indicate that Congress desired the ARA to involve itself in local economic planning and economic development. Necessarily, the problem of developing community Overall Economic Development Programs (OEDP) was first on the ARA's agenda —after it had designated areas as eligible for assistance—since a community could not qualify for financial assistance unless it had submitted such a program. To help communities prepare OEDP's, the ARA gave priority to the preparation of a special brochure of instructions.[18]

The brochure explained the need for the preparation of an OEDP and outlined the essential elements of such a community program. The designated areas were first directed to establish a duly authorized economic development group, to be known as a Redevelopment Area Organization (RAO). The ARA required that the OEDP list the members of the RAO, who should be representative of major community interests, business, agriculture, labor, public officials, and others. The OEDP was to contain a general description of the area, present labor-force data by industry and occupation, describe the extent of unemployment and underemployment and the factors that had contributed to economic decline and stagnation, and summarize and evaluate past attempts to rehabilitate the community.

The OEDP was then to list the past obstacles to economic growth and development of the community. The OEDP was to concentrate on problems related to the availability of venture capital and entrepreneurial initiative, the availability of sites for new or expanding industry, the need for retraining of available labor, the appraisal of public utility services, and the financing capabilities of the local government. Finally, the ARA admonished that each designated area "should establish goals and a program to guide its planning and action. Every move by local groups, every investment in new buildings and facilities should be a well-calculated move taking the community along the path leading toward these goals. The goals and program should be consistent with the area's possibilities and limitations. . . ." [18]

The completion of an OEDP proved to be not too burdensome upon communities. By 1961 there were more than 3,000 local economic development corporations in existence, according to a Small Business Administration estimate, and the bulk of the designated areas had some community economic or planning organization. Economic setback or stagnation, of which practically all of the designated areas were victims, had frequently served as stimuli to organized economic development activity. However, in most of these communities the economic development groups were either adjuncts or special committees of some other local business, agriculture, or governmental group. Since the ARA required that OEDP's be produced by a group representing the broadest views of the community, and not just those of businessmen and bankers, it was necessary in some cases that public officials, and union and farm-group representatives be included in the RAO's. This was not specifically spelled out in the Act, but there was ample justification for this requirement in the legislative history of the OEDP provision. The assumption was that a community's economic plan might be narrow in scope and self-serving if prepared by representatives of special-interest groups. An effective community plan, according to this view, must represent the consensus of various conflicting groups and interests in a community.

This thesis has not yet been proved. Heretofore, successful community economic development had usually depended upon one or a few businessmen who acted as the movers and shakers, and who worked in close harmony with the business community. Whether the introduction of new elements will bring broader perspective to community development, or introduce frictions and dispersion of responsibility, remains to be seen. No conclusive judgment can be made on the subject based on the rather brief ARA experience.

In most cases, the established local economic development group was

[2]A revised edition of the instructions to communities to prepare an OEDP was published in the spring of 1962 under the title *Planning for New Growth—New Jobs*.[20]

designated as the formal Redevelopment Area Organization, and apparently, where necessary, new members were added to satisfy the ARA requirement of "broad representation." [3] Except for a few regional conferences, the ARA could do little to educate communities in preparing OEDP's.

Communities hoping to benefit by the ARA lost no time in filing their OEDP's. By the end of 1961 about a quarter of the designated communities had filed such reports, and two-thirds of all designated areas had filed them by the end of 1962. As of May 1, 1963, 81 per cent —850 areas, including 42 Indian reservations, in 48 states—of all the designated areas had sent in OEDP's.

An examination of a broad random sample of OEDP's on file revealed that their preparation normally involved only limited thoughtful analysis of community resources and contained little that would provide a blueprint for future community economic development. Many of the OEDP's were poorly conceived and failed to contain essential economic data needed for future economic planning. Information having no bearing upon the purpose of the OEDP was commonly included. Since many of the Redevelopment Area Organizations were direct successors of the established local economic development groups, it was not surprising to find that the OEDP's followed the long-established tradition of such groups by basing the "plans" for future economic development on attracting new manufacturing plants. With manufacturing employment on the decline, the ARA could scarcely conclude that the sound economic future of the bulk of its customers would depend upon the expansion of manufacturing plants.

The community OEDP's also emphasized the need for additional public works and public facilities. A good many of the "needed" public works scarcely had any relationship to the future economic development of the community. And even in cases where the suggested public facilities were relevant to economic development, little attention was paid to the potential cost of the proposed projects; rarely, for example, was any attempt made to compute a cost-benefit ratio to justify proposed public works.

It was quite apparent that many designated areas did not take the OEDP preparation seriously and wanted to complete this preliminary requirement as quickly as possible in order to qualify for ARA bene-

[3]An unpublished ARA-sponsored study of a community in New York reported that the local labor representative on the RAO stated that he saw no reason for attending the meetings because "all they do is talk and there was no vote on any action to be taken."

fits. The ARA had anticipated that a locally conceived OEDP would be technically inadequate and incomplete, but in some cases local communities and state economic development agencies made a complete mockery of the congressional and ARA desire for grass-roots participation. For example, most if not all of the OEDP's for the designated areas in Kentucky were prepared by the State Area Programs Office in Frankfort, Kentucky. Practically all of the OEDP's were stated in such general terms that without basic changes they could have described almost any area. An OEDP prepared for an agricultural county in the extreme western part of the state was almost identical with one filed for a coal mining county in the eastern part of the state, except for different brief descriptions of the topography and resources of the respective areas. The sections of the respective OEDP's calling for a "program for action" were also almost identical, except that the western county called for the development of agriculture, while the eastern county substituted coal for agriculture.

In brief, while many of the community redevelopment plans submitted to the ARA were superficial in content, poorly conceived, and of little potential value to the areas concerned, others stimulated economic planning and action. Some of the plans were the products of consultants and indicated little community effort—except for the payment of consultant fees. Other plans, as exemplified by those received from Kentucky and southern Illinois, were drawn up by state agencies, reflected little or no participation at the local level, contained few realistic plans for action, and little analysis of community potential.

The cavalier attitude of some communities toward the preparation of OEDP's is readily understandable. Spokesmen for eastern Kentucky have asserted that their area had been "studied to death" and that they were looking to ARA for action and not further studies. By action they meant the building of roads, reservoirs, dams, houses, libraries, and other public facilities needed to make the depleted communities attractive to their residents and to new economic activity. The spokesmen for this area knew that unless they succeeded in achieving the proper infrastructure for their communities, there would be no hope of expanding the economic base of the area. But above all, the unemployed in eastern Kentucky were apparently led to believe that the ARA would supply them jobs. "They don't seem to realize in Washington," according to a spokesman for Perry County, East Kentucky, "that what we need is some sort of WPA program to put our people back to work."[11] The types of projects which they had in mind included reforestation, constructing fire trails, paving dirt roads, and cleaning streams. Of course, the ARA did not have sufficient resources to fulfill even a small part of these needs.

But it would be a mistake to assume that the preparation of the OEDP's was a futile exercise. In some communities the preparation of the OEDP's served to stimulate an appraisal of the community's economic status and to initiate the preparation of realistic plans for the development of specific industrial, commercial, and public-facility projects that "made sense" in the light of the community's resources, location, and organizational structure. The press in some depressed areas published the OEDP's in part or in whole, thus making them available to the local citizenry. It is difficult to evaluate the impact of this type of economic education upon the community, but it may be assumed that a greater awareness of the economic problems of an area and a better understanding of existing economic potential may have an indirect impact upon the future development of the area's economy. In fact, some communities have reported positive results from the preparation of the OEDP. The Benton County, Tennessee, Area Redevelopment Committee reported that "the OEDP itself has stimulated thinking along the lines of economic development even in areas not envisaged by our original plan." The committee listed some dozen projects which have resulted from planning and concluded that "the OEDP has had a catalytic effect and gives evidence of proving even more so."[2] Similarly, the Avery County, North Carolina, Planning Board asserted that as a result of implementing its OEDP the economic stagnation of the community would be reversed.[1] Similar expressions of optimism were found in other OEDP progress reports.

But the spirit of optimism was hardly universal; some communities could not show any tangible results emanating from the preparation of the OEDP's. An illustration of this is the frustration experienced by community planners in Yancey County, a neighbor of Avery, North Carolina.[4] The local planning group recognized the importance of developing and implementing the OEDP, but found that the county lacked adequate resources to take advantage of the help offered by ARA. The planners of Yancey County thought that their mountain area had already been studied extensively. According to the local ARA group:

[4]The wide divergences in the views of Avery and Yancey counties might have been due to the individual perspectives of the reporters rather than to actual developments. The factors that contributed to the differences in the reports could not be ascertained, but were likely due to differences in community leadership.

Yancey County has in the past made some very creditable efforts—at considerable sacrifice to our citizens—to lift us out of our economic rut. The failure of these efforts has contributed to skepticism and apathy regarding the present efforts. The slowness of ARA benefits to materialize in the western North Carolina counties is now serving to enforce this defeatist feeling . . . the optimism with which we started off has faded perceptively; at the last planning board meeting only three members attended. What these depressed counties in western North Carolina need is some tangible "bricks and mortar" to show for their efforts.

The Yancey County redevelopers were pessimistic about the future. The Yancey planners thought that outmigration (the 1950 population of 19,500 dwindled by 1960 to 15,000) had sapped the vitality of the community and that those who left the area "included all those with ability and initiative for developing business." According to the Yancey County spokesman, the ARA did not have adequate resources to help the poor isolated rural counties and therefore its help would go by default to areas which need help least. The Yancey folks volunteered that they found the state and federal agencies sympathetic, but "the wide dispersal among so many agencies of the possible sources of help is from our standpoint an unfortunate, time-consuming handicap."[24]

The Processing of OEDP's

From the time the first OEDP's began to flow into the ARA, it was clear that these documents could hardly serve as "blueprints for progress." Most of the established local economic development groups had concentrated their efforts on luring industry. The activities of these organizations had been largely centered on real estate development, including the development of industrial sites, construction of new plants, and various forms of financial assistance to new or expanding firms. It would require a complete reorientation in the thinking of the local development groups to interest them in sophisticated long-range planning for developing the economic potential of their areas.

The ARA, therefore, was faced with the dilemma of either approving inadequate plans or disqualifying designated areas from receiving financial assistance under the Act until better plans were worked out. The agency resolved this dilemma by accepting each OEDP submitted by communities as a token of good faith and an indication that the community desired to plan its economic future on a sound basis. The ARA was no less anxious to help communities than the latter were eager to receive federal aid. However, since many of the OEDP's could not qualify as realistic programs for action, the ARA decided to give the plans "provisional" approval, with the understanding that the communities would continue to develop more comprehensive plans.

The ARA intended to review each OEDP and prepare appraisals of the provisional program to help the communities work out more comprehensive plans. But this policy turned out to be unrealistic. The ARA had developed neither the expertise nor the staff to appraise the validity of the local programs and to offer sound suggestions for the development of better plans. To augment its meager staff, the ARA turned to consulting firms for critical appraisals and suggestions. Again this turned out to be an exercise in futility. It could hardly be expected that a technician sitting in Washington, no matter how expert, could prepare sound economic development programs for the hundreds of communities which sent in OEDP's. And because the ARA had only meager funds for the appraisal of the OEDP's, its consultants could not afford to devote sufficient time to their revision. Despite heroic efforts by the ARA staff and the consulting firms, the reviews usually did little more than summarize the OEDP and offer a few general suggestions for further work and study.

For a while the ARA toyed with the idea of assigning the review and critical appraisal of local OEDP's to its field staff—which presumably possessed a more intimate knowledge of local economic problems in the areas to which they were assigned. But by May 1, 1963, the ARA had only about sixty field staff people, many of whom were green in the business of economic development and planning. These field staff personnel were charged with stimulating and processing applications for financial and other assistance from their areas. To divert the ARA's meager field resources to assisting communities in the preparation of OEDP's would have postponed the processing of applications for financial assistance.

Further reflection also convinced ARA technicians that the concept of a "comprehensive" OEDP had inherent weaknesses. The underlying assumption had been that once a community drew up an adequate and acceptable program, its formal planning would be completed. This was a static approach; the economic conditions of a community are always in a state of flux, and planning for community economic growth requires continuing adjustment to changing economic conditions and needs. The ARA staff therefore began to view the OEDP as a program which was never completed but always in a dynamic state of suspension and change.

After more than a year and a half of searching for more effective means to review OEDP's, the ARA dropped the two-step—"provisional" and "comprehensive"—process for the development of community economic development programs and substituted a new procedure instead. Each community is still required to prepare an OEDP in order to qualify for assistance under the Act. Within a year after the ARA suggestions for improvement of the OEDP are submitted to the community, local authorities are requested to submit a revised program reflecting either modifications and improvements in the community's planning or a progress report indicating the status of, and accomplishments under, the program.[19]

This new procedure recognizes that the ARA can offer communities only limited help in preparing comprehensive reviews and meaningful "critiques" of community plans. At the same time, the new approach encourages communities to pursue their economic planning program as a continuing process that is undertaken with a minimum of assistance from the ARA. In short, the ARA formally recognized that community planning must be initiated and carried on locally, and that Washington can only extend technical assistance in helping with this process.

Technical Assistance for OEDP's

In a number of cases the ARA decided to use part of its technical assistance funds to help communities develop their economic planning programs. This undoubtedly was an attempt to examine more closely the dynamics of community economic planning processes. It was hoped that some of the techniques developed in the selected communities might be transferrable to other designated areas. In addition, the ARA recognized that in some communities there was little hope of developing local leadership to undertake the task of economic planning. In other instances, the ARA hoped that financing community economic development plans through subsidies to local universities would generate interest by local academicians in the economic progress of their communities, and that such assistance to the Redevelopment Area Organizations would continue after the ARA aid expired.

Since the ARA did not have sufficient staff—altogether less than a score of technicians were assigned to the division charged with reviewing OEDP's—it resorted to utilizing outside help in this phase of activity. Where universities had the talent and interest to participate in such a program, preference was given to the local talent; in other cases the ARA contracted with economic consultants to prepare—and in some cases also attempt to implement—the local programs. During the first two years the ARA contracted for the preparation of twenty-five community and regional projects at an average cost of $26,500. Regrettably, most of the reports were not available for the preparation of this study.

The ARA was urged by its National Public Advisory Committee to utilize task forces, whose function would be to assist Redevelopment Area Organizations in developing their economic plans. As visualized by the NPAC, these task forces would consist of a team of experts from various disciplines that were related to community development. Included would be an economist, a manpower specialist, a land-use planner, an architect, a natural-resource developer, and an industrial developer. Of course, the composition of the task force would vary in accordance with the needs and potentials of each community. It was contemplated that the ARA would collect a group of experts in these fields who would be supplemented by experts from other federal agencies or by private consultants. Teams selected from the above group would then be sent to the various communities for periods of a week or two to consult with the community leaders and technical experts; they were to help the Redevelopment Area Organizations appraise and perfect their plans and prepare comprehensive economic development plans.

Solomon Barkin, a member of the National Public Advisory Committee, was the strongest proponent of ARA assistance for economic planning. ARA officials sympathized with this position but had strong reservations about assuming responsibility that should normally be handled by the communities. Moreover, the ARA believed that unless planning were stimulated at the community level, it would have little chance of actual implementation. Barkin countered that unless the ARA stimulated such planning, it would never be accomplished in those communities lacking adequate leadership.

The ARA Planning and Research staff made some efforts to follow this recommendation, but with little success. The labor market during the first two years of the ARA's existence was not auspicious for securing the type of experts needed to staff the contemplated task forces, and the ARA chose to be selective in attempting to acquire whatever talent was available at the going government rates. Other government agencies were not too enthusiastic about allocating their manpower resources to implement ARA objectives. In addition, some ARA policy-shapers were skeptical of having teams of experts roaming the country and dispensing advice on the basis of only cursory knowledge about problems in specific communities.

The ARA was also criticized in some quarters for its failure to utilize the body of knowledge developed by the so-called regional scientists. Economists might disagree about the feasibility of applying techniques developed by regional scientists to specific area redevelopment programs. However, a close examination of the type of projects which various disciples of this discipline offered the ARA seems to justify the reluctance of ARA staff to divert its limited technical assistance resources to this type of activity. The propensity of regional economists to use an esoteric and rather confusing terminology and to engage in building models without vital organs—to borrow Professor Jacob Viner's *bon mot*—sharply restricted any usefulness that the techniques of the new discipline might have had for the ARA and for helping depressed areas develop their economic potential.

REGIONAL PLANNING AND DEVELOPMENT

In economic planning and development, the ARA placed emphasis upon the activities of each designated area. However, ARA planners were fully cognizant that single designated areas or counties do not necessarily constitute economic entities and that an effective program for many designated areas would depend upon the development of the surrounding economic region. The goal of ARA planners has been to encourage regional planning without sacrificing local activity, because a regional plan will normally overlook basic economic needs of local communities and could lead to the non-involvement of local authorities.

Even where the rehabilitation of a designated area is dependent upon an economic plan for the whole region, problems usually remain which are primarily local in character and which do not lend themselves to effective analysis or solution on a regional basis. For example, the raising of local money, development of sites for industry, and local community improvements, such as local land-use planning, zoning, and land-use adjustments, are strictly local in nature and can best be accomplished at that level.

The ARA therefore required that each designated area develop its own economic planning and program. But at the same time it also encouraged contiguous designated areas to band together to attack mutual problems whose solution appeared regional in nature. Such problems may include a regional highway and other transportation facilities and services; water-resources control and development in river valleys; region-wide gas and electric power systems; labor training and retraining; expansion and diversification of wood industry to utilize the full allowable cut of timber in a multicounty market region; regional exploitation of mineral resources; and regional promotion to attract industries and tourism.

The ARA requirement that each county prepare its own OEDP was a source of controversy in some areas. For example, the thirty-three counties of southern Illinois originally filed a single OEDP. At the ARA's urging, most of the counties prepared separate OEDP's. However, four counties—Jackson, Williamson, Perry, and Randolph—banded together to file a combined OEDP, and the state agency urged the ARA to permit the four counties to continue with a single OEDP. The local paper editorialized: "County lines, while convenient at first glance do not accurately reflect economic realities of the area."[8] Professor Richard C. Wilcock, who studied ARA activities in that area, found that a majority of the persons connected with local economic programs (he interviewed economic developers, businessmen, ARA "clients," and professional developers) favored the four-county committee. He reasoned that because the four counties had common problems, there would be greater efficiency and less friction with a combined group. The advocates of single-county OEDP's in the area contended that a larger committee would be unwieldy and that single-county development groups would bring about better results, since each group would be able to concentrate on the specific problems relating to the development of its respective county. Wilcock concluded that "the apparent solution is a four-county OEDP with single-county subcommittees,"[22] but the ARA technicians finally agreed with the majority favoring a single OEDP for the four counties.

The ARA did get involved in two regional planning programs—the Appalachian region and the Upper Peninsula of Michigan. In one case, the ARA launched what may prove to be a major effort for the redevelopment of Appalachia; the other is still on the drawing board. Both regions are among the most depressed in the United States.

In 1960 the governors of the Appalachian region, which includes West Virginia and parts of Pennsylvania, Maryland, Virginia, Kentucky, Tennessee, North Carolina, and Alabama, formed an informal organization to discuss mutual problems. The Council of Appalachian Governors (CAG) had no legal authority to effectuate any plans it might develop, and its major function was apparently to present programs to the federal government which would be beneficial to the member states. After the ARA was formed, CAG turned to the new agency for technical advice and assistance, since the governors had no staff of their own. The ARA responded by employing a regional planner to work with the aides of the several governors and, after some delay, commissioned a firm with a national reputation in regional planning to outline the elements of a viable program for Appalachia. When this contract did not produce the desired results, the ARA and the consulting firm parted company, after the latter collected its fee.

At this stage, Dr. Harold L. Sheppard, assistant administrator for ARA Operations, stepped in to head a federal interagency committee that was to plan with CAG a long-range program for Appalachia. But Sheppard could devote only part of his time to this project, and there is little that an interagency committee below the assistant-secretary level can accomplish. The committee lacked authority and prestige to influence federal agencies to allocate resources to Appalachia.

Recognizing the committee's inadequacy, the ARA recommended to President Kennedy that he establish a Joint Federal-State Committee on the Appalachian Region, to be chaired by the new Undersecretary of Commerce, Franklin D. Roosevelt, Jr. The new President's Appalachian Regional Committee was launched in April, 1963. The functions of this committee closely resemble those of its predecessor, but it is composed of federal and state representatives, and it has more influence behind it. The major staff support for this committee is supplied by the ARA. The staff activities in 1964 were directed by John L. Sweeney, who was, at that time, also concentrating on developing public and congressional support for the contemplated program. The committee was ordered to present an over-all plan for the redevelopment of Appalachia for the President's approval by December, 1963.

In addition, President Kennedy directed that all federal agencies concerned devote more of their resources to Appalachian development and then submit an assessment of their activities to the committee. The ARA response to this directive was to grant $300,000 to th᷄ University of Pittsburgh for technical assistance to the President's Appalachian Regional Committee (PARC). This committee, in co-operation with CAG, was to examine the feasibility of establishing an Appalachian Institute to serve as a center for dispensing technical assistance to the region—a proposal considered earlier by the Sheppard committee. PARC was also charged with developing a program for Appalachia which would serve as a suitable basis for a legislative program scheduled for proposal by the Administration to Congress in 1964. Meanwhile, the Roosevelt committee was attempting to resolve conflicts among the members of CAG and to co-ordinate federal interagency policies relating to Appalachia.

But all this assumes that a realistic and viable program can be developed for Appalachia. The basic question, whether Appalachia is an integrated region whose deep-seated economic problems can be solved by any approach, has not been answered.

ARA involvement in aiding the Upper Peninsula of Michigan was of much lesser magnitude. The area's economy has declined during recent decades both because of its isolated location and because of its inability to exploit fully its resources—primarily iron, timber, and tourist potential. There is little value added to the resources in the region; historically, the Upper Michigan Peninsula's natural resources have been extracted and shipped elsewhere for processing.

The economic difficulties of the region have given rise to several economic development groups. The most active of these is the Upper Peninsula Committee on Area Problems (UPCAP), which is composed of representatives appointed by county boards of supervisors. Fourteen of the fifteen counties in the Upper Peninsula are members of UPCAP at the present time.

Shortly after its formation in 1961, UPCAP applied for an ARA grant to help plan an economic development program for the region. The request was granted, and the ARA secured the services of an economic consulting firm, Robert Nathan Associates, to provide technical assistance for UPCAP. The firm has had considerable consulting experience in underdeveloped countries, and it was hoped that it might apply the source of its successful experience abroad to the domestic Point Four program. The firm established an office in the region, and while the ARA picks up the tab, the consulting firm works directly for UPCAP.

The initial hope of UPCAP was that the consulting firm would design an action program for immediate industrial promotion and that the ARA would help finance the group's plans. But the firm's representatives dampened the enthusiasm of the local economic developers by suggesting that the proposed program would have to be delayed until more was learned about the physical and human resources of the area. To this end, UPCAP obtained an additional technical assistance grant from the ARA to conduct an aerial survey of the area's forests; other applications to finance other resource studies were pending in 1963. The rationale of conducting these studies is that the added information will help develop information needed to attract prospective entrepreneurs. It should be noted that UPCAP and its technical assistance office have not completely neglected "action" programs. The technical assistance office has helped local companies in planning expansion programs and in preparing applications for ARA loans. But these activities were subsidiary to UPCAP's major role of long-range planning.

Whether the ongoing and planned studies will help bolster the Upper Peninsula's economy has yet to be seen. UPCAP is confronting a deeply entrenched problem which has left the Upper Peninsula apathetic to redevelopment efforts. Although some, including an influential newspaper editor in the Upper Peninsula, believe that UPCAP and the technical assistance have failed to obtain the support of the bulk of the Upper Peninsula's inhabitants, the local developers involved in the work believe that the UPCAP approach will eventually bear fruit. But it is still too early to predict whether tangible results will come from a program designed for a long-run payoff.

BREAKING BOTTLENECKS WITH TECHNICAL ASSISTANCE

During the first two years of the ARA, Congress appropriated $7 million for technical assistance. The Act authorizes an annual expenditure of $4.5 million for technical assistance; but since Congress delayed making the first ARA appropriations in 1962 until three months after the start of the fiscal year, it reduced the technical assistance appropriation by a fourth. For 1963, Congress appropriated $3.6 million for technical assistance.

Originally the ARA's technical assistance staff planned to stress programs and devices for upgrading community facilities and for the development of new products and processes. Accordingly, the technicians recommended that the total technical assistance resources be allocated to three broad areas of activity. Half of the funds were to be spent for local and regional development plans. Based on the hypothesis popular in the ARA that many distressed areas are "sitting on undiscovered gold mines," 30 per cent of the funds was to be allocated for unlocking bottlenecks, to be identified by local development plans. And the balance (20 per cent) of the technical assistance funds was to be devoted to the study of methods and experiences used by communities in overcoming economic setbacks. The successful techniques were to be made available to all depressed areas so that they could adopt whichever techniques are transferable to their own communities.[21]

In actual practice, this plan did not work out. Upon further reflection, the administrators of the program decided to put greater emphasis on studies which would hopefully lead directly to generating employment in depressed areas rather than on longer-range planning. The technical assistance staff was not in a position to design or plan projects to break bottlenecks which retard economic development in the designated areas. It therefore relied upon proposals submitted to the ARA by the communities or consultants. There is no evidence that the technicians attempted to establish priorities, and projects were approved on a case-by-case basis, occasionally depending upon the persuasiveness of those who submitted proposals and the political pressure they could muster to influence ARA decision-makers. Altogether, during its first two years, the ARA approved 145 technical assistance projects at an average cost of $32,000 per study, exclusive of the 25 community and regional planning studies mentioned earlier.

Most of these projects were approved within a year, prior to the completion of this study, and the final products have not yet been released, except in a few isolated instances. It is, therefore, impossible to evaluate the fruits of the ARA technical assistance program. The following discussion attempts only to list types of projects which the ARA approved. These are divided somewhat arbitrarily into the following three categories: (1) feasibility studies for the development of resources located in depressed areas, including area engineering studies; (2) feasibility studies of tourism potential; and (3) feasibility studies concerning the location of new commercial and industrial activities and their market potential.

Resource Feasibility Studies

Sixty per cent of the total of the $5.3 million in technical assistance funds obligated by May 1, 1963, was spent for feasibility studies related to the development of local resources. Wherever it proved practical, the ARA tried to involve the research facilities of local universities in resource feasibility studies, as it did in the other aspects of its research work.

Twenty-five projects, accounting for a fifth of the total technical assistance expenditures, were devoted to mineral and ore processing. The costliest project in this category was the study of a new method for processing large deposits of low-grade non-magnetic ore in the

Mesabi Range near Itasca, Minnesota. Because the better-grade ores in this region have been depleted, it was hoped that the studies would demonstrate the feasibility of exploiting lower-grade ores through the new Udy and Krupp processes recently developed in the United States and Germany. A commercially successful application of these processes to the remaining Mesabi Range ores might have helped not only to rehabilitate these highly depressed areas, but also to improve the balance of payments situation for the United States.

Eighteen studies, costing $300,000, were concerned with the utilization of forest products. For example, a survey of the timber resources of Missouri attempted to identify the special kinds of woodworking concerns that might be attracted to exploit the timber resources of the state. The study was to supply information concerning the availability of materials, markets, vocational factors, and competitive costs. The timber resources of two Indian reservations were also to be inventoried with the hope that the survey might justify increased timber cut and thus supply jobs to Indians on Flathead, Blackfeet, and Rocky Boy's Reservations in Montana. In addition, the ARA financed thirteen technical assistance projects designed to help the Indian reservations in several parts of the country. Altogether, the Indian Bureau in the Department of the Interior used almost a fifth of the total technical funds the ARA had in fiscal 1962.

A different type of feasibility study involved the possible utilization of aquatic plants as animal feed at Caddo Lake in Harrison and Marion Counties, Texas. This research was based on the hypothesis that the aquatic plants are superior to dehydrated and ground alfalfa as an ingredient in livestock feeds. Texas A & M College and several commercial firms undertook this study for the ARA.

The feasibility of storing liquid petroleum gases and other petroleum products in the massive shale formation near Jim Thorpe, Pennsylvania, was financed by the ARA with the hope that it might lead to the development of new petrochemical production in the area.

Some ARA resource-development and feasibility studies embroiled the agency in regional conflicts and were subject to congressional controversy. The ARA financed a technical assistance study investigating the feasibility of growing and processing sugar beets in Cayuga County in central New York. The ARA anticipated that the growing of beets in the area and the establishment of a sugar beet refinery would help increase the income of farmers. Beet producers from other areas, not to mention their congressmen, complained that in light of long-standing restrictions on beet production, it would be most inappropriate for the government to finance experimental projects for the raising of sugar beets when there was already, according to their claims, proven overcapacity in the industry. A congressman from Minnesota complained that the beet producers in his own state, the Dakotas, Texas, and Washington "have the potential of going into beet production without one penny of expense to the federal government . . . but now we are going to deny them that privilege, if you will, by moving that opportunity into other areas at government expense."[7]

A congressman from New York saw the situation in a different light. He thought that the farmers in his own state should have the same opportunity to raise sugar beets as farmers in other areas. According to the New York legislator, the farmers in Cayuga County

. . . saw a chance once and for all to prove that sugar was not a crop automatically reserved to one particular geographic section of the country, that it could be grown and should be grown in the northeastern section of the country which uses the greatest percentage of sugar and which has already been losing all too many of her jobs and her industry to the southern and western areas of the nation.

This congressman concluded:

This little case, which was supposed to show a mistake on the part of ARA, turns out when you really know the facts, to be a classic example of the ARA doing precisely what Congress expected it to do. It has been helpful to a county that desperately needs help. It could create a new $20 million industry in Cayuga County that would pay out some $6.5 million to farmers in the county every year and maintain an annual payroll of some $1 million. . . .[7]

The major purpose of the area engineering studies was to expedite the development of public works, if the studies proved the feasibility of the proposed projects. Twenty-seven such studies, at a cost of $1.1 million, were approved. An illustration of this type of project was the study for the feasibility and design of a multipurpose reservoir in the Willapa River Basin in the State of Washington. It was anticipated that the construction of a reservoir would make feasible the development of cheap power and promote the tourism potential of this area.

The largest chunk of technical assistance money allocated to a single project went for the planning and designing of a reservoir in southern Illinois, where the depressed economic conditions originally gener-

ated the idea of federal legislation. The Army Corps of Engineers has
considered for several years the building of a multimillion-dollar
reservoir to supply industrial water to the area and to make possible
the attraction of new industry and tourism facilities. As early as 1949
the House Committee on Public Works adopted a resolution urging
the Corps of Engineers to study the feasibility of building such a reservoir on the Big Muddy River, but the Corps of Engineers has priority
lists which normally postpone development of such major public
facilities, sometimes for many years. It was expected that the ARA
feasibility study would expedite the realization of this project. The
House Appropriations Committee took a dim view of using ARA
funds to expedite public-works projects before these projects are approved by Congress. The committee reasoned that ARA advances
might seem to commit the federal government to further financing
of the project and directed the Corps of Engineers and the Bureau of
Reclamation not to accept funds from the ARA without prior approval by the Appropriations Committee.[13]

Developing Tourism Potential

A special type of resource development, to which the ARA contributed $662,000, involved the development of tourism. In many of the
rural depressed areas the only immediate potential for economic
growth is the development or expansion of tourist facilities. The ARA
approved a score of different technical assistance projects dealing with
the feasibility of potential development of tourism in these areas.

The New River Gorge area of south-central West Virginia is a classic
depressed area. Its economy has been based largely upon the mining
of bituminous coal, and employment has been declining steadily. In
recent years about one of every six persons in the labor force of the
four-county New River Gorge area has been unemployed. The only
apparent resource of this area, besides its coal deposits, seems to lie
in the development of tourist facilities. The ARA financed a study
to determine the feasibility of establishing a national parkway in the
New River Gorge area which was conducted by the Bureau of Public
Roads in the Department of Commerce. Another study, undertaken
by a private economic consultant firm, concentrated on pinpointing
the facilities needed in the area to attract tourism. The study recommended the development of resort facilities adjacent to the three
lakes in the area at a cost of about $8.6 million, to be financed
through combined private and public investment. It was estimated

that such facilities would be able to attract about 42,000 tourists a year, who might be expected to spend close to $5 million annually in the area, adding about seven hundred part- or full-time jobs. The survey of the area also indicated that if the resort projects were to succeed, the ARA would have to invest some $3.6 million in the construction of public facilities to make the development of resorts more attractive investments for private capital.

The ARA did not wait for private capital to develop tourist facilities in the area, and a closer examination revealed that the original estimates about the cost of developing such facilities in the New River Gorge area were on the conservative side. In June, 1963, just prior to the closing of the fiscal year, the ARA invested most of its uncommitted public-facility grant and loan funds—a total of $14.4 million—in the development of tourism in the New River Gorge area.

Marketing Studies

The ARA also financed marketing studies which dealt with the possible expansion of specific locally produced products. Scallop and flounder fishing is an important resource of New Bedford, Massachusetts, accounting for approximately one-fifth of the city's total payroll. The ARA financed a study designed to develop plans for expanding the market for New Bedford scallops and flounder, improve the distribution methods, and develop more efficient handling techniques in the industry.

Another study was concerned with the marketing of Georgia peaches. In this case the problem was due to shifts in consumer habits, brought about by technological changes which have increased the demand for processed, rather than fresh, peaches. As a result of this changed consumer purchasing habit, the demand for fresh Georgia peaches has declined sharply during recent years. The problem in this case was to stabilize the market demand for peaches by developing new means of processing the product. Of course, not all of the Georgia peaches grow in the designated depressed areas, but technical assistance under the Act can also be offered to non-designated areas.

A technical assistance program for the largest state in the Union, Alaska, was aimed at expanding the market for Alaskan native arts and crafts. Apparently the sale of arts-and-crafts products is an important source of income to some remote Alaskan communities where other economic opportunities are extremely limited.

The ARA also invested money in selling iceboxes to the Kotzebue

Eskimos, who reside just 50 miles from the Arctic Circle. This was one of several ARA studies involving the economic feasibility of developing various community facilities. The case of the Kotzebue Eskimos dealt with developing refrigeration processes for reindeer meat and fish, and a tannery for the processing of fur products. Cold as it may be in that part of the world, the marketability of the products is extremely limited due to lack of modern storage facilities. The project was to develop methods by which the Eskimos would be able to process these products for commercial export.

Refrigeration is not exclusively an Alaskan problem. In Puerto Rico, an appreciable proportion of the total food consumed on the island is brought in from the mainland. The cost of many items of food, particularly perishables, is therefore considerably higher in Puerto Rico than on the mainland. The ARA allocated some of its technical assistance money to develop improved processing, storage, and marketing facilities of agricultural products in Puerto Rico.

The ARA also financed a number of marketing feasibility studies related to the products of specific firms. These studies were either outgrowths of applications for ARA industrial loans or attempts by the ARA to help expand home-grown small industries. ARA investment in cases where feasibility studies related to a specific firm was contingent on assurance from the firm that the federal outlays would be repaid if the project materialized and proved successful.

LONG-RANGE RESEARCH

In contrast to the types of projects which deal mainly with unlocking the potential resources of specific depressed areas, the ARA also invested some funds in long-term and general research. Technically, the Area Redevelopment Act distinguishes between "technical assistance" (Section 11) and "research" (Section 27). In the 1962 Budget, Congress did not appropriate specific funds for the implementation of the research section. In the absence of specific congressional appropriations, ARA authorities were somewhat reluctant to allocate funds which, in the words of the Act, would "assist in the long-range accomplishment of the purposes of the Act. . . ."

After considerable soul-searching, ARA policy-makers apparently decided that since economists have failed to establish sound criteria distinguishing between short- and long-term, it could hardly be expected that the Congress could do better; it therefore subsidized some research to implement Section 27 of the Act. The ARA sponsored a Labor Department study dealing with the characteristics of workers undergoing training. The research was also to follow-up the work experience of those who completed ARA-financed training courses. At the time the ARA financed this study, Congress had already approved the Manpower Development and Training Act, though it did not appropriate any funds for the Act until several months later. The Labor Department suggested that a study of the ARA training experience would be most helpful in setting up the MDTA, and the ARA authorities agreed. Another study by the University of Michigan Research Center investigated patterns of labor mobility. The ARA also supported the University of California's study of depressed-area legislation and the experience under such legislation in western European countries. It was hoped that some of the successful European experience might be transferable to the United States. The ARA also approved a study of Nashua, New Hampshire. This community was one of the first to suffer from the closing of textile firms and the migration of industry southward. However, it soon diversified its industry and has succeeded in maintaining a level of unemployment below the national average during most of the post-World War II period. The objectives of the study were to examine and evaluate the specific techniques and programs employed in Nashua and to appraise the transferability of such techniques to currently depressed communities.

For fiscal 1963 Congress appropriated $500,000 for long-range research. As in the case of technical assistance, most of the research projects financed by the ARA were generated by outside sources and were not instigated by the ARA. There is also no evidence that the ARA has developed an internal research program.

About a fifth of the total long-range research funds appropriated for fiscal 1963 was allocated to regional economic studies undertaken in another bureau of the Department of Commerce. The project, when completed, will provide comprehensive and detailed information about county and regional economic growth characteristics between 1940 and 1960. The data will offer useful tools for county and regional planning.

Three major studies dealt with general economic conditions in depressed areas. One study was to measure the extent of structural unemployment in the United States, to evaluate past proposals for reducing structural unemployment, and to develop new methods of coping with the problem. This study will presumably be an addition to the growing literature on the currently fashionable debate among economists as to whether creeping unemployment during the past decade has been a function of inadequate expansion in demand or due to technological or other "structural" changes in the economy. A related study was proposed to measure the impact of technological change on depressed areas. The study was to investigate the hypothesis that technological change by itself is unrelated to the presence or absence of depressed areas and does not create depressed economic conditions. The third study was aimed at examining the hypothesis that the cause of depressed economic conditions in many communities is the lack of adequate entrepreneurial talent. The objective of this study was to develop techniques for increasing the supply of entrepreneurs in depressed areas.

Two ARA-financed studies were aimed at evaluating the activities of the agency. One project proposed to analyze the characteristics of workers who were employed on ARA-financed projects. The goal of the study was to reveal the extent to which labor-surplus areas are able to meet the manpower needs of the new enterprises and the effectiveness of the federal retraining programs in satisfying skill requirements of the new or expanding firms. The purpose of the other study was to appraise the short-run impact of ARA-financed projects in five selected rural communities.

APPRAISAL OF TECHNICAL ASSISTANCE AND RESEARCH

The above discussion of technical assistance and research indicates that the ARA did not develop a carefully designed program in these areas. It is doubtful if such a program could have been devised and, if devised, whether it could have been effectively implemented. Basically, the ARA had to start from scratch in studying and developing techniques for economic development of communities. Whatever academic research was done in this area had extremely limited practical application to the ARA, and most of the community economic planning was mainly addressed to the luring of plants and dealt little with the unlocking of community resources and the development of long-range community potential. The ARA needed research which would address itself to investigating the socioeconomic characteristics of depressed areas, the factors that have caused economic stagnation or decline of communities, and to problem solving.

Harold W. Williams, deputy administrator of the ARA, pointed out the complexity of ARA research in connection with the agency's role in the development of tourist potential:

There is more to tourist development than writing colorful folders and enticing ads to persuade tourists to come to a state. Even more important is the planning and development of tourist facilities and tourist attractions. . . . Roads are needed. Historical sites need restoration and identification. Special scenic values need to be preserved. Roadsides have to be cleaned up. Recreational facilities have to be improved.[23]

The ARA was largely placed in a pioneering position in stimulating and planning such integrated economic activity programs. It attempted to try a variety of techniques and approaches which would help achieve its mission of combating chronic unemployment and underemployment. For example, the ARA participated in financing an input-output study which the Mississippi Industrial and Technological Commission and a few Harvard professors thought would aid that state's economic growth and development. The ARA technicians had considerable misgivings about the potential benefits that Mississippi would get from this type of study, but they thought that all available techniques should be tried in the development of sound economic planning, ARA finances permitting. This shotgun approach by the ARA to research and technical assistance has been criticized by some. It has been suggested that the ARA would have received greater value from its meager resources by concentrating its technical assistance and research support in a few specific areas, which would have helped the ARA to more effective planning and administration. But, of course, underlying the rifle approach is the assumption that the ARA was in a position to pinpoint the areas of study and place priorities on subjects to be investigated.

While experts have differed about the approach that the ARA should have used in designing and implementing its research program, it is difficult for an outside observer to appraise the ARA failure to develop its own research capabilities. It would appear that ARA policy-shapers must certainly have appreciated the need to devise appropriate data to rationalize, if not to evaluate, the experimental programs of the agency and to present the activities of the agency in salable package. No doubt this failure of the ARA to develop an adequate research arm did considerable harm to the agency's image as well as to its program. Opponents of the ARA could always point to horrendous examples of real or apparent mistakes of judgment. During its first two years the ARA failed to develop even basic operational statistics which would have given some ammunition to the friends of the agency in explaining and defending its activities.

Most of the technical assistance research projects financed by ARA were not completed at the time this study was prepared. The results of the projects for which partial or complete returns are available are mixed. An ARA-financed project to test the suitability of a salt strata for use in the chemical industries in Monroe and Washington Counties, Ohio, was completed successfully. The Pennsylvania Railroad, which has been interested in the project and whose geologists conducted the surveys, suggested that the finding of the "vast salt bed . . . may mean the opening of a new industrial frontier. . . ." The railroad company stated that without ARA technical assistance "the hard-pressed railroad company was in no position" to finance the project.[9] Preliminary reports on the New Bedford marketing project, mentioned earlier, have already resulted in expanding the market for the area's flounder. And, according to these reports, further financing of the project will be taken over by the community.[12]

It is only to be expected that some of the projects turned out to be duds. An economic consulting firm which was supposed to have come up with bright ideas for the development of several depressed areas in east Kentucky filed a report which a researcher could have obtained from a perusal of Census data. A technical assistance project which was supposed to have developed a plan for the creation of new industries tailored to the specific problems of a depressed area in Virginia came up with the startling proposal that the townspeople and the ARA should finance a factory which would produce hamburger-frying machines. The study left it a mystery as to why this particular town in Virginia should become a center for the production of hamburger machines. The proposal also failed to appraise the adequacy of the available labor force, the availability of a market for the product, and the methods by which it might be financed and distributed—if a market were available.

No doubt the ARA technicians anticipated that some of their projects would be failures; this is a part of the cost of the learning process. There was no way to foretell the results of research projects that appeared promising. It is to the credit of ARA researchers that they were willing to take chances in exploring research projects, rather than to play safe and avoid mistakes.

The ARA did try to get the academic community interested in

ARA problems by announcing that it was ready to encourage and sponsor research on broad problems relating to needed capital investment in depressed areas, causes of persistent labor surplus and their impact upon communities, and case studies of communities which have had success in re-establishing stable economies, including the techniques and programs used by these communities which might be transferable to existing depressed and similar areas.[10] It also organized a seminar of experts in economic development to involve them in the area redevelopment program. The response of the academicians and commercial firms was not overwhelming. Faced with research addressed to specific problems and their solution, the academic community had apparently little to offer. But in fairness to the academic community, it must be added that ARA technicians had neglected to follow-up and evaluate promising proposals made by academicians.

The ARA was also amiss in policing those projects which it did approve and in critically appraising completed projects. The contracts signed by the agency with technical assistance or research consultants normally provided for an escape clause that final payment would be withheld until the project was approved by ARA reviewers. But in most cases it is difficult to prove that a contractor had not delivered an acceptable product. There are no precise, effective standards for evaluating the quality of research projects.

ARA policy-makers succumbed too easily to pressures for immediate "earth-moving" projects, at the cost of neglecting the development both of a philosophy and a long-range plan for the agency. A top official of the ARA was reported to have proudly proclaimed that he was not interested in research, as long as he could get "projects."

However, there is evidence that, by the end of its second year, the ARA has become conscious of the weakness in its organization and has made serious efforts to improve its research and technical staff. Hopefully, some of the technical assistance and research projects may yet develop new paths and techniques to aid in the economic development of depressed communities.

REFERENCES

1. Avery County, North Carolina, Economic Development Committee. Letter to the ARA. February 2, 1963.

2. Benton County, Tennessee. *OEDP Progress Report.* Belmont County: The Committee, May, 1963, p. 8.
3. *Congressional Record.* March 9, 1963, p. 3385.
4. *Congressional Record.* March 28, 1961, p. 4746.
5. *Congressional Record.* March 29, 1961, p. 4948.
6. *Congressional Record.* April 20, 1961, p. 6015.
7. *Congressional Record.* June 12, 1963, p. 10109 (Congressman Odin Langen); p. 10105 (Congressman Samuel Stratton).
8. "Counties Should Be Allowed To Plan Together," *Southern Illinoisan* (Herrin, Illinois), February 6, 1963.
9. "Drilling for Salt," *The Pennsy* (published by the Pennsylvania Railroad Company), November–December, 1962, p. 3.
10. Industrial Relations Research Association Newsletter. Madison, Wisconsin, Spring, 1962, p. 2.
11. Luigart, Fred W., Jr. "Aid Plans Disappoint East Kentucky," *The Courier Journal* (Louisville, Kentucky), April 7, 1963.
12. "Sales Test on Flounder A Success," *The Standard-Times* (New Bedford, Massachusetts), July 18, 1963.
13. U.S. House of Representatives, Committee on Appropriations. *Public Works Appropriations, 1963.* Report 2223, 86th Cong., 2d Sess. Washington: Government Printing Office, August 14, 1962, p. 3.
14. U.S. House of Representatives, Committee on Banking and Currency. *Area Redevelopment Act.* Report 186, 87th Cong., 1st Sess., March 22, 1961, pp. 3, 4, 24, 14.
15. U.S. Senate, Committee on Banking and Currency. *Hearings on Area Redevelopment.* 87th Cong., 1st Sess., 1961, pp. 172–75.
16. ———. Report 61, 87th Cong., 1st Sess., March 8, 1961, pp. 19–20.
17. U.S. Senate, Committee on Labor and Public Welfare. *Hearings on Area Redevelopment.* 84th Cong., 2d Sess., 1956, pp. 844, 741, 254, 1074, 866, 188, 806.
18. U.S. Department of Commerce, Area Redevelopment Administration. *The Overall Economic Development Program.* Washington: Government Printing Office, August 1961, p. 11.
19. ———. "The Overall Economic Development Program—Policies and Procedures," December 20, 1962. (Mimeographed.)
20. ———. *Planning for New Growth—New Jobs.* (ARA Publication 62-A.) Washington: Government Printing Office. Undated.
21. U.S. Department of Commerce, Office of Planning and Research. "Technical Assistance Under Section 11," November 13, 1961. (Mimeographed.)
22. Wilcock, Richard C. "An Evaluation of ARA in Southern Illinois as of June 1963." Memorandum to the author.
23. Williams, Harold W. Speech before the Annual Conference of Association of State Planning and Development Agencies. Scottsdale, Arizona, November 29, 1962, p. 8. (Mimeographed.)
24. Yancey County, North Carolina, Planning Board. Letter to ARA. March 7, 1963.

Chapter 8

+++++++++++++++++++++++

The Package of Tools

++

During the six years that Senator Paul H. Douglas crusaded for his program to aid depressed areas, he often indicated that the package of tools he had put together constituted only the minimum meaningful program which he considered marketable on Capitol Hill. It is quite evident that Senator Douglas preferred a much more comprehensive and costly program, but had little hope that Congress would pass legislation of such scope.

In December, 1960, President-elect John F. Kennedy appointed a task force under the chairmanship of Senator Douglas to develop a program to aid depressed areas.

In the report which the task force submitted, legislation similar to the bill that was later approved by Congress was only one of seven major points in the total program to aid depressed areas.[21] Other measures recommended by the task force included granting special preferential treatment in government procurement contracts to businesses in depressed areas; measures to improve the educational levels of persons residing in depressed areas, as well as the expansion of employment and placement services in these areas: a comprehensive public-works program, including highways and recreational facilities; special tax-amortization inducements for expanding and new firms locating in depressed areas; and the establishment of a youth conservation corps.

The task force also recommended measures to alleviate hardships resulting from unemployment—expansion of the food distribution program, raising the level of benefits and extending the duration of unemployment compensation, and the inauguration of a federal general assistance program to aid unemployed who had exhausted their unemployment insurance. Finally, the task force favored the development of special regional programs to help combat underemployment and unemployment in the depressed areas.[1]

The first two years' experience under the Area Redevelopment Act tended to justify the opponents' fears that the program would be only the proverbial camel's nose. Some of the programs proposed by the 1960 task force have already been enacted.

The first official act by President Kennedy was to expand the surplus-food distribution program. The monthly number of beneficiaries of this program averaged more than 6 million a month, many of whom resided in depressed areas. The Kennedy Administration also initiated a food stamp plan which subsidizes food purchases of eligible needy families in forty-five counties and three cities, the bulk of which are also eligible for ARA assistance.[24] The legislation authorizing this program had been passed under the Eisenhower Administration, but Ezra Taft Benson, the Secretary of Agriculture, chose not to implement it. The estimated cost to the federal government of the two food distribution programs in fiscal 1963 was close to $400 million.

In 1961 Congress permitted states to extend aid to cover cases where the unemployed father of a "dependent child" was at home. By mid-1963 fifteen states had enacted legislation which qualified their eligible residents to receive benefits under the program. The estimated federal outlays for the program in fiscal 1963 amounted to $100 million.

An accelerated public-works program, largely, though not exclusively, directed to depressed areas, was approved in 1962 (Chapter 5). This program alone authorized the expenditure of $900 million, and the appropriations for fiscal 1963 amounted to $850 million, more than double the total expenditures authorized under the Area Redevelopment Act.

1963 AMENDMENTS TO THE ARA

Contrary to Douglas' fears, Congress was most generous in allocating funds to the ARA during its first two years and granted the agency practically all the funds that the Bureau of the Budget recommended.

[1]No doubt, this multibillion-dollar program might have been a little too rich for Senator Douglas' Scottish blood. Members of the task force were all of liberal persuasion, and the program perhaps included some proposals which Senator Douglas might have preferred to defer or eliminate. But officially he endorsed the total program.

There is even ample reason to believe that if the Secretary of Commerce and the Bureau of the Budget had originally requested additional funds to build up the ARA staff so that it would have been able to do its job more effectively, Congress would have appropriated the needed funds.

The appropriations committees of Congress blocked the provision in the Area Redevelopment Act that authorized the ARA to borrow loan funds directly from the Treasury and instead appropriated more funds for the agency during the first two years than the total four-year authorization called for.

During each of the first two years the ARA did not utilize the full amount of funds authorized for industrial, commercial, and public-facility loans. Only during the last month of fiscal 1963 did the ARA obligate nearly the full amount of grants provided for that year. During fiscal 1962 it expended only a seventh of the $40 million appropriated for grants. The slowness of communities in taking advantage of the assistance which the ARA was ready to offer was understandable; it certainly was not due to a lack of need for additional private ventures or improved public facilities. Rather, it represented the time lag needed for community officials to become familiar with, and to take advantage of, the new program. Even counting all pending projects at the end of fiscal 1962, the total was considerably below the appropriations made by Congress, and during the second year of the ARA, the accelerated public-works program provided, in most cases, more liberal grants than the ARA could offer.

By the second year of the ARA, the program started to pick up steam and the applications exceeded available funds. However, difficulties of raising local funds and slowness in processing applications —it took about half a year from the time an application was filed until it was approved—prevented the ARA from committing the total loan funds appropriated by Congress. By May 1, 1963, the ARA had more than three hundred applications for industrial and commercial loans at a total estimated value of close to a quarter of a billion dollars. The number of applications at that time was almost double the amount of those approved, and the funds requested were almost five times the total approvals. Pending applications for public facilities were more modest and barely exceeded prior approvals. However, the value of the applications for grants exceeded three times the amount approved.

To provide for the ARA's projected needs, the Administration requested, in the spring of 1963, that ARA authorizations be increased.[17] The bill called for increasing the $200 million authorization for commercial and industrial loans to $500 million and for raising the limit on authorized loans for public facilities from $100 million to $150 million. In addition, the Administration proposal urged that the grants for public facilities be raised from $75 million to $175 million. The ARA had found that the $4.5 million annual authorization for technical assistance was far from adequate and proposed that this figure be increased to $10 million a year.[2]

Once the ARA decided to seek additional authorizations for expenditures, it also moved to request substantive amendments to the Act. The ARA was not ready in 1963 to urge Congress to reconsider the whole kit of tools designed to help depressed areas, but hoped that Congress would remove those provisions which had proved to be serious operational impediments. The first amendment desired by the ARA was to remove the requirement for deferred repayment of the 10 per cent local equity capital which a public or semipublic body must supply in connection with commercial or industrial loans. The ARA considered this a very serious obstacle to its program because most communities found it difficult to raise equity capital when repayment had to be delayed for as long as twenty-five years. The ARA proposed that the local capital be placed on an equal footing with the ARA loan and be repaid concurrently. It is very doubtful whether the advocates of the original legislation appreciated the difficulty that the 10 per cent requirement would place upon communities in raising funds in order to benefit from ARA loans.

Another amendment proposed by the ARA was purely administrative in nature and was designed to correct what was obviously a "goof" in the 1961 legislation by some staff member. It dealt with the securing of services of experts. Executive agencies are normally authorized either to procure the temporary services of experts or consultants for as much as one year of continuous service, or to use the services of such consultants intermittently for an unlimited period of time. For some unknown reason, the Area Redevelopment Act (Section 12[10]) limited the ARA to procuring the services of consultants for half a year regardless of whether they worked continuously or intermittently. This sharply hindered the utilization of expert consultants, which the ARA badly needed to develop and to implement its program.

---

[2]Reportedly, the ARA proposed a $25 million annual authorization for technical assistance, but this amount was cut to $10 million by the Bureau of the Budget. Apparently, the BOB did not share the ARA's faith in the potential value of the approved projects and "persuaded" the ARA to reduce its sights in this area.

The ARA also proposed that the training provisions of the depressed-area act (Sections 16 and 17) be made comparable to those provided under the Manpower Development and Training Act of 1962. The amendments sought by the ARA provided that the maximum period of subsistence payments be extended to fifty-two weeks and that trainees be given a traveling allowance, not exceeding $5.00 a day, when training courses could not be provided in the immediate community. In many cases, designated areas do not have appropriate vocational training facilities. Under the provisions of the Area Redevelopment Act, unemployed persons enrolled for training could not receive reimbursement for travel to other areas for training.

The Budget Bureau favored even further expansion of ARA training provisions and considered recommending that the maximum duration of training courses and subsistence payments be lengthened to seventy-eight weeks and that special provision also be made for the training of the functionally illiterate unemployed. The training provisions proposed by the Bureau of the Budget would have at least tripled the current $14.5 million annual authorization. But representatives from the Department of Labor charged with administering the ARA training program were not ready in the winter of 1963 to reopen the training program and to subject their activities to congressional scrutiny. The Manpower Development and Training Act had been in operation at that time for only a few months and most of the funds appropriated for fiscal 1963 had not been committed. Thus, the amendments to the Act finally proposed by the Administration did not contain any training provisions.

The House rejected the proposed amendments to the Area Redevelopment Act (H. R. 4996) by a narrow vote of 209–204.[10] Fifty-seven Democrats, all but one from the South, joined 152 Republicans in voting against H. R. 4996, while 189 Democrats and only 15 Republicans voted for it. Two weeks later, on June 26, 1963, the Senate approved the companion bill (S. 1163) by a better than two-to-one vote.[11] Fifty-three Democrats and 12 Republicans voted for the bill, and 21 Republicans and 9 Democrats voted against the Administration proposal.

The wide disparity in the House and Senate vote deserves comment. Some pundits suggested that the House rejection of the Area Redevelopment amendments represented a retaliation by southern Democrats against the Administration's civil rights proposals—the bill came up in the House just after the Administration proposed its expanded civil rights program. A closer scrutiny of the vote suggests that the civil rights issue explained only part of the defections. In 1961, when the Act was originally approved, forty-three Republicans voted for it, but only fifteen voted for the 1963 amendments. The Administration's civil rights proposals did not appear to be the only cause for the rejection of the ARA amendments.

It is usually suggested that congressional debate has very little impact upon the final vote on a bill. Whether this is true in other cases may be debatable, but the evidence indicates that the generalization is not applicable in this instance. An examination of the lengthy House debate [10] shows that the defenders of the ARA either lacked the needed ammunition to prove their case or failed to use it effectively, while the attack of the opponents was rather persuasive. The argument of the ARA's opponents that the program was politically motivated was sufficiently convincing to sway earlier supporters of the program. In 1961 only two Republicans from Pennsylvania and three from Massachusetts voted against the Act. Two years later, all the Republicans from Massachusetts and eight from Pennsylvania voted against the amendments.[3] Even the lone Republican congressman from West Virginia voted against the bill. Apparently, the program had lost its luster and even some congressmen from depressed areas felt safe in voting against it.

In the Senate the situation was entirely different. There, Senator Douglas, with ARA assistance, led a number of colleagues in preparing a most convincing defense of ARA, and his work was sufficiently persuasive to secure overwhelming support for the increased authorization. The Douglas victory in the Senate has encouraged ARA supporters to attempt a second vote in the House. Whether they will be successful is not known at this time.

Meanwhile, by the end of fiscal 1963, the ARA lost its authority to make any grants for public facilities. The Act provided that $75 million may be appropriated for grants. The House Appropriations Committee had taken the position that the ARA had exhausted all the public-facility grant funds authorized under the Act, despite the fact that the agency actually used only $40 million of the authorized $75. The enabling legislation limits the amount of outstanding ARA loans at any one time to $300 million. Acting on overoptimistic data submitted by the ARA in February, 1963, which estimated that total outstanding loans by the end of fiscal 1963 would amount to $168

[3]Congressman Daniel Flood, of Pennsylvania, a major supporter of the area redevelopment program, once boasted that in his state an opponent of the ARA could not qualify for church burial.

million (actually the ARA had committed only $112 million for loans), the House appropriated $132 million for loans, the presumed total remaining amount from the originally authorized $300 million.[11] Thus, unless the House reconsiders its vote on the Area Redevelopment Act Amendments during fiscal 1964, the agency will not have any authority to make grants for public facilities, and the authorization of additional loans will virtually expire by June 30, 1964. The extension of the ARA will, under such eventuality, be revived as a political issue in the 1964 presidential and congressional elections.

ADDITIONAL PROGRAMS

The 1963 proposed amendments were limited to changes within the framework of the original Act. But the legislation itself is scheduled to expire in 1965, and at that time Congress must review the Act and its implementation. It may then determine that the experiment is not worth continuing, or it may decide to extend the life of the ARA. Congress could also decide that a more diversified set of tools and programs is needed to aid depressed areas. The remainder of this chapter is therefore devoted to an examination of additional tools that the Administration and Congress may desire to consider. These tools might include extending preferential treatment to businesses located in depressed areas in securing contracts on government procurement, special tax-amortization provisions and subsidization of worker mobility from depressed areas, and the extension of special provisions to depressed areas in the various current matching programs financed by the federal government.

Procurement

Since the Korean War the federal government has had a policy of granting preferential treatment to labor-surplus areas in procurement. The policy dates back to February 7, 1952, when the Director of Defense Mobilization issued Defense Manpower Policy No. 4, which was designed to channel Defense and General Service Administration contracts into labor-surplus areas.[4] The policy statement directed the procuring agencies to take all practical steps consistent with other procurement and military objectives to locate procurement in labor-surplus areas.

[4]Since the bulk of federal procurement is done by the Defense Department, the following discussion is limited to the Defense Department policies and practices.

As interpreted by the Office of Defense Mobilization, the policy authorized procuring agencies to award contracts to firms located in labor-surplus areas even if the firms did not initially make the lowest bid. If the original bid of a firm located in a labor-surplus area was within 20 per cent of the lowest bid, the firm was given another opportunity to obtain the award by meeting the otherwise acceptable lowest proposal. A hypothetical example will illustrate how this policy was supposed to have worked. Let us assume that the Defense Department advertised bids on a hundred units of a given item and that six firms, all located in non-labor-surplus areas, offered bids on twenty units at prices ranging between $1.00 and $1.10 per unit, with an average for the five lowest bidding companies of $1.05 a unit. At the same time, a company located in a labor-surplus area offers a bid of $1.15 per unit. The company in the labor-surplus area would be offered another opportunity to match the qualifying bids and thus "win" the contract from the firms which had initially made the lower bids.

In July, 1953, the Senate voted to prohibit the Defense Department from granting any preferential treatment to firms located in labor-surplus areas.[5] The House defense appropriation bill did not contain this prohibition, but the conference report contained a provision which prohibited the Defense Department from using any funds "for the payment of a price differential on contracts hereafter made for the purpose of relieving economic dislocation."[6] The Senate adopted the weaker language contained in the conference report only after Senator Knowland, then majority leader, promised to inform the President of the Senate's wishes in the matter.[7]

The next year the Senate majority had its way and the Congress voted that no funds appropriated for the Defense Department were to "be used for the payment of a price differential on contracts hereafter made for the purpose of relieving economic dislocations."[26] This provision has been repeated annually since 1954 in the Defense Appropriation Act.

As a result of the congressional action in 1953, Defense Manpower Policy No. 4 was amended. A new policy issued November 5, 1953, which was still in effect in mid-1963, required that the Department of Defense comply with the following provisions: [5]

1. It should attempt to award negotiated procurement to contractors

---

[5]On July 6, 1960, Defense Manpower Policy No. 4 was further revised. This revision urged the Defense Department to give "first preference to firms in persistent labor surplus areas. . . ."[14]

located in labor-surplus areas, provided that these firms can meet the same prices as those offered by contractors in other areas.

2. Where appropriate, portions of negotiated procurement should be set aside for firms located in labor-surplus areas, provided that the latter firms can meet the prices paid on the non-set-aside portion of the procurement.

Since about 85 per cent of the total Defense Department procurement is negotiated,[18] the admonition to encourage the placing of contracts and facilities in labor-surplus and depressed areas might have had a significant impact of bringing jobs to these areas. However, there is little evidence that the Defense Department has made any special effort to implement this program, and the above-quoted appropriation provision clearly prohibits the Defense Department from considering the social cost of unemployment in determining where Defense procurement should be filled. There is some evidence that under the Kennedy Administration special efforts were made to place contracts in depressed areas, particularly West Virginia. But this was accomplished informally because of the congressional admonition against the use of awarding defense contracts for "relieving economic dislocation." It is therefore impossible to measure quantitatively the extent to which preference has been given to labor-surplus areas in the location of Defense Department contracts under the Kennedy Administration.

This does not apply to the "set-aside" provisions. Under this provision, the Defense Department is required to retain the competitive aspects in procurement because of the limitation prohibiting price differentials in placing contracts in labor-surplus or depressed areas. Also, there are no fixed percentages in connection with the specific procurement that is set aside for labor-surplus areas. The extent of what is set aside is determined by the procuring agency separately for each case. The Comptroller General has ruled that even in cases where there is a reasonable expectation that bids or proposals would be obtained from a sufficient number of responsible labor-surplus firms to insure fair and reasonable prices, the Defense Department may not set aside a total procurement action for a depressed or labor-surplus area. The Comptroller General reasoned that the fair and reasonable competition which may be secured from firms located in labor-surplus and depressed areas is no substitute for ascertaining the lowest possible bid which might come from a firm located in a richer area.[4]

The procuring agency is therefore required to determine the optimal quantity which would probably result in the most favorable price, considering the manufacturing processes involved and the quantity required for an economical production run. Bids are then solicited for the non-set-aside portion. After the award of the non-set-aside portion, procurement for the set-aside portion is negotiated with firms in the labor-surplus areas. Special conditions must be met if a firm in a labor-surplus area is to be eligible to participate in the set-aside portion of the procurement. First, the firm must have submitted a bid upon the items not set aside; and second, its bid must be within 20 per cent of the highest award made with respect to the quantities not set aside.

Altogether, Defense Manpower Policy No. 4 has accounted for over $400 million worth of orders placed in labor-surplus areas between 1953, when the policy was inaugurated, and the end of fiscal 1962. This amounted to about 3 per cent of procurement orders placed by the Defense Department in these areas and has ranged in recent years between .1 and .4 per cent of total annual procurement awards made by the Defense Department.

An attempt to eliminate the congressional prohibition against granting any preferential treatment in procurement to the depressed areas was made in the House in 1962. Radical shifts in defense procurement had a deep impact upon the economies of certain areas following the Korean War. Michigan, which accounted for almost a tenth of the total defense procurement during the Korean period, had only 2.7 per cent during fiscal 1961. Other states which lost heavily in their share of defense procurement were Illinois (from 5 to 2 per cent), Indiana (from 4.5 to 1.6 per cent), and to a lesser extent New York, Ohio, and Washington. On the other hand, a number of states made major gains in their shares of the defense procurement as a result of these shifts. Between 1953 and 1961, California's share of the total defense procurement dollars increased from 13.6 to 23.9 per cent; Massachusetts from 2.8 to 4.8 per cent; and Texas from 3.2 to 5.1 per cent. In addition, new defense complexes grew up during the eight-year period. As a result of these developments, Colorado, Florida, New Mexico, and Nevada increased their share of the total defense procurement by percentages ranging from 450 to 1,500.

The major factors responsible for these changes were the relative decline in procurement of tank-automotive vehicles, aircraft, and other hardware, and to the sharp rise in missile procurement. Analysis of 1961 Defense Department awards for research and development and experimental work indicated that the radical changes which followed the Korean War are due to continue in the years ahead. In 1961 California received two-fifths of the total Defense Department contract awards in these fields. Colorado, Utah, Massachusetts, and Connecticut accounted for another sixth of the Defense Department research, development, and experimental awards. Since there is a considerable amount of linkage between experimental and research work and prime contract awards, it may be expected that defense procurement dollars will tend to be concentrated even more during the years ahead, barring further radical shifts in defense procurement.

This geographic imbalance in defense procurement has caused considerable concern among the policy-makers, and in 1962 a number of congressmen attempted to make it possible for the Defense Department to give depressed areas a better break in defense procurement by ending the appropriation provision which prohibits such action. Those who favored preferential treatment of depressed areas argued that defense procurement should take into consideration the economic and social costs of unemployment and not just the immediate contract costs: ". . . with the expenditures of a relatively small increase in funds, . . . we could accomplish a great deal more and much more cheaply in terms of helping our unemployed areas than if we had to put money out for unemployment insurance and through the provisions of the Area Redevelopment bill."[9]

Others retorted that "the nation's defense should not be made to serve a secondary purpose, such as aiding economic recovery," and that it would be a "dangerous attempt to place our nation's security in the toolbox of economic repairmen."[9] Another congressman argued that it is not the job of the Defense Department personnel to become "sociological reformers and economic rehabilitators."[9]

But aside from the rhetoric, the clinching argument against authorizing the Defense Department to give preferential treatment to depressed areas was that the policy initiated under President Eisenhower was supported by President Kennedy. The motion to strike out the provision prohibiting the Defense Department from paying price differentials on contracts for purposes of relieving economic dislocation was defeated by a teller vote (108–36).[9]

At about the same time the Kennedy Administration was also giving consideration to strengthening Defense Manpower Policy No. 4. President Kennedy indicated his concern over the limited amount of contracts, both defense and civilian, going into labor-surplus areas. He speculated that it was partly due to insufficient plants in those areas. In a press conference he indicated his inclination to approve a plan which would permit 100 per cent setting aside of government procurement awards.[13] During the spring of 1962 a number of drafts proposing revisions of Defense Manpower Policy No. 4 were circulated among executive agencies. But apparently it was finally determined that, in view of the congressional prohibition, little could be done by executive order to grant meaningful preferential treatment to depressed areas through government procurement. And additional exhortations would be politically unwise unless they could be accompanied by active implementation.

The original 1955 Douglas bill carried a provision dealing with federal procurement. Aside from general exhortations encouraging procurement agencies to award negotiated contracts to firms located in depressed areas, it would have provided legislative sanction to the original intent of Defense Manpower Policy No. 4. The bill would have allowed the firms located in depressed areas to match the lowest bid after the bids for procurement were made. The effect of this provision would have been to allow firms in depressed areas to obtain preference over the original low bidders. In addition, procurement agencies would have been directed to award contracts to firms located in depressed areas in the event of tie bids. However, before the Senate considered the depressed-area bill in 1956, Senator Fulbright indicated that he would interpose objection to Senate action on the basis of jurisdiction. He asserted that the bill was not properly before the Senate Committee on Labor and Public Welfare, since it contained provisions dealing with credit which were within the jurisdiction of the Senate Committee on Banking and Currency. One of the provisions in the bill to which Senator Fulbright objected was that dealing with procurement. An understanding was reached between the proponents of the bill and Senator Fulbright under which the former agreed to withdraw the procurement provision (Chapter 1). In view of the lopsided 1953 vote against such a provision, it is highly doubtful whether it could have ever been approved by the Senate.

The only procurement provision which was left in the bill when it was finally enacted in 1961 authorized the ARA Administrator to furnish federal procurement agencies with a list of firms in depressed areas which desired government contracts (Section 10). It required a great deal of detailed work to implement this provision, and during the first two years of its activities, the ARA did not develop the capability to prepare the list. It did maintain a small section of procurement experts in its Office of Operations whose function it was to help firms cut through the maze of red tape connected with procurement.

The ARA decided to limit the list of firms which it would furnish to federal procurement agencies to those capable of performing on a contract of $100,000 or more. This limited the list of firms to about 12,000. Preparation of a complete list of firms operating in designated areas would have involved more than 300,000 names and was beyond the ARA capability; the vast majority of these firms could not have benefited from government procurement. The list of 12,000 firms was in the process of preparation when this study was completed.

A major function of ARA procurement experts was to persuade government procurement officers to carry out the intent of the Armed Services procurement regulations which require prime contractors

. . . to establish and conduct a program which will encourage labor surplus area concerns to compete for subcontracts within their capabilities. In this connection the contractor shall—
(1) Designate a liaison officer who will (i) maintain liaison with duly authorized representatives of the Government on labor surplus area matters (ii) supervise compliance with the "Utilization of Concerns in Labor Surplus Areas" clause, and (iii) administer the Contractor's Labor Surplus Area Subcontracting Program.[25]

The Economic Utilization Staff of the Defense Department agreed in April, 1962, to advise the ARA of pending procurement actions in excess of $500,000; the ARA was then to advise the Department of Defense of firms in designated areas which might be desirous of bidding on the pending contracts. But this had only limited application since about seven out of every eight defense procurement dollars is spent on negotiated contracts and since Defense Department regulations prohibit issuing advance information to potential bidders on negotiated contracts. This obstacle, of course, did not apply to advertised bidding.

To channel more of the advertised contracts to labor-surplus areas, the Department of the Army devised a plan for selecting procurement actions on a trial basis which lend themselves to a substantial amount of subcontracting. These procurement actions are open to bidding by any firm, regardless of its location, but the lowest responsive bidder must agree to produce or subcontract a given percentage—from 20 to 50 per cent—of the total cost of the contract in labor-surplus areas. The results of this experiment were not available at the time this study was completed.

It is not likely that an effective government procurement policy can be developed to aid depressed areas as long as a loose labor market exists generally throughout the country. Even in 1953, when full employment prevailed, the use of federal procurement to assist labor-surplus areas was defeated by more than a two-to-one vote. Aside from purely regional interests, many congressmen and senators believe that federal procurement, particularly defense procurement, should not be used as a tool to aid depressed areas.

However, these objections might be mitigated under conditions of sustained full employment. In Germany, firms located in depressed areas receive preference in federal procurement. In cases where a bid from a firm located in a depressed area is within 5 per cent of that of firms located outside of such an area, the contract is awarded to the firm in the depressed area. It is highly doubtful that such an approach would ever be acceptable to Congress. But under conditions of full employment, effective aid to depressed areas might be obtained by energetic attempts on the part of procurement officials to find suitable productive capacity in depressed areas and award contracts to these firms under negotiated awards.

Accelerated Tax Amortization

It has been mentioned earlier in this study that during the first two years of the ARA the program failed to attract "blue-chip" corporations. No doubt a number of major U.S. corporations have expanded or built new facilities between 1961 and 1963 in the thousand designated areas. However, there is no evidence that the ARA program played a significant role in attracting these companies into the depressed areas.

It would appear that the package of tools provided by Congress to bring jobs to depressed areas had no appeal to established corporations. An established corporation which desires to expand normally experiences little difficulty in obtaining credit from traditional lending institutions and would consequently not qualify for an ARA loan. Nor would such a corporation be likely to turn to the ARA for technical assistance.

Federally subsidized training and subsistence payments made available under the ARA exclusively to redevelopment areas might have offered an incentive to firms to locate in depressed areas, but the Manpower Development and Training Act, which was passed in March 1962, barely a year after the ARA came into existence, made even broader training facilities available to all parts of the nation. This removed any advantages which depressed areas might have had over non-designated areas in offering free training facilities to new or expanding firms.

The original Douglas bill did contain a special carrot which might have induced successful corporations to locate or expand facilities in depressed areas. Section 14 of S. 2663 (Eighty-fourth Congress) would have permitted qualifying firms to write off the cost of investment in new plant and equipment in five years, instead of the longer normal depreciation period. But Senator Douglas had opposed the rapid tax-amortization program which was enacted in 1950 and dropped the provision from the bill before it was reported out by the Senate Committee on Labor and Public Welfare, which in 1956 handled the first Douglas depressed-area bill.

Accelerated tax amortization was used during World War I, World War II, and the Korean War as a financial incentive to expand industrial productive capacity to meet defense requirements. As it was applied during the Korean period, qualifying firms were permitted to depreciate for that portion of their total plant investment which was certified by the Office of Defense Mobilization (ODM) as related to defense production over a five-year period. From the beginning of the accelerated tax-amortization program, manpower availability was considered a factor in evaluating applications, though it played only a secondary role in defense needs.

Accelerated tax-amortization policies, as practiced during the Korean period, permitted defense contractors to write off the cost of new investments in plant and equipment within sixty months. Based on the assumption that at least part of such investment in plant and equipment would not be fully useful to the contractor after the emergency, the ODM allowed contractors to write off within five years from 40 to 50 per cent of the cost of buildings and 65 to 75 per cent of the cost of equipment. In exceptional cases, a full 100 per cent of both building and equipment was allowed to be rapidly amortized. This policy, which dates back to the Internal Revenue Code of 1939 (Section 124A), was adopted in the Revenue Act of 1950. More than three years later, in November of 1953, the Office of Defense Mobilization supplemented this policy and placed additional emphasis upon the availability of surplus manpower by providing for a larger percentage of rapid tax amortization on new or expanded defense facilities that were located in chronic surplus areas. Almost a year later, in September, 1954, the "chronic" requirement was eliminated and the incentive was extended to firms locating or expanding in any labor-surplus area—a labor market with 6 per cent or more unemployment. Firms locating or expanding in such areas were allowed to increase the application of the rapid tax amortization to an additional 10–25 per cent of investment costs. For example, under the 1950 Revenue Act, a firm building a new plant might have been allowed to amortize 50 per cent of the total cost in five years. But if it built the plant in a labor-surplus area, the proportion of the rapid tax amortization might have been increased by an additional 10–25 per cent. As stated earlier, the special tax-amortization privileges were dependent upon the existing defense expansion goals. Thus the controlling factor in the administration of the rapid tax write-offs has been national defense needs rather than availability of surplus manpower.

The policies granting additional accelerated tax-amortization incentives for firms locating in labor-surplus areas were adopted after the program had passed its peak. By that time the vast majority of the nearly two hundred defense expansion goals were completed. The program to aid labor-surplus areas was further limited by plant location requirements inherent in products which offered no long-range job opportunities in specific areas (pipelines). Special tax-amortization considerations were given to firms locating in labor-surplus areas only if new job opportunities were developed on a long-range basis. The accelerated tax-amortization program continued after the Korean War and expired officially at the end of 1959, but few rapid tax-amortization certificates were issued after 1956, and about four of every five of these certificates were issued prior to November, 1953, when the special provisions relating to chronic or labor-surplus areas became effective.

Altogether, of more than 4,300 such certificates issued after November, 1953, only 74 received special consideration and additional write-off privileges because they were located in labor-surplus areas. The exact additional tax-amortization write-offs which ranged from 10 to 25 per cent of the total capital investment for buildings and equipment were determined on a case-by-case basis. The 74 certificates represented a total new investment of $320 million and accounted for only one-tenth of 1 per cent of the total cost of facilities which were certified for rapid tax amortization and about three-tenths of 1 per cent which were certified after the inauguration of the special provisions made for labor-surplus areas. The Office of Defense Mobilization, which administered the program, estimated that more than 17,000 jobs were added in labor-surplus areas under the 74 certificates.

An ARA survey disclosed that all but one of the firms which received accelerated tax-amortization privileges for locating in labor-surplus areas remained in operation by the end of 1961. And some had expanded their operations since they received the original certificates. The extent to which rapid tax amortization determined plant location cannot be ascertained. The National Industrial Conference Board concluded that "the government's accelerated tax amortization program has been of considerable importance as an instrument for the expansion of defense facilities."[2] However, the companies surveyed by the Conference Board did not think that the accelerated tax-amortization policy had been a dominant influence in the choice of location for plant expansion. But the Korean experience is far from conclusive on this point, since the policies granting additional incentives for labor-surplus areas were adopted after most of the tax-amortization program had been approved, and firms qualifying for rapid tax-amortization certificates received only a partial additional incentive to locate in labor-surplus areas. A program which would be limited exclusively to chronic labor-surplus areas should be much more effective.

The Committee for Economic Development, in its program for distressed areas, favored the granting of rapid tax amortization on investments in plants and equipment to firms locating in depressed areas. The CED thought that such a program might constitute a major potential aid to these areas: "Special rapid amortization privileges should be made available to firms expanding or building new plant or installing new equipment in distressed areas. The type of incentive to industry has proved effective in the past and can stimulate an increase in employment in these areas."[3]

Reaction to the inclusion of a rapid tax-amortization provision in a program to aid depressed areas was mixed. In 1956 Senator John F. Kennedy considered the provision as "one of the most important" in the bill.[22] William L. Batt, Jr., later administrator of the program, referred to rapid tax amortization as "a most valuable provision."[22] He pointed to the rapid tax-amortization experience during the Korean period and estimated that more than 11,000 jobs were brought to depressed areas under the program. In the same vein, Governor George M. Leader, of Pennsylvania, testified that in his "considered judgment, based on extensive industrial development contacts . . . this device will attract a wide variety of new industries to distressed areas. Like other provisions of the bill, this may seem to some to be extreme, but it is not."[22]

But the rapid tax-amortization provision had its opponents as well as its skeptics. The Office of Defense Mobilization objected to the provision on technical grounds. In the Douglas bill, it was offered as an amendment to the Defense Mobilization Act. Though the ODM did not object to the use of tax amortization as a device to aid depressed areas, it suggested that such a provision should be considered apart from the defense program.[22] Professor Seymour Harris, of Harvard, did not oppose the accelerated amortization provision, but doubted whether it would be of much help to depressed areas.[22] Solomon Barkin, a major lobbyist for the depressed-area aid program, considered the provision "of minor importance," though he believed that it should be included as part of a package to help depressed areas. "In combination with a broader program of planning for economic growth," he thought, the accelerated rapid amortization provision "may prove most useful."[22]

Once the rapid tax-amortization provision was dropped in 1956, it was not revived as an active issue in subsequent discussions. However, the issue was raised tangentially in 1961, when the House Republican minority in the Committee on Banking and Currency suggested that a rapid tax-amortization program could be effectively substituted for the provision giving financial assistance to firms expanding or relocating in depressed areas. In opposing commercial and industrial loans to new or expanding firms in depressed areas, the Republicans argued that "Congress does not need to tap the taxpayer for any such sums as that." As an alternative, the Republicans on the committee thought that an accelerated tax-amortization program would be much more effective than the establishment of the loan funds in aiding depressed areas. In arguing in favor of the alternative, the Republican minority suggested that their proposal "would leave the business decisions to private enterprise. No worthwhile opportunity for a sound business venture would be overlooked. It would avoid all the pitfalls a federal loan program would encounter in federalized plant location. No new Federal lending bureaucracy would be required."[16] But during the debate on the bill on the floor of the House, the Republicans failed to offer an amendment embodying their proposal.

A number of other industrial countries have used rapid tax amortization to aid their depressed areas. For example, West Germany permits accelerated tax depreciation to firms locating in depressed areas. The accelerated depreciation applies to 30 per cent of the cost of building and to 50 per cent of machinery and equipment. The total amount eligible for accelerated depreciation is limited however. Belgium and Italy do not use tax amortization but permit a variety of tax incentives to induce industry to locate and expand in economically depressed areas.

The use of investment tax credit has also been suggested as a supplementary or alternative device to rapid tax amortization in aiding depressed areas. According to this proposal, new or expanding businesses in depressed areas would be permitted a higher investment tax credit than the 7 per cent permitted under existing federal legislation. Under this proposal, the firms investing in depressed areas would receive either a flat or a flexible tax credit differential on their investment. The obvious advantage of a flat differential is that it would provide administrative simplicity, but a flexible differential would permit the Treasury Department to consider the national need for expanded capacity in a given product or service as a criterion in administering the program.

However, some economists would object to any use of the tax structure to aid depressed areas on the premise that it constitutes undesirable fiddling with the federal tax structure and results in damage to the equity and efficiency of the federal tax system. According to this argument, if assistance is to be given to new or expanding firms in depressed areas, it would be preferable to give direct subsidies to these firms instead of attempting the same thing through tax gimmicks.

Relocation

Possibly the most obvious omission in the Area Redevelopment Act is any direct reference to relocation of unemployed. The Act is directed entirely toward bringing jobs to depressed areas. During the first Senate hearings on the legislation, a number of witnesses urged that the program make provision for relocating unemployed from depressed areas to communities where there is need for their skills. Professor William Miernyk recognized the reluctance of unemployed workers to move but thought that mobility could be stimulated by providing unemployed workers in depressed areas with information about living conditions and job opportunities in other areas. He also favored federal financial assistance to aid relocation.[22] Similar views were expressed by Frank Fernbach, of the AFL-CIO, but he believed that provisions for relocation should be carefully qualified to balance the prevention of "undue hardship" with "economic and social values of family life and of the communities."[22] [6] Solomon Barkin proposed a more modest program. He would have limited assistance to interest-free loans to cover the cost of relocation.[22]

Relocation provisions were not only favored by academic representatives and spokesmen for labor groups. Charles Taft, testifying

[6]Regrettably, a memorandum in which Fernbach presumably spelled out criteria which would aid in achieving such a balance was not included in the hearings.

for the National Trade Policy Committee, though expressing preference for a program which would bring jobs to depressed areas, urged
also that the program be combined with relocation assistance where
it was economically unfeasible to bring jobs to a depressed area. "It
is a question of helping the unemployed worker to adjust in the way
that he would normally want to adjust if he could."[22]

But powerful bipartisan forces were arrayed against relocation
assistance. Senator Hubert H. Humphrey favored freedom of mobility,
"but it is quite another matter to take as public policy the encouragement . . . of mobility."[22] Senator Douglas lost no opportunity to
remind those who favored relocation allowances that "investment in
houses and schools, in community facilities . . . would be wasted if
the population dried up and went away, and, furthermore, there is
such a thing as sentiment in the world, too."[22] And his colleague
from Illinois, Senator Everett M. Dirksen, invoked hearth and fireside
against subsidization of mobility and argued that "as the Indians were
reluctant to leave the graves of their ancestors . . . and rather than
leave [their lands] were willing to fight it out. . . ," so later Americans
are reluctant to leave their homes.[20]

With the rise of unemployment throughout the country after 1956,
support for subsidized migration lost much of its appeal and little
testimony was offered in favor of such legislation during subsequent
hearings. It was revived, however, by Robert P. Lee, who testified for
the U.S. Chamber of Commerce in 1961. Though Lee opposed federal
loans or grants for depressed areas, he grudgingly suggested that
federally guaranteed long-term loans to help relocate unemployed
might be tried: "If we must have the Federal Government doing
things for more people, maybe that is one that is not so harmful."[21]

Again, the opposition was bipartisan. Congressman Wright Patman
considered the suggestion "cruel" and Congressman (later governor)
William Scranton, of Pennsylvania, described the Chamber recommendation as "callous and inhuman."[8] Somewhat later, Senator
Joseph S. Clark, of Pennsylvania, deplored congressional opposition
of subsidizing mobility but thought that the blame was to be placed
upon spokesmen of depressed areas who "hollered" about relocation.
"This was considered unpatriotic," the Senator commented.[23] Congressional views on relocation have apparently undergone some trans-
formation during recent years, however. In 1961 and 1962 Congress
enacted three pieces of legislation which touched directly on aiding
the unemployed in finding jobs: the Area Redevelopment Act, the
Manpower Development and Training Act, and the Trade Expansion

Act. In the first piece of legislation there was complete "official neglect" of relocation provisions. The manpower development and training bill did contain a provision for relocation which was approved by the Senate Committee on Labor and Public Welfare, but the provision was dropped on the Senate floor. The House Committee on Education and Labor did not report the provision out. Unlike the two earlier pieces of legislation, the Trade Expansion Act does make allowances for relocation. The Act provides that unemployed heads of families who have little prospect of finding suitable gainful employment in their communities and who have been offered long-term employment elsewhere are eligible to receive relocation allowances which cover moving expenses for himself, his family and his household goods. In addition, the worker receives a lump-sum payment of 2.5 times the average weekly manufacturing wage (close to $250 at present wage rates) to defray other costs of moving.

As mentioned earlier, the Budget Bureau favored in 1963 the expansion of a federally financed training program in depressed areas. In addition, one of the provisions proposed by the Budget Bureau included the application of the relocation allowances under the Trade Expansion Act to the Area Redevelopment Act. But the Labor Department objections to reopening the ARA training provisions prevailed, and the proposal regarding financing of relocation was not submitted to Congress.

Federal Grants

The federal government is currently (1963–64) spending some $10 billion on various grant programs.[19, 1] The subsidy programs include a wide diversity of activities: highways, public assistance, educational activities, hospital and airport construction, post office, and others. Without arguing the merits of each of the subsidy programs, it is generally recognized that some have helped poorer states by granting them proportionately higher subsidies than those received by states with higher than average per capita income. But normally, the subsidy programs do not take into account the needs of individual communities. Section 15 of the Area Redevelopment Act is an exception to this rule. It qualifies designated urban (5[a]) areas to receive federal grants covering 75 per cent of the cost of planning urban renewal projects, instead of the normal two-thirds. The legislative history of the Act fails to explain why the urban renewal program was singled out to offer special assistance to ARA areas.

The Small Business Administration has made special provisions on its loans in designated areas. The interest paid on loans made by the agency in designated areas is 4 per cent instead of the normal 5.5 per cent which the agency charges in other areas.

An effective and comprehensive area redevelopment program should take into consideration the special needs of depressed areas. This would require recognition of the fact that frequently depressed areas cannot benefit from federal grant programs because they cannot contribute their share of total costs and that special provisions have to be made for these areas if they are to partake of the benefits offered by the government to other areas. The approach of the Area Redevelopment Act regarding urban renewal planning grants should be made equally applicable to other federal grant programs, for example, airport and hospital construction. Similarly, in computing cost-benefit ratios relating to the development of resources financed by the government, the cost of labor which would otherwise have been wasted in depressed areas should not be considered in the cost of any proposed project. A recommendation along this line was made by the President's Water Resources Council, but it has not yet been implemented.[15] Legislative action may be necessary to effectuate this proposal.

APPRAISAL OF ARA TOOLS

In mid-1963 the ARA suffered a serious setback. Authority to expend funds for public-facility grants was terminated, and loan funds were curtailed during House consideration of additional funds for ARA. The infant area redevelopment program was facing a serious crisis. But it was not likely that Congress had said the last word on the program. The Administration was marshaling its forces to mobilize the House to reconsider the mayhem it committed.

Congress will have to take another hard look at the program before June 30, 1965, when the present enabling legislation is due to expire. At that time Congress may well consider that the tools provided for area redevelopment are inadequate to meet the pressing problems of depressed areas. It could then consider means of strengthening the program, or it could kill the ARA altogether. The latter alternative would be unfortunate, since the program would not have had adequate testing. But if Congress is to decide that the area redevelopment program deserves further life to prove itself, the alternative of strengthening the tools of the ARA would face formidable obstacles. The ARA is too overextended to permit experimentation with new programs, since whatever new tools might be added would be spread too thinly to have a real impact on depressed areas, and since the costs of effective tools to aid all designated areas would be prohibitive.

The four additional programs considered in this chapter cannot be effectively utilized to benefit all designated areas. A rapid tax-amortization program or other tax incentives, which would include some of the major industrial complexes in the nation and 1,000 other areas designated by the ARA, would distort the tax structure and would create serious inequities for the other 2,000 counties. The same would also be true of granting designated areas preferential treatment in procurement. And even among the designated areas, the rich choice given employers to locate or expand in designated areas is likely to benefit the more viable communities, which should never have been designated, rather than the most severely depressed areas.

It is not likely that Congress would be able to withhold assistance from the areas that have already been designated. A possible approach to the dilemma would be to tighten designation criteria and to limit the benefits of any additional tools that might be added to the program to areas which would qualify for eligibility under the more restricted criteria.

Relocation allowances present special problems. Encouragement of mobility would tend to further hinder the rehabilitation of depressed areas. As noted earlier, a major problem of these areas is that outmigration saps these areas of their younger and better-educated population. Relocation assistance should therefore be used only sparingly and with considerable flexibility lest it speed up the deterioration of human resources of depressed areas and thus further impede their rehabilitation. However, the redevelopment tools, even if they should be broadened, will be of little help to depressed areas whose economic base has vanished. In such cases, the interests of individuals cannot be ignored, and their only hope may lie in relocation.

Finally, it must be recognized that a program to aid depressed areas can have only very limited success so long as high levels of unemployment prevail throughout the nation. A program to aid depressed areas is no substitute for over-all measures to stimulate economic growth and employment. Only under conditions of relatively high employment will the special tools to aid depressed areas become effective. When the cup runneth over for other areas, can the overflow be channeled with a minimum of waste to chronic labor-surplus areas? When a high level of employment and economic activity is achieved, over-all monetary and fiscal policies to expand demand in depressed areas can be used only at the cost of fanning inflation. And only under such conditions will the tailor-made programs to aid depressed areas, including tax incentives, preferential treatment in procurement, and others, come into their own.

REFERENCES

1. Benson, George C. S., and McClelland, Harold F. *Consolidated Grants.* Washington: American Enterprise Association, 1961, p. 4.
2. "Fast Write-Offs Spur Defense Expansion," *Business Record,* February, 1956, p. 74.
3. Committee for Economic Development. *Distressed Areas in a Growing Economy.* New York: The Committee. June, 1961, p. 66.
4. Comptroller General. Letter to the Secretary of Defense. March 3, 1961.
5. *Congressional Record.* July 22, 1953, p. 9817.
6. *Congressional Record.* July 28, 1953, p. 10397.
7. *Congressional Record.* July 29, 1953, p. 10519.
8. *Congressional Record.* March 29, 1961, pp. 4910, 4906.
9. *Congressional Record.* April 18, 1962, p. 6394 (Congressman Samuel S. Stratton); p. 6393 (Congressman James C. Corman); p. 6393 (Congressman Gerald R. Ford, Jr.).
10. *Congressional Record.* June 12, 1963, pp. 10122–23, 10085–123.
11. *Congressional Record.* June 18, 1963, p. 10397.
12. *Congressional Record.* June 26, 1963, p. 11061.
13. *New York Times.* February 22, 1962.
14. Office of Civil and Defense Mobilization. Defense Manpower Policy No. 4. (Revised, June 6, 1960.)
15. The President's Water Resources Council. *Policies, Standards and Procedures in the Formulation of Water and Related Land Resources.* U.S. Senate. 87th Cong., 2d Sess. Document 97. Washington: Government Printing Office, 1962, p. 5.
16. U.S. House of Representatives, Committee on Banking and Currency. *Area Redevelopment Act.* Report 186, 87th Cong., 1st Sess., pp. 21–22.
17. U.S. Congress. H. R. 4996 and S. 1163. 88th Cong., 1st Sess., 1963.
18. U.S. Congress, Joint Economic Committee. *The Economic Aspects of Military Procurement and Supply.* 86th Cong., 2d Sess., October, 1960, p. 25.
19. ——— (Julius W. Allen). *Subsidy and Subsidy-Like Programs of the U.S. Government.* 86th Cong., 2d Sess., 1960, p. 19.
20. U.S. Senate, Committee on Banking and Currency. *Hearings on Area Redevelopment Act.* 86th Cong., 1st Sess., 1959, p. 63.
21. ———. *Hearings on Area Redevelopment Act.* 87th Cong., 1st Sess., 1961, pp. 55–63, 311.
22. U.S. Senate, Committee on Labor and Public Welfare. *Hearings on Area*

Redevelopment Act. 84th Cong., 2d Sess., 1956, pp. 343, 1088, 258, 12, 328, 806, 155, 1067–68, 807, 769, 92, 605.

23. ———. *Hearings on Nation's Manpower Revolution.* 88th Cong., 1st Sess., Part 2, 1963, p. 694.

24. U.S. Department of Agriculture Press Releases. August 2, 1962, and October 26, 1962.

25. U.S. Department of Defense. *Armed Services Procurement Regulations, 1962,* pp. 1–805.

26. ———. *Defense Appropriations Act of 1954* (Section 644).

Chapter 9

++++++++++++++++++++++

Concluding Observations: The Policy Dilemma

++

Two years of operations hardly provide sufficient experience to evaluate a long-range program such as area redevelopment. Only a small proportion of the funds committed by the ARA have actually been disbursed, and little brick and mortar have been used. Most of the jobs which will be generated by loans and grants exist thus far only on paper. Few of the technical assistance projects which may hopefully unlock community resources have been completed, let alone put into practice.

The ARA has faced serious obstacles which prevented the effective execution of the program. The administrative structure impeded efficient operation of the program. Placing the ARA in the Commerce Department, and the subsequent parceling out of the processing of applications to other agencies, presented critical and experimental problems which were especially bothersome to an infant agency.

Aside from the administrative roadblocks, the package of tools which Congress gave the ARA to combat unemployment in depressed areas is in itself extremely limited. There is nothing in the Act which offers any real incentive to channel blue-chip or established industry to depressed areas. Four per cent interest on venture capital is not an effective carrot to dangle before successful corporations. The requirement that the local citizenry chip in at least 10 per cent of the required funds in any venture, without expectation of repayment until the ARA loan is repaid, has proven to be a real handicap to the program.

The Act in effect prevents successful corporations from receiving ARA financial assistance by restricting ARA loans to corporations

246

which cannot receive credit from conventional lending institutions; few, if any, established corporations could claim this inability during the first two years of the ARA. In effect, the law therefore limits ARA assistance to new or marginal firms which cannot obtain credit from private lending institutions.

The training program might have become a significant factor in attracting industry to redevelopment areas. In cases of new plants employing several hundred workers, a government-supported training program might have been a sufficient inducement for prospective employers to locate in ARA areas. However, the passage of the Manpower Development and Training Act, within a year after the area redevelopment program was established, made superior training programs available throughout the United States and thus reduced the attractiveness of the earlier program.

The ARA operations indicate the appropriateness of providing for borrowing from the Treasury for long-range economic development programs. The insistence of the House Appropriations Committee that ARA funds be appropriated annually acted as a pressure upon the administrators of the agency to expend the funds, which are "lost" to the agency if not committed by the end of the fiscal year for which they are appropriated. Borrowing from the Treasury, as the need arises, would have eliminated the pressure to approve applications and commit funds by a given deadline and would have permitted the agency to husband its funds more carefully. At the same time, Treasury borrowing would not have denied the congressional appropriations committees an annual scrutiny of ARA expenditures as part of their review of ARA requests for operational funds. As an alternative to Treasury borrowing, Congress could appropriate ARA funds without restricting the use of the funds to a single year. This is now done for other programs.

Aside from the inherent weakness of the package of tools put together under the Area Redevelopment Act, its effectiveness has been diminished by the slack economic conditions which prevailed in the country. It is difficult to defend government financing of new capacity when established firms operate below their optimum level because of inadequate demand. Given the prevailing economic conditions, it is not surprising that the biggest demand for ARA assistance came from the most rapidly expanding industry—recreation and tourism. However, financing tourism as a major part of the program involves inherent limitations. Tourism is a capital intensive industry, which means that the cost of generating new jobs is relatively high. Moreover, tourism normally yields only seasonal jobs at low wages. Despite these objections, the ARA could ill afford to reject applications for financial assistance for the promotion of tourism because it did not have enough applications from other sources. And in some areas, tourism offered the only immediate possibility of promoting economic development.

During its first two years the area redevelopment program has been a focal point of controversy. Given the obstacles to the ARA and the type of long-range economic development program that the agency was supposed to promote, it is hardly surprising that the ARA got off to a slow start. Those who had opposed passage of the plan were quick to attack with an "I-told-you-so" argument. Instead of viewing with alarm the vast new federal expenditures, some now blamed the New Frontiersmen for not spending enough to aid depressed areas.

Attacks came from friends and foes alike. During the prolonged legislative hassle over the enactment of the program, its potential benefits were oversold. When the anticipated benefits were slow in coming, grumblings about the ARA came from all quarters. A major southern newspaper suspected a Yankee plot and suggested that other states, such as West Virginia, had been favored while the ARA "dragged its feet on Georgia projects."[1] But West Virginians complained with equal vehemence that the long-expected help from the ARA was not coming to their state either. So the blame was put on government bureaucracy in general and especially on the Small Business Administration and the Community Facilities Administration, which processed ARA applications; presumably the ARA administrators wanted to help West Virginians, but the Washington bureaucrats in the other agencies which processed ARA applications made such help impossible. The ARA, according to a West Virginia newspaper, became a captive of federal bureaucracy and was "losing touch with its original set of objectives."[7] Others, however, blamed the Administrator of the ARA for the slow start of the agency. According to this view the agency got off on a slow start due to excessive caution on the part of its Administrator.[2]

Even the Secretary of Commerce, Luther Hodges, who was officially responsible for the program, stated in a press conference that he was not satisfied with the speed with which the ARA was progressing: ". . . there is so much checking and double checking, both internally within the government agencies, and back and forth with the states and municipalities, that it is very slow."[4] Senator Paul H. Douglas is reported to have expressed the hope that the administrators of the program would move faster "now that they have gained some experience."[6]

If the criticisms of the foes of the program were to be anticipated, the impatience of its friends was also understandable. So many promises had been made concerning the potential benefits of the program that its friends were expecting rapid results. For practical politicians, this meant that they would be able to "point with pride" to the ARA's accomplishments by election day.

ARA spokesmen contributed substantially to the confusion that existed in the public mind about the operations of the program and the frustrations of its friends concerning its progress. Instead of explaining and clarifying the real problems it faced, spokesmen for the agency displayed great dexterity in issuing exaggerated press releases about its accomplishments. Thus Secretary Hodges, testifying before the Joint Economic Committee on February 2, 1962, in connection with the President's Economic Report, talked about $30 million reserved for projects which "have been advanced to the final stages of review and action . . . some 17,000 permanent new jobs are involved in these projects for which funds have been set aside by ARA."[8] On the same occasion, William L. Batt, Jr., the administrator of the ARA, inserted into the committee record unsubstantiated conclusions from what was purported to be a case study of the impact of one ARA loan.[8] According to these claims, an ARA loan of about half a million dollars was supposed to have resulted in hundreds of new additional jobs in the community and the savings of millions of dollars in terms of welfare and unemployment insurance benefits and taxes. All these claims were at best imaginary, since at that time the plant had not actually begun operation. Yet a study prepared by the Department of Labor technicians suggesting that the multiplier effect of ARA-financed projects in depressed areas would be rather negligible due to existing underutilized capacity in service and trade industries never saw the light of day because the study was contrary to official ARA claims.

On another occasion, three months later, Batt expressed the hope that by the end of the fiscal year (June 30, 1962), the agency would be able to "point to some 50,000 jobs, directly and indirectly, that we have helped create."[5] At about the same time, a national magazine reported Batt to have claimed that the agency expected to approve, before the end of the fiscal year, some one hundred more projects which would be "enough to provide some 75,000 jobs."[3] Three months later the ARA reduced its claims somewhat and announced that 30,000 new jobs would be provided in areas of chronic unemployment by projects approved during fiscal 1962. This, according to newspaper reports, was the claim of Secretary of Commerce Luther Hodges.[9]

In reality, it would have been a minor miracle had the ARA exerted any real impact during its first two years of existence. The agency was not designed as a pump-priming type of organization. Its function was "to help achieve lasting improvement" in depressed areas (Declaration of Purpose, Section 2 of the Act).

But possibly the worst mistake committed by the ARA was its futile attempt to help too many communities. More than a third of the 3,100 counties in the nation have been designated as redevelopment areas eligible to receive ARA assistance. Needless to say, the majority of the areas will never receive any benefits of the program; some had not sought any help, and many more have no claims on the program and should never have been designated. The designation of over a thousand counties has overextended the ARA's meager resources.

The blame for the overextension of the ARA can hardly be placed on the shoulders of the agency's policy-makers alone. Only a few score communities would have been eligible for assistance under Senator Douglas' original plan. As the program went through the legislative mill more and more communities laid claim to eligibility, and their wishes were honored. When the Area Redevelopment Act was passed, Batt and his staff succumbed further to pressures from congressmen, state and community officials, and others to designate additional areas. The result is the 1,070 redevelopment areas designated by mid-1963.

The overextension of areas eligible for assistance raises the question of whether an effective program is politically feasible. The basic economic justification for the ARA is that depressed economic conditions in an area force people to migrate from their communities in search of a livelihood, which in turn creates pressures on growing communities to find adequate housing, schooling, recreational, and religious facilities for the immigrants. At the same time, the social facilities in depressed areas, poor as they are, go to waste and contribute further to the deterioration of the economic fabric of communities.

There are no precise data about the total social capital invested in communities, but it is conceivable that the amount of such capital equals corporate outlays in plant and equipment. According to Census Bureau estimates, capital outlays for schools, roads, hospitals, water supply, and related public facilities by state and local governments alone amounted in 1962 to $16.7 billion, nearly one-half of total corporate investment in plant and equipment. The amounts invested in community social capital by the federal government, private organizations, churches, fraternal organizations, utilities, and others is not known, but may well exceed the investments of state and local governments.

These data suggest that a decline in the population of communities involves the waste of significant proportions and that sound conservation of resources requires that social capital invested in communities should not be abandoned when it is ..asible to save such capital. A federal program to aid depressed areas should therefore focus on the needs of declining communities. But more than half of the larger designated areas with a labor force of more than 15,000 have experienced a growth in population between 1950 and 1960. Similarly, the population of a third of the smaller designated areas (5[b] counties) increased between 1950 and 1960, despite the fact that many of these areas are predominantly rural and would be expected to reflect the sharp decline in agricultural employment. During the same decade the population in half the counties in the United States declined. More than one of every four 5(a) areas eligible for assistance under the ARA had actually experienced a larger growth in population between 1950 and 1960 than the phenomenal increase in population experienced in the United States during the same decade.

A realistic and effective depressed-area program must also recognize that not all depressed communities can be "saved." The solution for most of the unemployment in depressed areas whose resource base has been depleted may lie in equipping the unemployed with skills which would be marketable elsewhere. Many resource-based depressed communities are located in isolated areas where new economic activity can be introduced only at prohibitive costs. Other depressed areas, particularly rural ones, have never developed an adequate economic base, and the social capital invested in such areas is normally insignificant.

This overextension of ARA designation places a burden upon the potential accomplishment of the modest program to aid depressed areas. The test of the program's success will be the extent to which it will bring jobs to declining communities in order to prevent the waste of social capital in these areas and obviate the need of people to migrate in search of a job. It can hardly be claimed that social facilities in communities are wasted when the population is increasing.

One may sympathize with the argument that change in the size of population is a poor indicator for the determination of a community's eligibility for assistance and that unemployment and underemployment are much better measures of want and deprivation. It might be argued that federal aid to attract industry to growing communities with persistent labor surplus might be more effective than extending aid to declining communities. But this assertion is hardly relevant in assessing the economic impact of a program aimed at helping depressed areas; it ignores the fact that major benefits will accrue from a successful program that should utilize social capital which might otherwise be wasted. Given the limited resources allocated to the program, a choice of priorities must be made. If too many areas become eligible to receive special assistance, it is not likely that truly depressed areas will be the beneficiaries of the program; relatively more viable designated areas are likely to reap the benefits of the program, and the economic gains that might be derived from federal aid will thus be reduced and minimized. This suggests that if growing communities are to be designated as eligible for federal assistance, the criteria establishing their eligibility should be sharply tightened.

The argument in favor of sharply restricting the eligibility of chronic labor-surplus communities to receive assistance under a federally financed depressed-area program does not suggest callousness toward the unemployed; it only recognizes the limitations of the program, particularly when the economy is operating at less than full employment. Forced idleness is deplorable wherever it exists, and national policy, as enunciated in the 1946 Employment Act, recognizes the responsibility of the government in the creation of an economic climate which will generate maximum production and employment. But it can hardly be claimed that the unemployed in a depressed area have greater claim on the federal resources than the unemployed in a growing community. The government properly provides direct forms of assistance to both; training, unemployment benefits, relief, and other forms of assistance are provided for the unemployed wherever they reside, and the disturbingly high level of unemployment which has prevailed in the U.S. during the past few years argues for strengthening these programs as well as for pursuing monetary and fiscal policies which will stimulate demand.

In contrast to the direct programs aimed at reducing unemployment and alleviating its devastating impact upon individuals, the depressed-area program focuses attention on community needs. Furthermore, its aid to the unemployed is based on a "trickle down" process: by inducing entrepreneurs to expand or locate in designated areas and by bolstering the capital investments in these communities to make them more attractive to business. By bringing new jobs to depressed areas, the program attempts to deter the waste of social capital and reduces added pressures for new investments in growing and more prosperous areas where the unemployed from depressed areas would otherwise be forced to migrate.

The above argument does not negate the basic economic justification of a federal program to aid distressed areas. It does suggest, however, that Congress and the ARA have drastically diluted the plan and that the compassion for the suffering of the unemployed shown by the administrators of the agency has dissipated their efforts.

A depressed-area program can be effective only when the number of depressed areas is reduced to manageable proportions and only when areas with a potential for development at a reasonable economic cost are made eligible to participate in the program. In short, the program must recognize that some areas are more equal than others. If such a selection were to be made, it would then be desirable to consider additional programs to aid depressed areas. It would make little economic sense to strengthen the ARA's tools if the program remains so thinly spread.

It is doubtful whether the medicines prescribed by Congress are sufficiently potent to cure the ills of depressed areas. Two additional tools which might be added are preferential treatment in securing government contracts and the offering of rapid tax-amortization or other tax incentives to induce business to locate or expand in these areas. In addition, special consideration might be given to depressed areas under federal grants-in-aid programs. At present, state and local shares of federally subsidized programs are either uniform or based on the per capita income of the state. Under the accelerated public-works program, the share that a labor-surplus community contributes to a project varies from 25 to 75 per cent of the project cost, depending upon the level of income and unemployment in the community. The same policy may be adapted to other federal grants, reducing the share that depressed areas would have to contribute in order to benefit from federal grants.

The Area Redevelopment Act is due to expire on June 30, 1965, unless Congress extends the life of the program before that date. At that time, the Administration and Congress will have to determine whether it is feasible to enact a more effective program to aid a relatively limited number of areas. However, under our political system, it is unlikely that Congress will enact a stronger area redevelopment program and limit the number of eligible areas. A realistic alternative would be to continue the present program with additional funds, recognizing that a diluted program to aid the unemployed in chronic labor-surplus areas is better than no action at all. By 1965 the present ARA program may have matured sufficiently, and its benefits have become adequately pronounced, to justify the continuation of federal aid to areas where chronic labor-surplus is a persistent problem.

REFERENCES

1. *Atlanta Constitution.* May 23, 1962.
2. Duscha, Julius. "Aid for Our Own Underdeveloped Areas," *The Reporter,* February 1, 1962.
3. "Depressed Areas Still Hungry for Work," *Business Week,* April 21, 1962, p. 85.
4. Hodges, Luther. Transcript of Press Conference. October 3, 1961, p. B-3. (Mimeographed.)
5. "Opinion in the Capitol," Metropolitan Broadcasting Company, May 13, 1962, p. 2. (Mimeographed transcript.)
6. *The Wall Street Journal.* April 24, 1962.
7. Stafford, Thomas F. "ARA Falls Short of Original Aim," *Charleston Gazette.* Reprinted in *Congressional Record,* June 4, 1962, p. A4038.
8. U.S. Congress, Joint Economic Committee. *Hearings on the 1962 Economic Report of the President.* 87th Cong., 2d Sess., 1962, pp. 429, 450.
9. *Washington Star.* July 10, 1962.

Postscript

++++++++++++++++++++++++

The statistics in this volume cover ARA activities during its first two years of operations, through April 30, 1963. During the succeeding eight months ARA-approved loans and grants more than doubled, and spokesmen for the agency claim that the projects supported by the ARA have already helped create 20,000 new jobs and will eventually expand employment in depressed areas by 61,000. In order to generate these new jobs, the ARA committed, by the end of 1963, a total of $215 million to be expended in designated areas:

Industrial and commercial loans	$111 million
Public facilities loans and grants	82 million
Technical assistance	8 million
Training	14 million

While ARA loan and grant activities have expanded during its third year of operation, the general scope and direction of the program has undergone little change. Before the end of 1963, the program was further extended when the ARA designated an additional seven large cities, including Philadelphia, Cleveland, and Buffalo, as eligible to receive the agency's assistance. Designation of these areas required that the ARA depart from its labor-market approach by designating cities rather than whole metropolitan areas. The authority to designate parts of labor-market areas is clearly spelled out in the Act. But it is not clear how ARA officials hope to aid the nearly 5 million persons, of whom about 156,000 are unemployed, in the seven newly designated areas, while hundreds of areas which had been previously designated have not as yet received any help from the agency. Without minimizing the serious unemployment problem faced by the seven designated core areas, it could hardly be claimed that the meager resources available to the ARA could be used more advantageously in these areas than in the thousand or more areas previously designated.

The future of the ARA still remains in doubt. A bill to authorize additional funds has been pigeonholed by the House Rules Committee since the summer of 1963. The Administration's preoccupation with the tax cut seems to have precluded any serious effort to get the bill out of the Rules Committee and thus permit the House to express its will. However, it is expected that authorization of additional funds to the ARA may be revived as part of the Administration's war on poverty.

President Lyndon B. Johnson's war on poverty—the details of the program are not as yet available—indicates the need for a great concentration of resources and a more diversified set of tools in order to help pockets of depression and deprivation and to combat widespread structural unemployment and underemployment. Since a major portion of the antipoverty programs will be concentrated in ARA communities, the new proposals to aid the poor, if enacted, will complement the area redevelopment program.

Prior to publication, a limited number of mimeographed copies of this study were made available to persons interested in the ARA. It was only to be expected that an evaluation of a controversial public program, such as the ARA, would be subject to distortion. Opponents of the ARA have already extracted some sections of the study, sometimes out of context, to support their attacks. On the other hand, ARA supporters have expressed criticism because the study fails to endorse all ARA activities. The temptation to comment on these partisan criticisms is strong, but it would hardly be cricket to defend one's own book before publication.

However, it might be in order to restate briefly the major argument of this study. Our economy is undergoing major structural transformations which have left pockets of depression in the midst of abundance. Exclusive reliance upon outmigration as a solution for the problems of the unemployed in depressed areas is as realistic today as the "let-them-eat-cake" solution proposed by Marie Antoinette. The ARA presents an action program, albeit a very modest one, to aid depressed areas. To the extent that the program is diluted, its accomplishments become difficult to measure. It is also impossible to quantify, at this early stage, the positive achievements of ARA, especially the role that the program has played in stimulating local economic planning and the development of unutilized resources. The success of the ARA mission can be measured only in longer-term developments, and the program should therefore be given a further chance to prove its potential as a tool to aid depressed areas.

March 9, 1964   Sar A. Levitan

COMMENT BY WILLIAM L. BATT, JR.

A study of any new government program covering only its first two years of experience, as Dr. Levitan himself states, is a difficult task. Since this opportunity for a short commentary does not allow a point-by-point "rebuttal," it might be useful to cite briefly a few observations:

1. Area redevelopment as a practicing art—in contrast to being only a theoretical subject of interest—is actually a new endeavor in the United States. In contrast, western Europe is far ahead of us, particularly Great Britain.

2. The concrete legislation of 1961, which made possible the practical application of that art, was not a simple blueprint. This book is clear on that point. The Act required much careful education and participation with individuals, businessmen, and communities, and also with the many agencies necessary for effective implementation of the Act.

3. These first two points made the economic development of distressed areas a complicated and difficult process to get underway. Perhaps because of the pragmatic, "trial-and-error" quality of so many innovations in American public policy and their related programs, ARA has been bound to be subjected to criticism, even from the most ardent supporters of its legislation.

4. Because of the pent-up demands in distressed areas for long-deferred action and economic progress, there was great pressure on ARA to act as quickly as possible, without an opportunity first to work out a completely "rational" scheme of priorities—as so earnestly desired by many academic economists and planners. In a less democratic political system, this may be possible. This does not mean that ARA, during the course of its actions, has developed no priorities (and criteria). But program priorities are largely based on community programs and on initiatives of businessmen.

5. For the same reasons (pent-up demand for action and the democratic nature of our society), ARA has responded to requests for assistance as they arise, despite the strain on its limited staff resources. Perhaps such responsiveness does not conform to "pure" public administration science.

6. The major goals established by ARA itself include (*a*) reducing the unemployment rate in distressed areas to the general national rate, and (*b*) the education, through experience, of communities in the funda-

mentals of "grass roots" economic development planning. On the first, unemployment has been reduced by one-third of the gap that prevailed in 1961 (by no means through ARA projects alone).* On the second, hundreds of communities are undergoing that experience.

7. Finally, I agree with Dr. Levitan that the ARA experiment was launched at a most difficult time, when unemployment was a general national problem, along with over-all retarded economic growth. Its real test will come as new trends and policies (including the effects of tax-reduction, expanded manpower training, youth development, etc.) come into being and restore the general economy to more desirable levels of economic well-being.

Limitations in space prevent a more comprehensive statement.

Washington, D. C.   WILLIAM L. BATT, JR.
March, 1964   Administrator
                             Area Redevelopment Administration

---

* In this connection, a study of the nearly 60 ARA projects operating for a year shows that actual employment was 105% of the anticipated figure at the time of their approval.

Index